UNSEENPRESS.COM'S

MW01506038

ENCYCLOPEDIA OF

HAUNTED

INDIANA

BY
NICOLE KOBROWSKI

Second Edition

Unseenpress.com, Inc. PO Box 687 Westfield, IN 46074

UNSEENPRESS.COM'S OFFICIAL

ENCYCLOPEDIA OF

HAUNTED

INDIANA

BY
NICOLE KOBROWSKI

Second Edition

Unseenpress.com, Inc. PO Box 687 Westfield, IN 46074

Copyright © 2008, 2017
By Nicole Kobrowski
All rights reserved.

No part of this book may be reproduced, transmitted in any form or by any means, known or unknown, electronic or mechanical, including photocopying, recording, or by an information storage and retrieval system-except by a reviewer who may quote brief passages in a review to be printed in a magazine, newspaper or on the Web- without permission in writing from the publisher.

For information contact:
Unseenpress.com, Inc.
PO Box 687
Westfield, IN 46074

Library of Congress Cataloging-in-Publication Data

Kobrowski, Nicole
  Unseenpress.com's Definitive Encyclopedia of Haunted Indiana/Nicole Kobrowski
        Includes index
 1. Ghosts Indiana; 2. Paranormal Indiana; 3. Indiana History; 4. Indiana Travel

Library of Congress Control Number: 2017900821
ISBN-13: 978-0-9986207-0-1

Printed in the United States of America

Published by
Haunted Backroads Books
an imprint of Unseenpress.com, Inc.
PO Box 687
Westfield, IN 46074

Although the authors and publisher have made every effort to ensure the accuracy and completeness of information contained in this book, we assume no responsibility for errors, inaccuracies, omissions or any inconsistency herein. Any slights of people, places or organizations are unintentional.

The Unseenpress.com, Inc. website is
http://www.unseenpress.com/

Cover design Unseenpress.com, Inc.
Editing by Emily Dickos-Carter
Cover photograph copyright: netfalls / 123RF Stock Photo

Notes

The persons, events, places and incidents depicted in this book are based on oral history, memoirs, interviews and accounts that were used as research for this book. The author makes no claim as to the veracity of the information. The author makes no claim as to the exact historical authenticity of the legends presented in this book. The author does not guarantee any location directions contained in this book. You visit these sites at your own risk. Although many sites are open to visitors during the day (and some in the evening), they all have an owner.

Additionally, this book is comprised of material that is intended for the entertainment of its readers. The author has paid particular attention to collecting legends that have been told, in many cases, for generations. The information concerning these legends may not reflect historical events. The author takes no responsibility for the veracity of each story except that she believes the storytellers. The author has attempted to research and locate each area as accurately as possible. Although we made every effort to ensure that the information was correct at the time the book went to press, we do not assume and hereby disclaim any liability to any party for loss, damage, or injury caused by information contained in this book. Furthermore the publishers disclaim any liability resulting from the use of this book. The publishers and author do not condone, advise, or recommend visiting these sites without obtaining permission first and taking safety precautions.

We apologize if there is inaccurate information presented in the book and will rectify future additions and editions if we are contacted by mail or email and provided the correct information.

Table of Contents

Other Titles by Nicole Kobrowski

Published by Unseenpress.com, Inc.
(print and ebook)

- Haunted Backroads: Central Indiana
- Haunted Backroads: Ghosts of Westfield
- Haunted Backroads: Ghosts of Madison County, Indiana
- Fractured Intentions: A History of Central State Hospital for the Insane
- She Sleeps Well: The Extraordinary Life and Murder of Dr. Helene Elise Hermine Knabe
- Unseenpress.com's Official Encyclopedia of Haunted Indiana
- Unseenpress.com's Official Encyclopedia of Haunted Northern Indiana
- Unseenpress.com's Official Encyclopedia of Haunted Central Indiana
- Unseenpress.com's Official Encyclopedia of Haunted Southern Indiana

Published by IUPUI
Distance Learning: A Guide to System Planning and Implementation

(by Merrill, Young, and Kobrowski)

Published by Bildungsverlag EINS
Metal Line (Instructor's guide and workbook)
Hotel Line (Instructor's Guide)
Englisch für Elektroberufe (Instructor's guide and workbook)
Supply Line (Instructor's guide and workbook)
Construction Line (Instructor's guide and workbook)

Coming soon!
Haunted Backroads: Ghosts of Hamilton County, Indiana
Audio books

Dedication

Stand up for what you believe in even if you are standing alone.
~Sophie Scholl

This book is dedicated to the
freedoms of speech, the press, and expression.

Long may they live.

About the Author

Nicole Kobrowski is the co-owner of Unseenpress.com, Inc., which was founded in 2001. She and her husband Michael started the business because of their interest in the paranormal and their love of history. She has written professionally under a variety of pen names for over 20 years, including books for ESL and dozens of articles on a myriad topics. Being a paranormal enthusiast for over 30 years, she has done investigation work in many areas including spirit photography, electronic voice phenomenon, and automatic writing. In addition to her work in the paranormal field, Nicole is an Adult Education Consultant. Currently, she lives in her "über haunted home" with her husband and Lyla, their rescued cat.

Second Edition Preface

Every book I write is a creative pleasure. With this particular book, I need to learn to cut the cord. In the development of the second edition, every time I was about to finish and send it off, someone (sometimes me) would let me know about another fascinating place that I think just has to be included.

When I originally wrote the book, I had been to about 33% of these locations. As of this writing, I have been to over 65%. By the next writing, I will have completed my goal of visiting every site listed.

It has taken nine years for second edition to come out. Some noticeable improvements include

- expanded information about many locations.
- revised listing methodology
- an improved index.

As always, the intent of this book is to educate and to serve as a guide for paranormal enthusiasts, investigators and anyone traveling around the wonderful state of Indiana.

Special thanks to Emily Dickos-Carter and to Megan Norris.

I hope you enjoy it as much as I enjoyed writing it.

Nicole Kobrowski
January 2017

We love hearing from paranormal enthusiasts and investigators about their experiences at these locations or from other "haunted' locations. Send all enquiries or story submissions for future publications to customerservice@ unseenpress.com.

Original Preface

Four years in the making hardly describes the amount of time that really went into this book. If truth be told, this book has been in the making for many more years. Not only has it been four years of development on the part of Unseenpress.com, Inc. but also years' experience on the part of folklorists, paranormal investigators, people interested in the paranormal, and people who have experienced this collection of hauntings.

Anyone can say their town is the most haunted town- I believe every town is haunted and no one town can earn the right to be "the most haunted" in any location. The proof of this is in this book, which is the most extensive collection in existence of haunted Indiana locations covering every county in Indiana.

This book is perfect for anyone interested in the paranormal, but it is especially helpful for the paranormal traveler, ghost hunter and paranormal investigator. It contains a legend to help you interpret the listings as well as an index to locations and types of sightings and hauntings. As you read this book, you might disagree with what you read and that's ok. I present the information for you and I want the people who read this book to interpret the hauntings in their own way.

Even after 20 years of writing in a variety of fields, I enjoyed every minute of this project including sifting through accounts, reading several accounts of one story- over and over, and talking with myriads of people. In writing a volume of this type, it is impossible to thank everyone by name. In no particular order, I want to thank all of the people who helped in the writing of this book: the archivists, librarians and researchers; all the reporters and authors, and the paranormal investigators and ghost hunters. I want to also thank the private individuals who trusted me with their stories and the people who supported this effort in other ways.

This collection of haunted places is a living document because the paranormal is infinitely popular- and long after media hype of the paranormal fades away- the paranormal, as always, will remain.

Nicole Kobrowski
August 2008

We love hearing from paranormal enthusiasts and investigators about their experiences at these locations or from other "haunted' locations. Send all enquiries or story submissions for future publications to editor@unseenpress.com.

A Guide to the Encyclopedia

This book is set up in order for you to find information quickly and easily. The book is set up by counties, which you'll find at the top of each page. For each entry, I've developed a legend for your use as follows:

Sample Entry

State Theatre	The name of the location.
Anderson: 1303-1316 Meridian St	The directions, address and supporting information.
This former theater sadly unused was built in the 1920s and was home to stage and screen stars. In the 1960s Anderson's downtown went downhill and took this theater with it. For a time in the late 90s, it operated as a live venue, but seems to have gone belly up with the rest of the town.	The section entry contains background on events around the history and haunting.
From at least the 1960s, the balcony of the movie theater was haunted by a man in a suit. He was known to sit down next to movie goers and scare them by disappearing into thin air. Later, when the balcony was closed due to safety issues, the man seems to have moved to the main seating area. After the theater closed, many patrons during the 90s claimed to have seen him in the upper restroom areas. Workers also saw the man backstage.	

Do-It-Yourself Investigations

Since starting Unseenpress.com, Inc. we've been approached by people and organizations on a weekly basis asking us if we'd investigate their home or asking if they can go with us to a "ghost hunt" or an "investigation". These aren't even including the places we approach for investigations. Unfortunately, we can't accommodate all requests- days only have 24 hours. As a result, we've referred some people to reputable paranormal groups so they connect with investigators in their area and we've worked with clients to find them reputable help in their area. Also, we have taken some experienced investigators on our investigations and had great success with it. We have also started education classes for people who want to take responsibility for their own hauntings. We'll talk more about that later.

Still, we find a fundamental difference in some of the requests- "ghost hunt" and "investigation". Both terms have very different meanings. Certain people want to go to haunted locations, be scared, talk about what they've experienced, make a quick determination it is haunted (or not) and move on to the next location. Other people want to conduct investigations that are scientifically documented, following set procedures.

Before you go

Your team should have a clear idea of who they are and how they should behave before they ever set foot on the client's property. Standards should be explained and reviewed before the investigation.

Before you decide to go, we recommend the following standards:

- Get permission (See Permission section).
- Walk the area before the investigation. If you're doing a daytime investigation, this is not so important. If you're doing a night time investigation, you should do this step to understand where you might encounter difficulty. You should always do a walk through to understand the temperature fluctuations and EMF readings (however, how will you really know what a baseline is? You could be experiencing paranormal activity on your first visit).
- Meet at the location and decide who will do what and with what equipment.
- Offer a blessing, protection, or prayer if you wish.
- Walk around to decide where to place equipment.
- Take pictures, videos and audio recordings. Make notes about any changes in temperature, feelings you had or sightings. If everyone on your team does this, you should have an accurate picture of the investigation when you're finished. It helps eliminate non-paranormal causes for suspected activity.

Once you've made the necessary arrangements, consider the following points during an investigation.

- Never roam alone in an unfamiliar setting. You need to be safe.
- Take ID with you. You might need to prove who you are.
- Take a cell phone with you and let others know where you are going.
- If you will be in the field for a long time, take adequate food and drink with you. Eat only in specific areas to minimize noise and contamination of evidence.
- If you are asked to leave, do so without making a fuss. It will benefit you in the long run. Respect everyone

living and dead.
- Don't smoke. It can contaminate photographic/video evidence.
- Use care when taking photos. Don't take photos when others are taking them. Note anything that could create false orbs in photos. Keep hair, fingers and camera straps away from the lens. You, equipment, or other items can cast false positive shadows so be aware of your location and equipment placement.
- Do not move audio recorders when speaking. It can create distortion.
- No drugs or alcohol before, during or after an investigation. If you're sick, stay home. Illegal drugs are a no. Drunk people on an investigation or after an investigation while still a part of the team is stupid and not good for the paranormal field or its image.
- Record any conditions that could affect data (humidity, dust, etc.).
- No noisy clothing, jewelry, keys, or change- these items affect what we hear.
- Apply no items that affect smell- cologne, perfume, etc. Do use fragrance-free deodorant.
- Dress for the field. Use your team's uniform or wear clean, weather appropriate clothes.
- Ensure hair is away from face- ponytails are good. Buns are even better.
- If you are frightened in a location- leave. Some of the most haunted places are in the middle of nowhere and you might have a bad encounter with a human. Use common sense.
- Have an emergency plan and make sure someone is on the team that is able to perform CPR and/or call for help quickly.

Paranormal Investigation

The Field
Much information is written about paranormal investigation. Some of it is stated in absolute terms. Paranormal investigation is a wide open field. I say field, because that is what it should be, however, to my knowledge, no one makes a living solely by investigating the paranormal- myself included. Certainly, research labs exist for parapsychology, which is completely different than paranormal investigation. Most investigators belong to organizations that support paranormal research, though, most everyone has a day job.

Education Options
Along these same lines, there are no accredited degrees in paranormal investigation. None. Zero. Nada. Niet, Kein. Don't even waste your time and money. Many paranormal organizations offer certificate courses to become "certified" in paranormal investigation. Many paranormal groups charge dues and ask you to take classes (sometimes paying extra) in order to be "qualified" to go on investigations. As a lifelong student of Adult Education, I can hardly argue about basic training needed to safely go on an investigation. However, each organization has its own policies and procedures for accomplishing an investigation. You have to decide if they are sound, if you agree with them and if you'd like to be a part of the organization.

Knowing the state of education in the paranormal field, this difference begs the question, "what does being a certified paranormal investigator (or obtaining a certificate) get me? Some people believe it doesn't really benefit you. As it isn't a recognized field of work or science (yes, we are considered pseudo-scientists), it isn't going to raise your pay (unless you latch onto the media). Some people would argue the benefit comes in being certified to investigate with the organization that certified you. Other people argue that being certified or recognized by a certain group is motivation enough. They believe that this certification might get them into more places or give them more of an advantage. Again, it is up to your interpretation.

Media, Myths and Absolutes

No one, no matter what experiences someone has had with the paranormal, knows what to expect or what concrete facts can be said about spirit activity. No one can concretely define what a ghost really is or if they exist. While I have definitions of some of the elements surrounding the paranormal and investigation, my take may be different than another investigator's definition. Also, I have most definite feelings about ghosts; I am a firm believer in them. Some people are out to disprove the existence of spirits.

The media also has its own take on the paranormal ranging from the cheesy "ghostbusters" type attitude to making it somewhat darker and more dramatic than what it really is. For example, shows exist for ratings. If television shows didn't have something scary and exciting, no one would watch them. Be careful what you consume.

Also, be careful about what you read and absorb. For example, an investigator on a popular television series said "A human spirit can only lift three to ten pounds." Really? How do we know this? Did this investigator have an interview with a ghost? Because if he did, I would love the transcript. Does this mean that when Arnold Schwarzenegger dies he is limited to lifting three to ten pounds? Or does he get to lift more because he was a body builder? Likewise another misconception is that the "haunting hours" are between 12-3am. If that were true, why do we have so many daytime reports of activity?

Absolute statements like the ones above are patently false until proven otherwise. If someone says conclusively, "Yep, you've got ghosts.", it is their own flavor and opinion- kind of like a certification that your house is haunted. Other investigators may disagree with the findings. While some people believe that ghosts can go home with you (as I do), there are other investigators who do not believe this.

If we can't prove anything what is the point?

All we can do is conduct inquiry based on common assumptions and draw our own conclusions. However, surrounding investigative inquiry is more than just our opinions and biases. We also must take scientific method into account. In scientific inquiry, we decide what we're going to study, decide on an explanation for what we're studying, define how we'll research it, muse on the types of results you think you'll get, execute and analyze the plan. Scientific method is scientific method, no matter what area you are in. I am a scholar in Adult Education and I apply scientific method the same as anyone who has learned it. The focus of my research in Adult Education is different than that of a Sociologist.

You might ask what the problem is, that scientific inquiry seems very straightforward. It is, but what is contained in each step is the difference between mainstream, accepted science and the assumed pseudo-science of the paranormal. We can't test against what we don't know. Our tools have only been test driven to a certain point. For example, many investigators believe EMF detectors can indicate spirit activity. How do we know they aren't picking up power inside the walls, under the floor, etc.? There is a scale for what is normal for certain types of electromagnetic fields, but have we been able to consistently replicate what we're seeing as "abnormal" to be able to say it is truly abnormal and paranormal?

Organizations and Investigations

Investigators employ several steps involved in paranormal investigation. Investigations aren't always exciting and many of them are hurry up and wait situations. Sometimes you get a hit and sometimes after hours of sitting or hours of analyzing, you get nothing. It can be frustrating, but also rewarding. The difference among investigators is how they conduct themselves, their groups and their investigations.

One bad experience can lead to a complete distaste for the paranormal in general. Two recent cases come to mind. First, the producers of a show about ghost children did an unauthorized ghost hunt and filming in Crown Hill Cemetery in Indianapolis, Indiana. While I believe there is much paranormal activity afoot in the cemetery, the cemetery staff made it quite clear that it wants nothing to do with the paranormal. The makers of the program misrepresented the history of the subject and also the history of Crown Hill. Additionally, they didn't ask permission to film on the grounds. They seemed to assume that because it was a cemetery, owned by the State (not true), it was fair game (also not true).

Another example is Central State Hospital also in Indianapolis. A "documentary" was produced on the premise that it would be historic in nature. It was historic all right, but not the historic documentary that was presented in the proposal to the city. Would you want to be affiliated with an organization that misrepresents itself?

Reputation

Moving to the practical, keep in mind that the reputation of your organizations, investigations, and personal behavior is under scrutiny from the minute you approach an organization or individual about conducting an investigation. How you conduct your organization, investigations and/or personal behavior determine how much credibility each element has and how the paranormal community is perceived as a whole. For example, a group of investigators trespassed on a site where a well known serial killer lived. They took pictures and video and posted both on their website and a video sharing site. They even boasted about it on television. When the owner saw this evidence, the police became involved. What do you think about this group's ethics or credibility? I certainly wouldn't want to work with this group. Another group trespassed at Central State Hospital, several times. They were told by the police to stay away from the site but didn't. Now, they have a bad reputation with the police and have given paranormal investigation a bad name. Would you want these people coming into your home or business?

Permission

Investigation doesn't mean glory. Too many times have I seen investigators jockey for position while investigating hauntings. With the exception of private homes, businesses, etc. any already known location has been investigated or hunted to some extent many time over. There is no "scooping" going on. For example, Central State Hospital in Indianapolis is the perceived as the Holy Grail of haunted locations. Who hasn't been out there? Most folks who have been here are employees, with the police or have done so illegally. What does claiming "first rights" do? Absolutely nothing. What does the trespassing do to the credibility of you, your organization and to the field? *Trespassing kills credibility.*

Many people say, "well how do you get in there?" or "I don't know how to get permission." Well, here's your guide. Find the owner and get permission. *Always get it in writing.*

Find the Owner
Property, including businesses, historic properties, "abandoned" properties, farms, woods, etc.

Go to the township or county recorder and ask for the name of the owner on record for the property. This is public information that they have to give you. You can usually get a phone number as well. Contact the owners and if they don't respond, follow up. If they still don't respond or you get a resounding, "No," let it go. Remember, what you do and how you act reflects on not just you and your organization, but on everyone. Think about how you can revisit it at a future time and maybe change the no to a yes.

Cemeteries
Go to the township trustee, who usually controls them. If your county has a cemetery commission, speak with them. If it is a large cemetery like Crown Hill that is run by an organization, talk to them. If it is a cemetery attached to a church, talk to the pastor, minister, priest, etc. Don't assume that because it is a cemetery that you can visit it any time you wish. Most cemeteries in Indiana close at dusk. Simply calling the police to let them know you're out there doesn't cover you. It is still under the control of others.

Roads and Highways
For your own safety, if nothing else, you must have permission to create an obstruction or to be on these roads. If you are walking on the road, you run the risk of getting yourself killed. If you're with several people, you increase your risk. Many of the haunted roads are in areas where people live.

Once an organized ghost hunting group decided to trespass on a fairly well known area in Hamilton County. They even posted pictures on the internet showing them trespassing. The police were alerted by the owner and they received a notice telling them to take down all photos, videos, etc and that next time they would be prosecuted. How would you like to ask the boss at your day job for bail money?

County Map

The map on the following page shows a numbered county map. On the next page, these numbers correspond with the correct county.

Use the names as a quick reference to find the correct county in the book.

County Map of Indiana

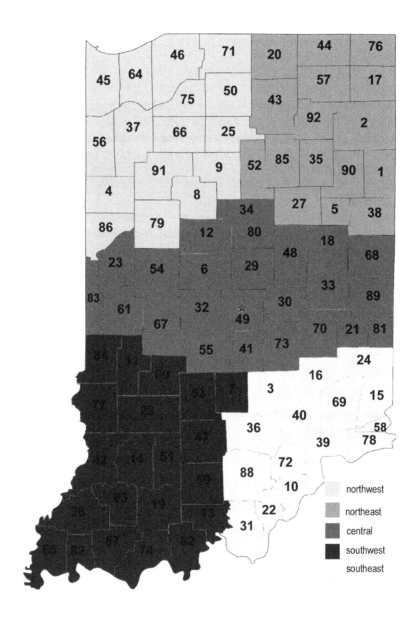

Alphabetical List of Indiana Counties

Number	Name	Number	Name
1	Adams	24	Franklin
2	Allen	25	Fulton
3	Bartholomew	26	Gibson
4	Benton	27	Grant
5	Blackford	28	Greene
6	Boone	29	Hamilton
7	Brown	30	Hancock
8	Carroll	31	Harrison
9	Cass	32	Hendricks
10	Clark	33	Henry
11	Clay	34	Howard
12	Clinton	35	Huntington
13	Crawford	36	Jackson
14	Daviess	37	Jasper
15	Dearborn	38	Jay
16	Decatur	39	Jefferson
17	DeKalb	40	Jennings
18	Delaware	41	Johnson
19	Dubois	42	Knox
20	Elkhart	43	Kosciusko
21	Fayette	44	LaGrange
22	Floyd	45	Lake
23	Fountain	46	LaPorte

Alphabetical List of Indiana Counties

Number	Name	Number	Name
47	Lawrence	70	Rush
48	Madison	71	St. Joseph
49	Marion	72	Scott
50	Marshall	73	Shelby
51	Martin	74	Spencer
52	Miami	75	Starke
53	Monroe	76	Steuben
54	Montgomery	77	Sullivan
55	Morgan	78	Switzerland
56	Newton	79	Tippecanoe
57	Noble	80	Tipton
58	Ohio	81	Union
59	Orange	82	Vanderburgh
60	Owen	83	Vermillion
61	Parke	84	Vigo
62	Perry	85	Wabash
63	Pike	86	Warren
64	Porter	87	Warrick
65	Posey	88	Washington
66	Pulaski	89	Wayne
67	Putnam	90	Wells
68	Randolph	91	White
69	Ripley	92	Whitley

ADAMS
COUNTY

Adams County Cheese Factory
(reported razed)
Decatur: In the woods east of the Kukelhan Mansion

(See Kukelhan Mansion entry, Geneva, Adams County)

This site was abandoned for many years then torn down. Active spirits are caretakers for the property. Some people describe experiencing feelings of uneasiness while other visitors feel a sense of peace.

Ceylon Covered Bridge
Geneva: Two miles NE of Geneva on CR W950S just east of US 27.

This bridge originally crossed the Wabash River. Since the river shifted, the bridge now spans a back channel. It is considered the last standing covered bridge over any part of the Wabash River. Built by the Smith Brothers Company, it is a Howe Truss structure. At 126 feet long (140 feet including the seven feet overhang at each end), the bridge is now surrounded by a roadside park and is on the National Register of Historic Places.

A group of teenagers performing a séance saw a man as tall as the bridge itself. The man left a blood stain on the pentagram they were using on the floor of the structure. Some people believe this pentagram was a portal and today strange occurrences still take place.

Kukelhan Mansion
Geneva: Just north of Decatur, east of US 27, not far from North Pointe sub-division

The house was owned by a wealthy banker who lost his mind. He was paranoid that people were after his money. Due to his illness, he killed his family and hung himself. Investigators report they are unable to be on the property for long periods of time because of uneasy feelings and the residual haunting replaying the hanging death.

South Adams Middle School
Geneva: 105 W. Line St.

Staff including cooks, janitors, teachers and administration report a full apparition seen in the rafters when arriving at the building early in the morning and during evening events.

Williams Covered Bridge
Williams: Huron and Williams Roads between SR450 and Port-Williams Rd.

Before the bridge was covered, a man went across on horseback and the horse jumped off. Also, an African-American man is said to have been hung on the bridge, ripping his head from his body.

Today, visitors see the rope swinging and hear screams. At either end of the bridge, a translucent apparition of a man is seen. You can hear horse hooves and the neighing of the animal. A phantom shadow figure also appears.

ALLEN
COUNTY

1530 North Harrison Street
Fort Wayne: 1530 N. Harrison St.

Former tenants report being physically touched by spirits that left marks. Growling noises and brown goo are reported. A demon rag doll reappears although it was burned.

Blue Cast Magnetic Springs Sanitarium
Woodburn: Blue Cast Rd.

Visitors see shadows and red and blue orbs. Investigators report cold spots, footsteps and voices.

Bostick Bridge
(aka Turner Bridge)
Fort Wayne: On Bostick Rd. between US 24 and US 27 just south of I-469.

This historic bridge is a Whipple truss (double intersection Pratt truss) bridge built in 1894 by the Canton Bridge Company. It spans 169 feet. Many people believe satanic activity performed here opened a portal to Hell. Investigators report hearing growling, seeing menacing red and white glowing eyes, and hearing the tortured cries of those unfortunates in Hell.

Luckily for you, now you can safely test out these theories. This bridge was rehabilitated into a pedestrian bridge and a new one was put in its place. The historic bridge was painstakingly restored with vintage techniques such as reproduced panels and in-kind hot metal riveting. In acquiescence to modern life, modern railing was added.

Bruick Road
New Haven: Bruick Rd. runs N/S between SR 37 and US 24

A white light appears, grows in size and even changes colors. If you follow, it seems to move farther away from you and disappears.

City Hall
New Haven: 428 Broadway St.
(aka Historic City Hall)

This building was built in 1913 and served as the courthouse, jail, fire station and a recruitment center during WWII. Investigators captured orbs and smells ranging from sulphur and sewer to cigars and perfume. Additionally, one visitor was chased out of the upstairs by rapid pounding on the wall around her. As she ran down the stairs, it followed her all the way out the front doors. When she exited, the doors closed behind her and she could still hear the pounding from the street. According to her, it went on for over five more minutes until it silenced. Some people believe these were the souls of the dead who were supposedly taken care of here when the building was used as a temporary morgue.

Carroll High School
Fort Wayne: 3701 Carroll Rd.

Old stories state one junior at the school dies every year and comes back to haunt the building. A boy took the seat of one of these unfortunates and was rudely pushed off the seat.

Cedar Canyons
(aka Griffin Rd.)
Fort Wayne: Griffin and Auburn Rds.

An old transparent man walks on this road near Cedar Canyons. The best time to see him is between 9:00pm and 5:00am.

Chapman Road
Fort Wayne: North of Cedar Canyons Rd. to Chapman Rd. Turn right on Griffin Rd. and stop at the bottom of the hill.

Cars seem to be pulled up the road when they are put in park or neutral.

Char's House of Oak
Fort Wayne: Was located on Wells St.
Out of business

This store used to sell oak furniture. There are reports of a man with messy black hair, an unshaven face, soiled undershirt and green workman's pants appears on the main staircase. He seems to be angry and takes his belt off, raising it to swing. People report a chilling cold and unsettled feeling when he passes through them.

Cold Water Road Wal-Mart
Fort Wayne: 5311 Coldwater Road.

Between 3:00am-4:00am, bagpipes play. A man in a plaid kilt paces the floors. When he passes by you, a cold feeling settles on you. Although he hasn't interacted directly with staff or shoppers, he is friendly. Additionally, when he makes his appearance, items fall off shelves.

Crossroads Cemetery
Fort Wayne: East side of Bethal Rd., south of Dupont Rd.

Visitors report moving lights, mysterious noises, feelings of being watched when in cemetery.

Devil's Dip
Georgetown: Unknown

Local legend states the house at the bottom of this hill was home to a little girl who was hit by a car. If you drive too fast, the girl appears next to the telephone pole across from the house or she is also said to get into your back seat, cry, and tell you to slow down.

Devil's Hollow
Fort Wayne: Two versions of the legend exist for this location. One is on Cedar Canyon Rd. between Canyon Run and Auburn Rd. The other is on Devil's Hollow Rd.

Orbs and faces have been caught on camera between 9 p.m. and 5 a.m. An old transparent man walks on this road near Cedar Canyons. ## Eel River Cemetery
Dunn Mill: Corner of Madden and Carroll Rds.

A tall, thin man in tan pants and a long coat walks the cemetery. When approached, he disappears. Sometimes he wears a dark hat and other times he smokes a cigarette. Investigators report the smell of smoke when he appears.

Embassy Theater
Fort Wayne: 125 W. Jefferson Blvd.

This glorious theater opened on May 4, 1928 as the Emboyd Theater. Top-notch in every way, it boasted a pipe organ, vaudeville shows and the nearby Indiana Hotel. In 1952, the theater was sold to the Alliance Amusement Corporation and the name changed to the Embassy Theater. It was a movie theater until 1971 when both the theater and the hotel were in danger of destruction by a wrecking ball. Over the last 30 years, the theater and hotel have been protected by the community. Renovation is a continuous process. Volunteers see a deceased maintenance man roaming the theater at all hours.

Ft. Wayne (Town)
Fort Wayne: Off I-69

All of Fort Wayne (or most of it) is built on Indian grounds. Many people think that Fort Wayne is haunted because of the ancient burial grounds and just being in old places downtown makes some people feel a presence.

Greenlawn Cemetery
Fort Wayne: Covington Road east of I-69

Floating orbs appear in the cemetery in front of visitors and in photos.

History Center
(aka Old Jail)
Fort Wayne: 302 E. Berry St.

Built in 1913, this building has been a city hall, a jail and a fire station. As it is under restoration, many employees have had paranormal experiences. The basement seems to have strange smells around it. Visitors report apparitions of an old man, orbs and transparent children. Some locals believe the basement was used as a morgue. A murderer haunts the old jail, walking through the halls and touching visitors on the neck. Noises like metal on metal are heard as well.

Jehl Park
Fort Wayne: West end of Bohnke Dr.
(aka Swinger's Grave)

A girl was strangled by the chain of a swing. If you swing at midnight at Jehl Park, she pushes you off.

Knee House
Fort Wayne: Between Hanna, Warfield, and John Streets and US 27
(aka Cement House; aka White's/Whites/Whities Mansion)
(Razed in 1988)

The home was built during WWII and construction was halted by the family when the sons went to war. The man built the house for his invalid wife, including a checkerboard pattern in the front entry of the home. He built ramps for her wheelchair. Before he could finish it, she died in 1951. He left the house unfinished because he didn't have the money to continue. The invalid wife walks the home with a light or a candle.

Lakeside Park Neighborhood
Fort Wayne: 1401 Lake Ave.

Located near a lake, this neighborhood was Native American land used for unnamed purposes. The land was also part of an amusement park with canals and a dance hall. Residents hear strange sounds and see apparitions in their homes.

Leo High School
Leo: 14600 Amstutz Rd.

A student died during a stage production and now haunts the auditorium. Lights turn off and on, doors open and close for no reason.

Main Street Bridge
Fort Wayne: Main Street over St. Mary's River

A woman in white walks the bridge but never interacts with people. She's been walking Main Street since the mid-1800s by some accounts and 1903 by others. Sometimes she races over the bridge in a horse drawn carriage.

Mason Long House
Fort Wayne: 922 Columbia Ave.

In 1965 the McCaffrey family moved in– tales of ghosts and all. The home's former life was that of a hotel, casino and drinking establishment. Visitors see misty figures– especially in August.

New Haven High School and Middle School
New Haven: Middle School: 900 Prospect Ave./ High School: 1300 Green Rd.

A ghost of a homeless man walks the tunnel.

North Side High School
Fort Wayne: 475 E. State Blvd.

A Miami chief who tried to stop building in Fort Wayne on the burial site of his tribe roams the halls and grounds of this school. A janitor who died of a heart attack is seen in the basement. A construction worker who died in the building of the school is also seen wandering in the school from the auditorium to the classrooms. The construction worker is often seen by people to warn them of school and personal dangers.

Old Bryon Health Care Center
(aka Stairway to Hell)
Fort Wayne: 12101 Lima Rd. (New facility attached to old)

A legend claims that the stairs to be the basement are endless and that no matter how many times you try to go down to the basement, you'll never get there. The ghost of a nurse who died while on duty walks the halls late at night watching over her patients.

Old Lutheran Hospital
Fort Wayne: 3024 Fairfield Ave.
(Razed, now part of Lutheran Foundation property)

This old hospital was built on the Ninde homestead property in 1903. Between 1906 and 1975, four additions were made. The current building at 7950 Jefferson Boulevard was built in 1992. The fourth floor of the old hospital had a male ghost that would walk through the silent halls and visit patients.

Pfeiffer House
Fort Wayne: 434 W Wayne St.

Charles and Henrietta Pfeiffer and their children Fred and Marguerite lived in the home. Charles made his money in meat packing and banking. Currently, Fred, who died at almost 100 years of age, inhabits the house still. Pots and pans move, lights turn off and on. Doors open and close. People refuse to go to the attic.

Snider High School
Fort Wayne: 4600 Fairlawn Pass

People hear a girl crying during the day. Legend states that a girl drowned in a pool on the site of the school. She still haunts the building.

U.S. 20
Brushy Prairie: Various areas of US 20

A pale woman in a white gown walks the road. When drivers stop for her, she disappears.

University of Saint Francis Library
Fort Wayne: 2701 Spring St.
(aka Bass, John H. Mansion, aka Brookside)

A student committed suicide in the library. Students and staff feel cold spots, hear moans, and see the lights turn off and on around the anniversary of his death. This building is no longer the library, but now houses administrative offices.

BARTHOLOMEW COUNTY

1130 25th Street
Columbus: 1130 25th St.
(aka Subway Restaurant on 46)

Shadow figures walk through the store. Patrons and employees hear voices when no one else is around.

Ceraland Recreation Area
Columbus: Off 525 E. south of SR 46 and north of SR 7.

In the 1970s, a woman drowned while crossing the creek during a flood. You can see and hear her crying on the edge of the banks.

Crump Theatre
Columbus: 425 3rd St.
(aka The Crump, Crump Opera Hall and Theatre)

According to Rovene Quigley, executive director of the Crump Theatre, she is never alone in the 1800s building. Many stories exist about this historic theater, including Quigley finding an extra $86.50 in her receipt box, and a helpful ghost finding a boiler inspection certificate and placing it on her desk.

Visitors see orbs, mists and apparitions in this theater. Temperature drops and spikes occur preceding these events. EVPs caught in the building include male and female's voices. Some topics of conversation include "That was fun.", "What was that", "I wish they'd leave.", and "What are they doing?"

Elizabethtown
Elizabethtown: Elizabethtown is located between US 31 and SR 7 on CR E475S (Legal Tender Rd./2nd St.)

At the edge of town by the welcome sign a woman in black will stare at you as you drive into town.

Hartsville College Cemetery
Hartsville: South end of East St.

This is the original site of the coeducational United Brethren school. It was founded 1850 as Hartsville Academy by a public act of the Indiana General Assembly. The campus moved four blocks south, circa 1865 and was destroyed by fire in January 1898. Many graduates became distinguished citizens in their communities throughout the state and nation.

Several serious looking young men walk through the cemetery in the day and night. One young man chases a woman in a hoop skirt into the woods on the south east side of the cemetery.

Haunted House
Columbus: House at west corner of SR 11 and CR W200S.

Visitors hear noises. Metallic clangs heard throughout home, especially on first floor. Whispers from male and female voices are also heard.

Haw Creek Baptist Cemetery
Hope: CR S200E at E. Stafford Rd.

Shadow people dart between headstones. One investigator was chased by a shadow figure through the cemetery and back to a nearby church. A vortex and white apparitions have also surprised visitors.

North High School
Columbus: 1400 25th St.

A child named "Mikey" was run down by a buggy on a road that used to be where the school is now. The auditorium is believed to be exactly where he was killed. Mikey runs on the stage, in the sound booth and up on the catwalk. He also turns lights on and off.

Old St. Louis Cemetery
Hope: South of 800 N on 670 E

Visitors captured orbs on film and video. One investigator left hurriedly after he saw a group of transparent people carrying a wooden coffin .

Petersville House
Petersville: Unknown. Rumored to have burned.

Orbs and a bright white female figure were seen at this location. The exact location of this house is unknown, but it is suggested that it was located anywhere from downtown Petersville to any number of empty country lots.

Quality Machine and Tool
Columbus: 1201 Michigan Ave.

An employee hung himself over a failed relationship with a woman. Employees and customers have seen his shadowy figure as well as other spirits. Employees find that things go missing, but are returned to odd places.

Roberts Cemetery
Edinburgh: CR W1200S east of CR S500W (east of Edinburgh) Bartholomew County/ Shelby County line.

Investigators captured orbs on film. An EVP of a woman asking where her husband has been heard.

Seventeenth Street Railroad Bridge
Columbus: Go into the park at the end of 17th St. Walk the path leading into the woods. You will see a tunnel that goes under the tracks with a steep gravel incline. Climb to the top of the tracks and the bridge will be to your right.

A woman in the 1920s had an illegitimate child and was driven to throw herself and her child off the bridge. They found her body but not the baby's body. A creature with two legs and yellow eyes haunts the bridge. Sometimes the cries of a baby can be heard. During a full moon the mother of the baby appears and she calls out to her baby. People report footsteps following them through the area.

BENTON COUNTY

Adams Mill / Adams Mill Bridge
Bolivar (near Cutler): Between SR 18 and SR 26; .5 miles east of Cutler on CR 50E

While this area has an annual Halloween party with haunted trails, some non-staged paranormal activity also occurs here. Psychics claim the area is a portal that allows spirits to cross between their world and ours. Ghost hunters have captured voices heard calling for help and investigators heard a man say "Are you there, Josie?" Investigators have also taken several pictures in which demons and faces have appeared. EVPs of spirits talking to investigators have also been reported. Also, a woman walks across the water and comes toward you. Down the stairs, into the woods, and across the Adams Mill bridge is a memorial. The woman who walks on the water is rumored to be buried at the memorial.

Built in 1845, this mill was originally called Wildcat Mills because of its location on Wildcat Creek. By 1913, this water-only milling operation was able to produce enough electricity to power Cutler, Sedalia, and Rossville. The bridge was built in 1872. The building is open for tours and features a slanting chimney that starts in a lower level office and continues all the way to the roof of the structure. The ownership and focus of the mill has recently changed, and they may no longer permit investigations to come in and set up equipment.

Fowler Theatre
Fowler: 111 E. 5th St.

Currently under restoration, this 1940s building entertained theater goers for 60 years. Patrons report feelings of being watched and seeing a gray-haired man. Another gray colored man in a fedora is seen in the lobby. Some people believe it is Dick Vlastos, the original owner of the building.

St. Anthony Cemetery
Earl Park: 7048 N. CR 200W

According to legend, this settler cemetery is home to a mist. Sometimes it takes the shape of an 8-9 ft tall, white bearded man who carries a large stick or club. This man is believed to be the ghost of a robber who killed another man for his money. He motions for you to come closer. If you don't approach him, he will come after you with his weapon. Although St. Anthony's Cemetery is not conclusively the cemetery, a man with a white beard has been seen at this location sans gun.

BLACKFORD COUNTY

Asbury Chapel
Montpelier: 8022 W 1100 S
(aka United Methodist Church)

Investigators caught unexplainable bright red, green, and white strands of light. Additionally strange blue, white, red, and green orbs were also captured. Red mists seeped out of the ground. A man who was not part of the investigation was surrounded by red light.

Montpelier
Montpelier: Montpelier town, especially around CR 800 N

A blond bank robber killed in June 1959 haunts the town. He's seen in various spots by law enforcement and private citizens. Usually he is seen trying to break into buildings. His apparition is solid as if he is still among the living. He wears jeans, white tennis shoes, a jean jacket or a leather jacket. When he's chased, he simply disappears. Police have chased this phantom for years.

BOONE
COUNTY

302 East Church Street
Thorntown: 302 E. Church St.

This second Empire home haunted by resident spirits who push visitors down stairs. Locals see lights from uncovered windows although there is no electricity connected to the home.

1424 Park Drive
Lebanon: 1424 Park Dr.

The ghost of a woman named Alexa haunts this home. It is believed she was murdered and buried in the sump pump well. She walks through the house and the basement as though she still lived there. This residual haunting seems to take place in the 1970s judging from her clothes. She is described as Latino and enjoys pets, especially cats.

Two other spirits inhabit the house. Jacob, a young boy sits in the bathroom and cries. Frank, a poltergeist who does not like the other two spirits, haunts the basement and throws things.

Additionally, a dark presence of an older man haunts the back yard. He looks in the windows from time to time and dislikes a messy yard.

7629 Stonegate Lane
Zionsville: 7629 Stonegate Lane

The Carolina Restaurant purchased an antique bar that is haunted by the spirit of a female bartender. She changes channels and music. She also enjoys making the lights flicker.

Abner Longley Park
Lebanon: 1601 Longley Drive

Abner Longley Park was named for the founder of Lebanon. Follow the trail into the woods. People into the occult have set up an altar of sorts. A negative presence permeates the woods. Dark, sinister shadow figures appear and follow visitors. One visitor was scratched across the face.

Boone County Courthouse
Lebanon: Bounded by SR 32, W. Main St., N. Meridian St., and W. Washington St.

Public hangings were held here. People hear the ghosts of several hanged victims screaming. Investigators see the corpses and ropes in mid-air, hear screaming and feel cold ghosts of wind in the basement.

Brown's Wonder Cemetery
Elizaville: Elizaville Rd. and 300 N

Since 1924, a seven foot tall man is seen between Elizaville and Lebanon. He is seen also in Brown's Wonder Cemetery. Legend says he is looking for something but can't find it. He has no issues with trying to take you back to where ever he stays. One evening, a visitor reported seeing the man and before he could move, talk, or leave, the mysterious figure came toward him. That is all the visitor remembered until he woke up, laid out on a grave in the cemetery. Digital movie and photo cameras with fresh batteries go dead.

Country Side Antiques
Thorntown: 4889 N. US 52

A customer swears that she went into this location and saw a series of pictures of a family ranging from the parents in high school to their wedding and the arrival of their children. She said she wanted to buy just a couple pictures but was overwhelmed with sadness when she picked just the ones she wanted that she put them down and refused to buy them. As she walked through the store, she was followed by one of the children in the picture and the boy held her hand.

Holiday Drive Bridge
(aka Screaming Bridge)
Zionsville: Located on the left side off of North Michigan Rd. past Willow Rd. Turn left on Neal Rd. (It is called Neal Rd., O'Neal Rd., and Holiday Rd.)

A lynching by the KKK took place on this isolated bridge. Screams, believed to be from the hanged man sound out in the late night.

Intersection of US 421 and SR 32
Lebanon: Intersection of SR 421 and SR 32

Several nuns died in a car accident. Investigators have seen their dark figures in a straight line moving from one side of the road to the others. One investigator was driving to the intersection when a truck in front of him slammed its brakes on. She didn't think she would be able to stop in time. She saw the nuns walk in between her car and the back of the truck. Her car immediately came to a dead stop.

Oak Hill Cemetery
Lebanon: Off E. Main St. south of E. Washington St.
(See Sylvia Likens, Indianapolis, Marion Co.)

The ghost of Sylvia Likens can be seen here. Sylvia was brutally killed in Indianapolis while in the care of the Baniszewski family. She was beaten and tortured for many months before her death. Sylvia walks through the cemetery and sometime leaves it, walking toward Indianapolis. Some people speculate she's walking back for revenge, although many of her torturers are long since dead. Other people theorize she's walking home to her biological family.

Old Indiana Fun Park
Thorntown: Intersection of SR 47 and I-65. Go west on to CR N350W and Kent Rd. (CR 700N)

Emily Hunt was paralyzed from the chest down and her grandmother, Nancy Jones, was killed after a train derailed at Old Indiana Fun Park. After a lengthy legal battle, the park closed. Today, it is a wildlife preserve.

Investigators report a residual haunting of the event with screams heard. In December 2007 a hunter saw "an older woman in white" walking through the park. He watched her come closer to him and as the hazy figure approached, she smiled and disappeared.

Old Lebanon High School
Lebanon:327 N Lebanon St.

Visitors claim to be trapped inside the building for several minutes to several hours at a time. Some people believe the building is conducive to time travel as they have seen people in clothes and heard music from other time periods.

Old Thorntown Graveyard
Thorntown: Bevel Rd. between N. Front St. and E. Pearl St.

People have been punched, scratched and touched in this cemetery. EVPs recorded document some unfriendly spirits asking people to leave "or else".

Witham Hospital
Lebanon: Hospital is at 2605 N. Lebanon St. The old Nurse's School is at 1122 N. Lebanon St. on the west side of the road.

Conceived in 1915, Witham hospital has been providing healthcare to the community for over 100 years. Staff and visitors report the ghosts of patient and former employees roaming the halls and in the old nurse's building, phantom nurses are seen often. Additionally, lights are said to turn off and on regularly with no explanation.

BROWN
COUNTY

Podunk (aka Brown County State Park)

Nashville: Brown Co. State Park off Bond Cemetery Rd.
(See also Bargersville, Johnson Co.)
(aka Brown County State Park)

A baby crawls on the road and sometimes it laughs and cries. Emotional outbursts, physical touches (pushing and scratching) plague visitors. One version of the stories at this location includes a phantom truck that will follow you. Many people have reportedly seen this truck and lights that appear and disappear just as quickly. Visitors have taken photos of strange mists and half apparitions. One investigator claims to have taken a picture of a satyr.

Story Inn

Nashville: 6404 S. SR 135

The Story Inn used to be a general store in what was once Storyville. Dr. George Story established the small town in 1851. The original structure burned down in 1915 and was rebuilt. Today, Story Inn is a restaurant, as well as four bed and breakfast units. It is also comprised of ten other little cottages.

Several paranormal events occur regularly at this location and many ghost hunters spend the night at the inn. In the Blue Lady room, one can summon the spirit by turning on a blue light next to the bed. She primps at the dresser. She interacts with guests, and has clawed one man in the shower. The Blue Lady also whispers to guests and hypnotizes them with her lovely blue eyes. Other occurrences include objects moving such as coffee pots and candles. Pictures slide off walls, tables, and shelves. Smells of baby powder and cherry tobacco fill the air. Visitors hear chatting and footsteps upstairs when no one is around. Guests experience severe temperature drops. Wine was thrown in the owner's face. A spectral man in brown has been seen in the kitchen. People are regularly pinched and poked. The staff hears whispers throughout the inn. Visitors and investigators report orbs and a picture captured a transparent woman looking out a window.

CARRROL L
COUNTY

Ball Hill Cemetery

Flora: West of IN 75 on CR W300S between CR S100W and CR S150W

Investigators report several types of mists, colored orbs, and temperature in this pioneer cemetery. During the day, visitors record wisps of white and grey mists. During the evening hours visitors might catch a white or even purple mist.

Old Flora Cemetery

Flora: End of Green Acre Dr. (The road also has a Flora Cemetery sign)

Flashes of light and colored streaks of spirit energy are seen regularly in the cemetery.

Old Flora School

Flora: Main Street east of Division St.

Voices can be heard asking questions if you can hear them. Levitating equipment were witnessed in the school. Locals believe that the people in the old graveyard behind it inhabit the school.

Old Sycamore Haunted Bridge

Burlington: West of US 31 in Kokomo. Take Sycamore Rd. past Malfalfa Rd. (CR N300W). The road will curve to the right onto Sycamore Lane but you want to take Sycamore Rd. (CR W80N). This road eventually curves around and turns into CR W00NS. At CR S440W turn left to get to the bridge.

Drive your car over the bridge, and a phantom white car will chase you to dish out death if it catches you. If you go, be sure to look for the bullet marks on the bridge- legend has it a jealous boyfriend shot at his girlfriend and her new boyfriend, killing them both. The white car appears on any given night. The murdered couple makes appearances in late May and in September.

CASS
COUNTY

Longcliff
Logansport: 1098 S. SR 25
(aka Logansport State Hospital- aka Northern Indiana Hospital for the Insane)

Modeled after Central State, this hospital opened its doors in 1888. In its heyday, the facility had in/out patient facilities, and surgeries. It produced its own food and was a small town onto itself.

Miami Cemetery
Adamsboro: East of S. Eel River Rd. on CR W100N

Two children who are buried here can be seen sitting beside their headstones. Sometimes they call to each other. Other times investigators have reported seeing them run and play tag.

Mount Hope Cemetery
Logansport: 1800 Grant St.

Visitors experience the sounds of horses' hoofbeats and someone whistling.

Shiloh Church
Logansport: 1047 N. CR 350W

A headless horseman haunts the area. If you circle the church and look in the basement windows, you will see an unkempt girl watching you.

Water Street
Logansport: West of Logansport. Take Water St. west (it turns into Delaware Rd.) The pond is on the left side of the road between Holland St. and Kiesling Rd.
(aka Delaware Rd. swimming hole)

This man-made pond is used by local kids for swimming. At one time, a child drowned in the pond. Several people report seeing a transparent little boy and little girl walking next to the pond and running around it, giggling. However, when the visitors approached, the children disappeared.

CLARK COUNTY

10 Penny Bridge

Charlestown: Tunnel Mill Rd.
(aka Tunnel Mill Road Bridge)

A man died on the bridge. As the story goes if you put 10 pennies on the bridge in a straight line (not stacked) the pennies will scatter over the bridge or disappear.

Blackston Mill Road

Utica: Blackston Mill Rd. (where road dips)
(aka Deadman's Hollow)

This road was the site where illegal slaves were hanged. It is called Deadman's Hollow because a man was found dead in the area. Investigators hear the scrape of rope on trees, hear unearthly moans and see several men hanging in the trees. When they saw these apparitions, it was as if they were in a time warp and they could see the crowd of people watching them hang.

Brick Church Road Cemetery

Sellersburg: Brick Church Rd. east of Tom Combs Rd.

This cemetery has a glowing green tombstone. Depending on the source of your story, the tombstone that glows changes throughout the cemetery. Some investigators have reported seeing transparent cloaked figures in the church and cemetery during the day and night.

Census Bureau Warehouses

Jeffersonville: 1201 E 10th St.

These buildings are full of paranormal activity. Boxes of heavy paper fall as if feather-light. Radios turn on and lights turn off and on at will. Local history indicates that the area was a holding camp for Germans during WWII and investigators have captured EVPs of men speaking German. Security guards sometimes refuse to go into buildings. (B66 was the infirmary and supposedly the most haunted.)

Charlestown High School

Charlestown: 1 Pirate Place
A girl fell from the catwalk and now haunts the auditorium. She turns lights off and on and walks though the auditorium. You can hear her footsteps on the floor and on the catwalk.

Colgate Palmolive Factory

Clarksville: 1410 S. Clark Blvd.

This factory used to be Indiana State Prison South. Prisoners were mistreated and the female inmates were prostituted to guards and prisoners. The basement is haunted by these prisoners. Apparitions of women chase you through the basement. Some male and female investigators have been scratched by unseen hands.

Dan's Run

Henryville: Corner of Pixley Knob Rd. and Mountain Grove Rd.

Daniel Guthrie was murdered and buried near Pixley Knob Road and Cemetery Hill (see Mountain Grove Cemetery entry). For over a year, the body remained there until it was found and reburied in Mt. Zion Cemetery. The original burial hole is about four feet deep and still can be seen near the edge of the woods.

People who live in the area see a young man with a handlebar moustache. Additionally, people in the area hear footsteps and experience other paranormal activity, including finding footprints outside windows, muddy shoe prints appearing inside the house, objects levitating and male voices whispering. Some investigators believe the negative energy from Dan's unsolved murder has created a portal for paranormal activity.

Investigators have captured EVPs with a male voice crying out for help and screaming until his voice fades away. Another similar EVP reveals a scream that is accentuated with what sounds like a knife being "pulled in and out of a pumpkin". Visitors to the creek have heard disembodied voices, and have seen mysterious shadows crossing the road in front of headlights at night, although no one is seen. One person ran away from the creek because she heard growling nearby. This unseen growling beast followed closely behind until the woman heard it give a "mournful cry" and then it was silent.

Haymaker House

Charlestown: 14 E. Market St.

Built by Isaac Haymaker around 1870, this home belonged to the family for many years. Close knit as this community is, the families stayed around Charlestown. Many are buried in the local cemetery. can be found in the local cemetery. Several family members had their funerals conducted in the home.

The sound of glass, such as a bottle, falling and rolling, is heard. Pets avoid the upstairs. Banging has been heard in the dining room. Lights turn mysteriously on and off, and light fixtures sway in an absent breeze. Temperatures change from hot to cold. Residents hear their names called although no one is around. The front porch swing sways with invisible visitors while no wind is felt. Items fall from shelves and out of locked cabinets. Phantom figures move around the back yard. Voices are heard in the kitchen. Moans as if someone is in pain are heard. Shades in the home all rolled up at the same time; another time, they went up, down, up, as if someone was pulling them manually. A former owner heard the phone ring and heard strange music playing on the answering machine. Even after she turned it off and unplugged it, the music continued.

Howard Steamboat Museum
Clarksville : 1101 E Market St.

James Howard stands in the basement wearing a top hat.

Jeffersonville High School
Jeffersonville: 2315 Allison Ln.

A woman roams the auditorium. She sits in a corner and when she is spoken to, she stares at you and disappears. Additionally, items in the auditorium move and people have been pushed and have fallen. At one time a construction worker was killed by falling off a ladder- some people believe he was pushed. He's been seen on a ladder on the right side of the auditorium.

Mountain Grove Cemetery
(aka Cemetery Hill)
Henryville: Corner of Pixley Knob Rd. and Mountain Grove Rd.

(See Dan's Run entry, Henryville, Clark Co.)

Investigators hear voices hissing incoherent words. Visitors speculate that this manifestation could be in connection with some of the activity from Dan's Run.

Mount Zion Cemetery
Henryville: At the east end of Henryville Bluelick Rd. and Mt. Zion Rd.

A green hazy lady walks through Mt. Zion Cemetery, sometimes jumping on cars and leaving a sticky residue. She is said to be a woman who was killed on Blue Lick Road after a car accident.

Old Man Ike's
Sellersburg: Stricker Road across from a meat processing facility; near the old Essroc Cement Corp.

Supposedly a man named Ike killed family members in the house. Ike worked at the meat facility and came home one day and chopped his family with a cleaver. Screams are heard at all hours of the day and night.

St. Joe Road Cemetery
Sellersburg: SR 111 east on St. Joe Rd.

There is a hanging tree in the middle of the cemetery. At night, you can see one, or several men hanging from it.

Sunset Grill Restaurant
Clarksville: 318 W. Lewis and Clark Pkwy.
(aka Strattos)

This restaurant was formerly the McCullough Steak House, but was a family home. Originally, guests and employees have heard weird noises in the building. Some mornings employees will come in the restaurant, and all the light bulbs will be unscrewed and sitting on the tables.

Theatre X
Utica : 4505 US 31 East
(Note: Theatre X is an adult entertainment venue.)

A mysterious, transparent man in old work clothes shuffles through the theater. Several of the patrons have also seen a pale woman with blond hair walk near the booths and disappear before their eyes.

Witches Castle
Utica: Upper River Rd. near Quarry Bluff
(aka Mistletoe Falls)

Allegedly witches lived in the house and a group of townspeople ran them out. A transparent apparition of a 7-8 year old girl has been seen and her laugh is heard in the woods. She is also seen as a mist in the home. She has long black hair that covers her face. Several sources claim this area is where Shanda Sharer died but this is untrue.

In a small shack behind the home: Male and female voices are heard. Many apparitions are seen peering out. Two investigators saw apparitions in the shack and its door opened. Two apparitions came out and started walking toward the investigators. Both of them (whether nerves or fact) felt that is was a malevolent force coming toward them and they ran away.

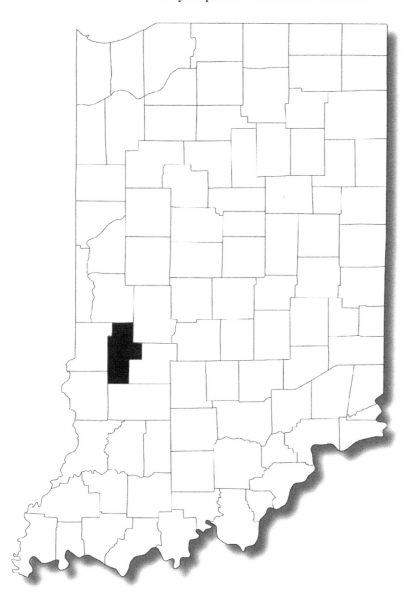

CLAY
COUNTY

Carpenters Cemetery

Brazil: West of SR340 and US40 on CR675. Located next to a jog in the road.
(aka 100 Steps Cemetery)

This cemetery dates back to the late 1860s. At night, count the steps as you ascend to the top of the cemetery. When you've reached 100 the old caretaker will float by you in a semi-transparent state. Some versions of this story say he will predict the future for you. He tells you to leave. If you count the same amount of stairs going back down, your future is supposed to be good. Otherwise, you might be joining the caretaker on the other side! If you avoid the steps, an unknown force pushes people and leaves handprints (or other marks) on them. During the day, you won't count 100 steps. However, visitors witness the figure of a slender woman in a white gown during the day.Strange, misty shapes appear on film.

Haunted Church

Brazil: 300W, in the opposite direction from Spooklight Hill
(See Spooklight Hill, Brazil, Clay Co.)

Lights and mysterious phantoms roam the church. Additionally, visitors feel chilling breezes when the trees are perfectly still.

Hell's Gate

Brazil: Take IN 59 north to CR1350. Continue on this road until you reach Rock Run Rd. Follow Rock Run Rd. until it turns. At the turn you should see the Hell's Gate.

For years, this old railroad underpass has been the source of legends for years. The most common one claims that a train crashed at the location killing, everyone. If you go through the tunnel and wait 10 minutes, a supposed method of death is scribbled on the wall. Mists and orbs collect in pictures. Numerous psychics, the curious, and investigators visit the spot in hopes of finding proof of paranormal activity. Some psychic have violent feelings towards themselves and the area in general. Other people hear screams, laughing, and loud crashes. EVPs of children crying and women speaking have been recorded.

Masonic Lodge

Brazil: Southwest corner of Sherfey and Jackson Streets
(aka Blue Lodge of Masons)

A singing ghost haunts the one time Masonic Lodge. Originally called "the Blue Lodge of Masons", visitors have been pulled, pushed, and touched a variety of times in a variety of places.

The Plantation

Brazil: From the SR 59 and SR 42 intersection, take SR 42 East about 7 miles until you come across Boy Scout Road. Turn north on this road and go about 1.2 miles and you will come to a lane on your right side.

The old shed to the left of the lane leads you back to the ruins of an old home and out buildings. At one time the barns had lofts that were said to be home to the ghosts of the people who used to live at the home. Largely friendly in nature, these ghosts would be doing work in the barn. If they saw you, they would smile, stare and then return to their work.

Poland Chapel

Poland: E. Ohio and Cherry Sts.
(aka Poland Cemetery)

A five year old boy buried here was taken over by "demons"- or at least he began speaking in tongues and acting age-inappropriately. His picture on his gravestone is said to have horns. Investigators who believe the child was possessed by demons think the physical manifestation occurred both inside and outside the child. Pictures taken at the cemetery do seem to have some anomalies, including the outline of horns, on his headstone, and the faces of the investigators are blurred. The woods to the rear of the cemetery are home to several transparent figures. including children, men and women. They do not interact, but walk slowly through the trees at night.

Spook Light Hill

Brazil: Take IN 59 north out of Brazil. About 5 miles out you will come to a gravel road that takes you to Carbon. Turn right. On this road, there are three hills. Go to the third and look back at the second. Some people believe any of these hills is Spooklight Hill.

Because this is legend, many people can't agree which of the three hills is the real Spook Light Hill. As the story goes, a ghostly father is looking for his daughter's head. She was decapitated in a car accident or a buggy accident. He appears in the form of a light coming down the road or in the woods. Others have seen him as a shadow figure walking to the left or right of the hill. For a couple of visitors, the man has been known to ask if you've seen her head. On occasion, the girl herself makes an appearance as a headless apparition to the west.

Zion Gummere Cemetery

Brazil: Zion Church Rd. between CR525 and CR100.
(aka Zion Church Cemetery)

A spectre appears and tells you to go back the way you came. Local people believe this is a bad omen. Investigators believe this is someone trying to warn you about something that has happened in the past. Unexplained lights, sensing presences, and hearing whispers are also a part of the paranormal activity here.

CLINTON
COUNTY

Clinton County Historical Society and Museum

Frankfort: 301 E. Clinton St.

(aka Old Stoney)

People hear voices and footsteps as well as see shadows and mysterious orbs.

Farmers Gravel Road

Frankfort: Farmers Gravel Rd.

In the early 1920s a school bus full of children was involved in an accident. Everyone on board died. If you stop and put your car in neutral, children push you up the hill (presumably to have you go down the hill and into the river). After, handprints are visible on your car.

Hamilton Road

Mulberry: Take SR 38 to Mulberry and CR 900W. If you are coming from Lafayette, go right on it and go through the next stop sign, which is Hamilton Rd. Three one-lane bridges are on this road. When you get to the third bridge, stop and flash your lights 4 times.

A church caught fire on this road in the 1800s and everyone inside was killed. Also, a set of railroad tracks are haunted by a boy named Danny, who was killed in the early 1910s. A cemetery near the railroad tracks is also haunted.

At the eastern-most bridge, you may be chased by an apparition of a man. Sometimes he's seen as a shadow and other times as a solid form. Park at the back of the cemetery, and you'll see flames from the woods and smell smoke. Visit the tracks, and you'll hear a train whistle and a very loud noise as if the train hit something. Sometimes Danny can be seen walking along the tracks as a transparent glowing apparition.

Main Street Pub and Eatery

Frankfort: 58 N. Main St. Frankfort (West side of courthouse)

A ghostly man sits at the bar. A chandelier light on the stairway to the upper floor swings wildly though no one can reach it. Lights turn off and on. Employees hear ghostly voices in the kitchen, back hallway, and upper floor as though unseen people are having a conversation.

Providence Cemetery

Mulberry: CR N580W outside of Mulberry

The church burned down years ago. Now, the church mysteriously reappears and screams are heard about 2 a.m. Visitors observe mists and experience physical contact (touches on neck, arms and shoulders).

Sleepy Hollow

Frankfort: Take CR 600W off Mulberry Jefferson Rd. (Wildcat Creek Bridge)
(aka Haunted Railroad Bridge/Trestle)

Kids were killed at this location. Their handprints appear on your car. The wooden railroad bridge is guarded by the ghosts of two dogs and a man. The man, who appears as a shadow figure, chases you out with the dogs.

A woman from the 1940s who killed herself because her husband was cheating on her. She ran in front of the train. On foggy and cold nights, you see her reenact this event and hear her scream as the unseen train hits her.

CRAWFORD
COUNTY

Carl Smith House
Marengo: Burned and razed. Used to be next to the post office.

Former owners report lights off and on. The house is rumored to be a portal. These events are attributed to many people dying in the home and area surrounding it, it burned and was razed.

Devil's Washboard
Milltown: E Rothrocks Mill Rd. east of Burgess Circle Rd. NW

Considered magical by New Age believers, people come from far and wide to capture a little of the water that flows through this area and give praise for the area. Because of these activities. Visitors report many shadows, fairies and other occurrences, due to these activities.

Marengo Caves
Marengo: IN 64 to SR 64 (400 East SR 64)

Two children, Orris and Blanche Heistand, found the cave in 1883. Public tours began that year. Men with pickaxes and work clothes have been seen in the cave. Investigators believe them to be diamond hunters who were killed shortly after the cave opened.

Old English
Old English: US 64 SW of N. Brownstown Rd.
(precursor to English, Indiana)

The Federal government moved Old English because it was in a flood plain. During the move, the old town was abandoned. All that is left are a few old houses and buildings and a new golf course. Investigations have uncovered paranormal activity in the woods behind the golf course. Fairies and will-o'-the-wisp abound in the trees and lush greenery. The fairies appear at twilight with the lights and they dance through the trees. The lights often burn brightly and as one comes closer to them, both they and the fairies disappear.

Proctor House
Proctorville: Old 64 east of Marengo
(and Proctor House Cemetery; aka Woods Cemetery)

This house was built by William Proctor in 1832. He operated a stage coach stop, store and post office here. The Crawford County Historical Society currently owns and maintains the building.

Visitors report pokes by unseen fingers. One volunteer remembers hearing children giggling on the second floor. When she went to investigate, she found one of the upper rooms in disarray. She left to get another volunteer and when she returned, the room was back to its proper state.

Shoe Tree
Milltown: 3826 S. Devils Hollow Rd.

Stories abound about this shoe tree that has been around for at least 60 years. Supposedly Larry Bird has a pair of shoes hanging from the tree. It was burned by lightening a few years ago. Maxine McFelea Archibald, who owns Maxine's Market in Milltown made signs to direct people to the location. However, nothing on the signs indicate the paranormal activity. Shadow figures and a child lit by a bright light walk down the road near the tree.

Wyandotte Caves
Marengo: Harrison-Crawford State Forest (off IN 462)

Henry Rothrock hired three men to dig trenches so visitors could come to the caves. He only saw the men except on payday. Andrew, Henry's 19 year old son, would spend hours exploring the caves. Work was progressing nicely and a tour guide decided to explore up to where they'd finished. He found a printing press for counterfeiting. The sheriff caught two of the three men, but the third holed up in the caves. After weeks of armed guarding, they assumed he was dead. Some people believe that the voices heard come from at least one of the men from the counterfeiting ring.

Years later, two men decided to explore the caves. They went very far into the caves and their oil lamp was extinguished by water. For three days they tried to figure a way out. Suddenly, a bright light shone in front of them and a young man guided them out. The men were so grateful they vowed to return and give him some sort of present. When they did return, they found no one at the cave. They went to the Rothrock home, which was the nearest home and asked about the young man. Rothrock told them that his son had been diagnosed with histoplasmosis- a condition that occurs from excessive exposure to bat droppings. Rothrock explained that Andrew couldn't be the person that helped them as he died in the cave when Rothrock took him in one last time. However, he changed his mind when the men pointed to a picture of his son, taken shortly before his death, and identified him. The light is still seen from time to time at the caves.

Wyandotte Woods Cemetery
Marengo: Harrison-Crawford State Forest (off IN 462)

The gate to the cemetery is known to hit visitors as they enter or exit. Campers and investigators report a dark figure jogging through the woods at night.

DAVIESS COUNTY

Alfordsville High School
Alfordsville: Unknown

Alfordsville doesn't have a school. Unless it is another school in the area or a school that burned down some time ago, the story of kids reported playing in a gym at night is pure legend.

Blue Hole
Washington: East of CR N300W (Oak Grove Rd.) along the railroad tracks about 1.25 miles west of town

Created during the flood of 1875, it remained quiet until March 27, 1913 when the Baltimore and Ohio work train moved the trestle that went over the blue hole. Four of the six men in Locomotive #401 died in the water. Within a half hour of this accident, the bridge over the West Fork of the White River collapsed leaving a total of 20 men trapped between the two bridges. On April 6, 1913 rescue crews found Locomotive #401. In Oak Grove Cemetery, a marker commemorates this event.

The Blue Hole is said to be bottomless, although some people believe it has a quicksand bottom. Today many people hear screams and cries for help coming from the area in which the accidents occurred.

Fairview Cemetery
Elnora: Off of SR 57 on CR 1500N

There are reports of several glowing tombstones.

Private Home
Alfordsville: Outside of town on Sugar Creek

A man killed his entire family and was found dead two days later. It appeared as if someone came back and killed him. Speculation is that the ghosts of his whole family came back to murder him. The house is full of cold spots even in the heat of summer.

William Hackler Farm
Odon: Home torn down by former owners

In 1941 the Hackler family experienced 28 random fires. They started from walls, a mattress, books, calendars, and other places. In one three hour period, there were nine separate fires. Firefighters from two communities waited to extinguish the flames. The house had neither electricity nor open flames to ignite them. During the time of the fire, the family's whereabouts was monitored. Traveler's Insurance Company paid for the damages stating they covered fires even of "supernatural origin".

DEARBORN
COUNTY

Greendale Cemetery

Lawrenceburg: Greendale Cemetery Association is across the street from the cemetery at 886 Nowlin Ave.

Milk white and grey figures walk by the Tebbs family graves. Visitors feel watched, cold and uneasy.

Guilford Park

Guilford: SW of SR 1 off of Main St. (York St.)
(Note: This location is largely credited to Sunman, Indiana, but Guilford Park is in Guilford, Indiana)

A woman was hit by train and knocked into creek next to the tracks. Investigators were unable to get her out of the creek because it started to rain. Her body was washed away and never found. Visitors hear her horrific cries and the sound of impact from the train.

Laughery Creek Road

Dearborn County: Laughery Creek Rd. is between SR56 (Ohio Scenic Byway) and SR 262

In 1941 Harvey Sellars discovered the body of his neighbor, Johnston Agrue and his eleven year old granddaughter, Mary Elizabeth in the barn. When authorities arrived, they found Mrs. Agrue in the kitchen-dead. A son, Leo, was later found dead on a hillside and his brother, William was found shot in the back near Wilson School House. A son-in-law, Virginius "Dink" Carter was held for questioning. Later, he admitted to having dinner with the family, arguing with the sons and shooting the family. In 1942 he was eventually executed by electrocution at Michigan City.

From the time of the family's death, the area has been disturbed by their residual haunting. Twenty-eight years later, the Agrue house burned to the ground. Laughery Creek Rd. remains haunted.

Lesko Park

Aurora: SR 56

Mary Enzweiler drowned herself in the river on January 31, 2007. She cries and walks toward the river from the park.

Riverview Cemetery

Aurora: 3635 E. Laughery Creek Rd.
(See Laughery Creek Road, Dearborn County, Dearborn Co.)

Virginius "Dink" Carter killed the Argue family and is buried here. His spirit is seen reenacting the murders. He is buried less than 100 feet from where he shot two of the family members.

Whiskey's Restaurant
Lawrenceburg: 334 E. Front St.

This family owned restaurant was originally two houses and later a button factory. One of the women who lived in the home now haunts the Malt Room. The staff feels apron strings tugged and smells the scent of perfume in the back of the restaurant when no one is around.

DECATUR COUNTY

Billings School

Greensburg: 314 W. Washington St. Old West End School has been razed.
(property housed Old West End School)
(Note: Now the area is a parking lot and has a building that houses city offices.)

The school was built in 1863. Later a mechanic died in the building. For many years, children lived in fear of being sent to the basement for punishment. They all knew the man continued to prowl the area. Some believe this ghost left when the Billings School was built in place of the Old West End School. Some staff and visitors believe the mechanic still roams the halls. A strange man dressed in work clothes walks in several halls. Visitors hear phantom footsteps.

Greensburg Courthouse

Greensburg: 150 Courthouse Sq.

Many staff and visitors to the courthouse feel the presence of a man. Other staff members working late at night experience breezes passing them or being touched by the spirit. In the basement, an ashtray moves on its own. The staff hears thuds and bumps around the stairway to the basement. In 1895 a janitor, Jack Thompson, was found dead on the stairs leading to the basement. Other people feel that the spirit may be a man who was hanged in 1879 by a mob, a block away. Another spirit has been seen on the second floor of the courthouse. A gentle looking woman in 1920s clothing has been seen sitting by several of the windows in the courthouse. When asked by staff if they can help her, she smiles, shakes her head sadly and disappears.

New Point Bridge

Greensburg: SR 46 (E Main St.) as you leave Greensburg

Like many bridges in Indiana, this bridge has a man encased in cement within a bridge support. He waves a lantern at night.

Sandusky Bridge

Greensburg: SR 3 just south of CR W680N

Like many bridges in Indiana, this bridge has a man encased in cement within a bridge support. He waves a lantern at night.

Scheidler Brothers Decorating

Greensburg: 318 S. East St.
(See South Park Cemetery entry, Greensburg, Decautur Co.)

Visitors and staff feel a presence in the building. Some speculate this presence may be connected to the South Park Cemetery ghost.

South Park Cemetery

Greensburg: On East St., south of E. McKee St. shortly before South Park Cemetery

On the historic stone bridge over Gas Creek, a well dressed man in a long silk top coat, and high silk hat appears to visitors. Sometimes they speak in passing to each other, but when people turn back to see the man again, they find he's disappeared. People speculate that this ghost could be President Lincoln visiting South Park Cemetery and Soldier's Circle. Activity usually happens at night, on foggy, cold nights, but also occurs (albeit less frequently) during the day.

Letts (town)

A baby is seen crawling and crying for its mother.

New Harris City (town)

A farmer is seen walking his bulls in the fields.

Old Railroad Bridge over Flat Rock River

St. Paul: Railroad tracks go next to E. Washington St. go SE over bridge

A man fell from the bridge during construction and died. A lantern moves back and forth on the bridge. Visitors also hear moans.

DEKALB
COUNTY

Abandoned farm

Butler: CR 75A north of SR 46 second curve before CR 42. Overgrown but a small path can be see back to the ruins. House has collapsed and may be unsafe. Close to Land of Moses/Gypsies Hill.

(See Land of Moses/Gypsy Hill, Butler, DeKalb Co.)

Shadow figures cross the road in front of cars and shape shift in the night air. Disembodied voices cry for help nightly. In the home, visitors are terrified by growling noises. A smell of rotting meat permeates the building.

One investigator walked through the backyard and heard "the most unholy laughter I've ever heard". Legend of this land is that two brothers lived on the property with their mother. One brother killed the other, and the mother hung herself in abject grief from a large oak tree in the back yard. Some visitors believe the sound of the rope is heard swinging from the tree and can be seen during the day and night.

Auburn Cord Duesenberg Museum

Auburn: 1600 S. Wayne St.

Mysterious footsteps and the smell of cigars haunt this building. The lights turn on and off by themselves. One staff member shut all the lights off and closed up the museum. Walking to the parking lot, the worker noticed the light in a former office was on. The worker went back into the museum and turned the light off. The next day, the museum staff received notice that the wife of the man who used to work in the office had died the previous evening.

Other interesting facts:
* Auburn Automobile Co. produced a model 666, known as "Satan's car."
* Race car driver, Scott Brayton donated a fully restored Italian Cisitalia. Weeks later, he died in a crash at the Indianapolis Motor Speedway.
* One of the cars donated to the museum is said to have been given to a daughter by her father. She later died in it.

Land of Moses

Butler: South of US 6 at CR 28 and CR 79.

(aka Gypsy Hill)
(See Abandoned Farm, Butler, DeKalb Co.)

Gypsies used to make camp here. According to a local legend, the gypsies kidnapped and raped a farmer's daughter, although it isn't clear if she died. Her father and other farmers killed the gypsies in retaliation. Over the next decade each farmer who participated was brutally killed with an axe. The spirits of the gypsies and farmers are said to haunt the area.

Investigations have uncovered EVPs that sound like screams and fighting. Moans and wails are also heard. Ethnic music has also been recorded when no music was playing at the time.

DELAWARE
COUNTY

1116 W. North Street

Muncie: 1116 W. North St.

Footsteps stomp up the back steps. In 1993-96, great evil spirits was sensed by the residents. They felt as something wanted in, but needed to be invited.

403 W. Washington Street

Muncie: 403 W. Washington St.

A man haunts the top of the stairs. He is believed to be Charlie, a man that died of old age in the mid-1980s. He turns lights off and on and growls in the dining room. Students who live there report feeling a hit to the front room like a car or something large crashed into it, but nothing is amiss. It was a loud enough noise and physical shock that several items on a bookshelf fell off. One person who lived there, Angie, seemed to have a good rapport with Charlie; however he didn't like her roommates. Ray, one of the roommates, would find his pencils missing. He wouldn't go into the dining room because of Charlie. Another roommate didn't last long either. When Angie moved, she invited him to come with her, but he didn't. Her boyfriend, now husband, felt Charlie on the stairs as an "ice cold breeze". The second time it happened he said "Excuse me, Charlie" and went around him. Charlie appears as a shadow at times.

Ball State University

Muncie: The university website has an excellent interactive map for finding these locations on campus.

- Edwards Hall: The elevator randomly stops on the 9th floor.
- Elliot Hall: A WWII veteran, Will Schamberg, was disfigured by burning during the war. When he returned to school, he hung himself on the fourth floor of Elliott Hall. He stirs cool breezes and walks through the halls. Students report hearing a table moved to the area where Will hung himself. EVPs are caught in the building and orbs found in pictures taken in the area of Will's death.
- North Quad: Mysterious footsteps follow lone visitors.
- Phi Sigma Kappa House: Ask any Phi Sig and they can tell you all about "Leonard".
- Shively Hall: Doors mysteriously lock.
- Statue of Beneficence (Benny): cries blood tears when a virgin graduates
- Underground Tunnels: These tunnels were used for food transportation between Elliot and Johnson Halls. A rapist haunts the tunnels. They are no longer in use for safety reasons.

Ball State University- Christy Woods

Muncie: West of the Cooper Science building on University Blvd.

Named for Dr. Otto Christy, a former member of the science faculty, this 17 acre tract of land is open to the public during the day. Used for biology studies, students and visitors alike report many types of hauntings. A girl in torn, ragged clothing is seen on the south end of the woods. Her hair is ratted and she is very dirty. She has a wild look in her eye as if she's trying to escape something. When approached, she disappears. As this area is well known for the natural setting, it is only fitting that creatures are also included in the haunts. Visitors report a satyr romping in the late evening and sprites dance in the darkness of the nature preserve. Some students use the trails to jog. One woman distinctly remembers running one early morning and the fog was thick. She went slower than normal but as she came upon a curve in the trail, she heard a voice say "Be careful!" She said thank you and turned to see who it was, but no one was there. She ran forward and called out, but no one answered.

Carole's Curve
Daleville: 6400 W. CR 550S
(aka Dead Man's Curve)

A little girl haunted the attic of this home. She switches lights on and off. Her laughter is heard often and she likes to move items to different places. She told one resident to get out of the house. The same resident started to make arrangements to leave and then pets started to die.

Guthrie Park
Muncie: South of CR 2600 on CR 3900

A girl drowned in the pond and she is said to reenact her death in the now empty pond on a regular basis.

Hotel Roberts
Muncie: 420 S. High St.

This hotel was built in 1922 by George Roberts. He commissioned Charles W. Nichol to make a "showplace of Muncie". Virtually every part of this historic hotel is haunted. Shadow figures are seen throughout the building. Specific rooms are haunted by different spirits. Hotel Roberts is a gem of paranormal activity, if not a gem of beauty. The most notable experience is that of a woman who was either thrown or fell out the window of one of the rooms. She is heard whispering and was captured on video walking through the suite. Additionally, she likes to play with investigation equipment by clicking buttons and tapping microphones.

(Note: This hotel closed in late 2006 and at this time has no plans for reopening. It may be turned into senior living facilities.)

Madison's
Muncie: 2617 S. Madison St.

A restaurant once known as the SkyLine, the former owner lived upstairs and died. He haunts the place and turns light off and on. Also, he is heard walking through the restaurant.

Muncie Central High School
Muncie: 801 N. Walnut St.

A boy disappeared in Muncie and later his cleaned bones were found in the elevator shaft. A small pocket knife was found nearby. He is often seen walking through the halls at night.

Muncie Civic Theatre
Muncie: 216 E. Main St.

Visitors see a solid apparition of a woman in the middle of the center and left hand sections of the balcony. Visitors also report a feeling of being watched. The sewing and costume rooms are also host to ghosts- staff and visitors see apparitions of both men and women, doors slam and equipment has an odd way of relocating.

Oakhurst Gardens
Muncie: Minnetrista Cultural Center; 1200 North Minnetrista Parkway

The gardens are part of the Ball family legacy. From time to time, a girl and her grandmother are seen playing with a doll house.

Shoe Tree
Albany: Edgewater Road

While on a walk, an old man saw something in an oak tree. When he looked closer, the demon in the tree cut his throat, killing him. If you touch this tree, the demon will kill you and take your shoes, putting them in the tree as a trophy.

Rail Road Tracks
Oakville: East of CR S50W The tracks are in the middle of town.

Slaves supposedly built this track, although Indiana was not a slave state. Dark apparitions are seen on the empty train tracks.

Shanholtzer House
Eaton: 2065 E. Eden Rd.
(aka Emery House)

This 1850s home was the first house in the township. At one time it was a blacksmith shop, a hardware store and a general store. One of the owners saw three people moving a piano from the living room to the parlor- when they didn't own a piano. A translucent spirit, nicknamed Fred, has been seen in the kitchen (which was being remodeled at the time). It is known that one person died on the property when it was a general store, although the building is no longer on the property. A man shot his father because he heard his dad had been molesting school children. In the early 1800s, a cemetery was located down the road from the house. Early in the 1900s two sisters looked out the window and saw the front gate swinging back and forth for 20 minutes. This was very odd to them as it was a weighted gate and there was no wind at the time. The property is next to a school. The two sisters walked home one evening after an event and knew they weren't alone.

Springport Train Depot

Springport: East of SR 3 on CR W800N. The depot is at the corner of W. Main St. and the railroad tracks.

This train station is haunted by the ghost of the old train station master. He is seen walking through the building.

Union Cemetery

Eaton: Corner of CR N100E and CR E1000N (Eaton Wheeling Pike)

Upon entering the cemetery, the temperature drops. Visitors smell fresh flowers when none are present. This scent is prevalent in February and March. An invisible entity pushes people in the cemetery.

Witches Circle

Daleville: South of old SR 67 on Honey Creek Rd., drive until you make a 90 degree turn right, when you make another 90 degree turn left, you'll see a path that will go uphill slightly. You'll see a circle with several stones in it.

A transparent woman walks the area. Rumor has it that there is a circle of stones in the cemetery used by witches, which seems to be false. Other rumors include a shack that was the place where witches practiced. Investigators have been pushed and knocked to the ground by unseen forces. Psychics report that the spirits are scared. A little girl and her brother haunt the cemetery. Both were killed by their mother after she learned their father had been killed in battle.

DUBOIS COUNTY

Devil's Road
Jasper: CR N175E off CR E300N

Legend says that a bus full of children was hit by a train, killing everyone but the driver. The driver, overcome with grief, eventually killed himself. The children visit the spot regularly. When you park your car on the tracks and put your car in neutral, the kids push you off the tracks. Another male apparition walks toward your car with a lantern and disappears. Some investigators speculate that this figure is the bus driver trying to find any survivors of the crash.

Merkley Family Home
Jasper: E Schnellville Rd. Between Jasper (CR S300E) and CR S400E

A few miles from Jasper a farm boasts a haunted barn and grain shed. One visitor smelled pipe smoke and perfume. Numerous items have been thrown at people, and there are knocks on the door when no one is around. The farm also has a ghost of a little girl who likes to play with other children. She is about seven years old, appears as a solid figure, and loves to make noise- especially if it keeps you awake! The story indicates a little girl died in the pond on the farm near a former Native American village. Drivers have accidents and hit a lot of deer along the road in front of the farm.Deer or drivers bolt after seeing the Native Americans walking along the road. At the creek behind the farm, two boys drowned and at night you can hear them splashing. Several investigators have captured orbs and EVPs of splashes in the water.

Shiloh Church
Jasper: 1971 W. SR 56

The church burned, killing several people. Their spirits haunt the church. Many times on clear nights, the sounds of wailing, screams and even singing of hymns is heard.

St. Anthony Home
St. Anthony: SR 64 and S. St. Anthony Rd.

A family of nine people was in a car that stalled on the railroad tracks. Six of the people died when a train hit them. The house across from the railroad tracks is now home to the ghost of a little girl and an older woman. Objects move around the home and visitors hear noises in rooms when no one is in them. Some visitors to the home are pushed or kicked down the stairs.

ELKHART COUNTY

Bristol Opera House

Bristol: 210 Vistula St.

(aka Elkhart Civic Theater)

This 100+ year old building is haunted by Percy, who seems to like the name Percival better. Legend has two stories about Percy. As the stories go, either he was a woodworker who squatted at the building with his family during the depression or his home burned by fire or he was allowed to live in the building. Staying in the lower levels of the theatre, he loves to appear to women (although he does appear to men). He likes to watch the action in the theatre. He has been known to help with set construction, and to hide tools. According to psychics and investigators, a little girl named Beth looks through the curtains on stage. A woman named Helen protects the theater. Two other spirits, Frank and Tad, have been identified as pranksters. Sometimes these spirits levitate objects. Some people feel taps on their shoulders in the theatre seats and costume room. Investigators have collected pictures with orbs and shadows and recordings of EVPs.

Cable Line Road

Jamestown: Near Jamestown (or Jimtown) (CR 26)

A troll lives under the bridge. If your car stalls on it, the troll will drag you under the bridge and kill you. At times, fog is seen at this location when conditions are right for it. Other mythical like creatures are seen dancing off the road nearby.

In the 1960s a motorcycle rider was killed when his bike crashed into a tree. The tree was said to bleed every year. In September 1999 a woman died at this same location when her car slammed into a telephone pole.

County Road 18

Middlebury: CR 18

An Amish man who was hit and killed by a car is seen walking along the road, trying to return home. A man on a motorcycle was also killed on this road and is seen riding his bike.

The Cross on Mill Stone

Bristol: The Bonneyville Mill, in the Bonneyville Mill Park on CR 8, just outside Bristol, Indiana is a popular tourist destination.

Home to the oldest operating gristmill in Indiana, this mill has a colorful history. Edward Bonney started the mill and had somewhat of a checkered past, dabbling in anything that was guaranteed to make him money. When he sold it and moved away, the mill became a place for the town to gather and talk. One child was killed when he fell in the inner workings of the mill and was crushed.

Legend states that a cross appears on the original stone at the mill (although some say it is a leveling mark). The boy has been heard and seen in the rafters of the building, laughing.

Goshen College–Umble Center
Elkhart: 1700 S. Main St.

The Umble Center, built in 1978, was named after John S. Umble. His wife Alice haunts the center. She prefers the fly loft and the catwalk, making walking and creaking sounds. She also likes to play with the lights, dimming them at her whim.

Haunted Farm
Elkhart: 23128 CR 28

Electronic issues occur in this house. Unplugged radios play music, and the TV changes channels alone. Lights turn off and off without help. A mirror in the home is said to show people from your past who have died. Blankets are pulled from sleepers. Misty apparitions are also reported. One apparition is said to wave at you and you can hear a voice faintly as if from a distance.

Jackson Cemetery
New Paris: West of US 33, north of Elkhart St. (CR 44)

Apparitions of African Americans are said to walk the road and haunt the cemetery. So far, no reasons have been found for these apparitions. It is an active cemetery with hours from 7am to 7pm.

Oakridge Cemetery
Elkhart: Grave is at back of cemetery. Bordered by N. First St., River Ave., N. Indiana Ave. and W. Wilden Ave.
(aka Michael Bashor's Grave)

Michael Bashor, founder of Bashor's Children home was a mason. A statue at the grave of Michael Bashor cries tears of blood. At night, a woman in a long wispy see-through white dress walks through the cemetery and stops at Bashor's grave. This same woman can be heard weeping. People have noticed figures darting among the graves at night- although this could be animals or teenagers who frequently trespass at night.

Old Elkhart Hospital
Elkhart: 126 N. Clark St.

Opened in 1899, the hospital was used until 1914 when the community built larger structure. Later, it became an apartment building where doctors still walk the halls. Some people have reported a stern nurse in a white dress and cap. Crying and whimpering are frequently heard.

(Note: Nursing was not an official profession as we know it today until 1921, well after the time this hospital was no longer in use.)

Ruthmere House Museum

Elkhart: 307 W. High St.

AR Beardsley built the home and was the president of the Muzzy Starch Company. He and his wife, Elizabeth, died in 1924. Items levitate to different rooms, lights go on and off and alarms sound for no reason. Elizabeth loved to entertain and is believed to be the one haunting the museum.

Stagecoach Inn Bed and Breakfast

Goshen: 66063 US 33

Lights come on at night without anyone turning them on. A white mist is seen in the building. Spirits have also been seen peeking around doors.

Union Cemetery

Elkhart: CR 11 and CR 50

The gravestone of Irwin Yoders weeps because of all the vandalism in the cemetery.

Winchester Mansion

Elkhart: 529 S. Second St.

Nellie (Knickerbocker) Winchester lived the life of a society girl and later matron. She kept her family's plot in Grace Lawn Cemetery pristine and became obsessed with her own arrangements. She eventually bought a solid copper coffin. Nellie died in her home in 1947. Although she came from money, her estate was meager at her death, amounting to about $11,000. Items in the home move and once, the back of a grandfather clock fell out. Office workers have experienced cold spots, and unexplained cool breezes. They have also heard footsteps in the empty building.
It is now a multipurpose building.

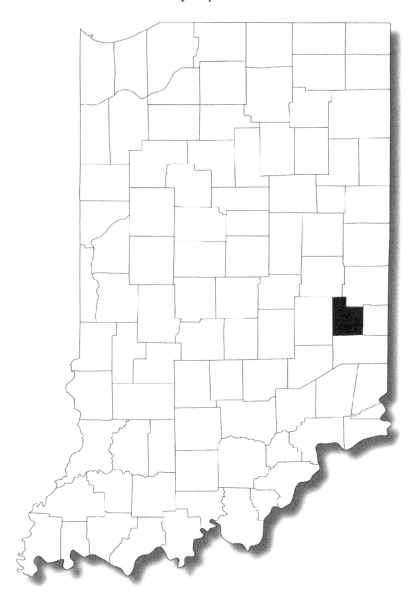

FAYETTE
COUNTY

Elmhurst

Connersville: South of Connersville on SR 121

(aka Old Elm Farm)

This mansion was built in 1831 by Congressman Oliver H. Smith and was occupied by other political leaders throughout the 1800s (including Caleb Blood Smith). Through this home's long history, it served the people of Fayette county, much as the original owner did. The house was part of the Underground Railroad as well as the Elmhurst School for Girls, and the Daum Annex, a sanatorium. It was also a military institute and a Masonic lodge.

Paranormal activity at this location include numerous orbs, EVPs of girls laughing, the sound of marching feet and singing. Small girls are seen skipping on the grass surrounding the building. Occasionally military buttons drop from no where in and around the building.

FLOYD
COUNTY

1311 E. Elm Street
New Albany: 1311 E. Elm St.

Children sing "Ring around the Rosie" in the kitchen. A little girl in the upstairs windows look out at the street. A strange man pour buckets of liquid into unseen containers. Another man in suspenders paces the living room and walks through walls.

1600 Block of Oak Street
New Albany: 1600 Block of Oak St. Seventh house on right.

Home has many ghosts including a child, who played ball with visitors by rolling a ball into various rooms. The woman who owned the home died of a heart attack in 1995 and is said to be seen looking out of the windows at many times of the day.

Budd Road Cemetery
Blunk: *(Shively, community of Buchanan- near New Albany)*: Knob Rd. and Budd Road

White, foggy masses are seen in the cemetery. Sometimes the masses come into yards and homes.

Captain Frank's Tomb
Elizabeth: Off River Rd. SE. Parking provided. You'll have to walk up to the tomb.

Captain Francis "Frank" McHarry was a successful riverboat businessman. In the 1850s he turned to ferryboats. When he noticed the animals and people he transported were upset by the riverboat wakes, he became bitter. His vertical tomb is rumored to be built so he can overlook the river, and possibly curse the boats going by. Visitors have captured orbs and some investigators report seeing a shadow figure skulking around the tomb.

Culbertson Mansion (State Historic Site)
New Albany: 914 E. Main St.
(See Mansion at River Walk, New Albany, Floyd Co.)

This home was built by William S. Culbertson in 1867 at a cost of $120,000. Built in the French Second-Empire style, it contains hand-painted ceilings, rosewood, marble and crystal.

On the third floor Culbertson's first wife walks the halls, supposedly because of her dislike of the new wife. Spirits have been sensed. The vacuum turns on and off on its own. The spirits like to put things like dried flowers on the floor to be swept up. The third floor where the children's rooms and ballroom are host other ghosts. The third floor staircase is haunted by an old woman with grey hair; she is seen at night and during the early part of the day. She is also seen through the house.

The twin's bedroom has a heavy sense of death and one staff worker who spend the night there smelled dead fish around the bed in the twins room. When she asked that the smell go away, it did. The private parlor holds the remnants of harsh words spoken about the Civil War. Many times people have heard men arguing in this room.

Some tour guides have admitted the spirits are angry because they don't like people walking through their home.

Mansion at River Walk

New Albany: 704 E. Main St.
(A Culbertson Family Mansion)
(See Culbertson Mansion, New Albany, Floyd Co.)

This home was built by William S. Culbertson in for widows of wars and other tragedies. It mirrors the Culbertson Mansion State Site.

A woman named Roberta, a former owner, haunts the house. On the back second floor veranda, solid forms of women and captains are seen chatting. In the autopsy room, a strange mix of energy is felt. Visitors have seen orbs in the home, especially the in autopsy room. The basement of the building is home to several wispy grey figures that glide from room to room. Visitors report hearing knocking on their doors during the day. The widow's meal bell rings for no reason and the phone rings when no one is on the line. The front gate opens and closes on its own.

New Albany National Cemetery

New Albany: 121 W. Spring St.

Colored orbs float through the cemetery. Soldiers from all time periods are also seen in the cemetery. An EVP saying "got a light?" was captured.

Pine View Elementary

New Albany: 2524 Corydon Pike

J.R. Hays died when his bike hit a truck on Corydon Pike. At 8:47pm, you will hear his bike tires, and the truck slam on its brakes. The truck appears at the stop sign. Visitors have also reported hearing voices and sirens and someone saying "Why don't you help? Help me!"

FOUNTAIN
COUNTY

Historic Attica Hotel
Attica: 126 N. Perry St.

Built in the 1850s, the hotel was once host to Al Capone and Teddy Roosevelt. A former employee named Vida (Mennie) Foxworthy was murdered by a clock salesman who lived in one of the rooms. He took a .12 gauge and shot her in Room 21.

Vida touches people and calls out their names. Visitors hear scratching on the walls. The water in the showers turns off when you are still in the shower. A misty white woman seen in corridor. Visitors smell the scents of different flowers. Vida is considered a protective spirit as she has run off people who intend harm to the building. She also provides extra pillows for workmen.

Some visitors claim to see phantom lights, hear music and see ghostly images of people in and outside the hotel.

Mudlavia Spa
(See Warren County)

FRANKLIN COUNTY

Brookville Inn
Brookville: 1049 Main St.

The inn was built in the early 1900s as a private residence. According to several visitors the Delft Blue room is active. A small child plays with jacks inside and outside the room.

Metamora (town)
Metamora: US 52 near IN 229

Metamora is an early canal town with an operating grist mill, wooden aqueduct and restored lock. The whole town has several spirits; some seem to move from location to location.

Metamora Inn
Metamora: 19049 Wynn St.

The inn was built in the 1850s. According to several visitors Clara's room is home to spirit activity. A man with loud work boots is seen pacing the room. A woman has been seen sitting in the Suite room looking out the window.

Thorpe Country House Inn
Metamora: 19049 Clayborne St.

Built between in 1840-1860, the inn is listed on the National Register of Historic Places. Investigators sense a comforting presence of a woman smelling of lavender and cinnamon.

White Hall Tavern
Laurel: Baltimore and Franklin Streets

The house was built prior to 1832 and was famous for hospitality and good food. Squire Isaac Clements did not allow hard liquor at the establishment. A newborn baby and its mother, who waiting for her husband to return, died shortly after childbirth. Her shushing noises to her baby are heard periodically. Guests hear a wailing baby too.

FULTON COUNTY

Antioch Cemetery

Rochester: West of SR 25 on CR S75W

A man in a dark colored suit holding flowers haunts this cemetery. He is often seen kneeling at various graves on foggy nights between 12-1am. Shadow people fly over and around vehicles. If you walk the cemetery at night, these shadows follow you around the cemetery.

Deadmans College School and Cemetery

Rochester: South of SR 110 at the corner of CR N500W and CR W700N
(often misspelled Dead Man's College)

This one room pre-1875 school building is on the site of a family cemetery. This location is linked to Prill School because "Sister Sarah's (McIntire)" baby was buried at this site. In the evening and early morning, people visiting this site hear children playing and they'll ask you to join them. People also see children running in the yard as well.

(See Prill School entry, Rochester, Fulton Co.)

Earl's Tree Cemetery

Rochester: Off SR 25 on CR 300S

A boy named Earl speaks to you about the tree next to his grave.

Fulton Cemetery

Fulton: SR 25 between CR E700S and CR E600S

A couple that died in a car accident were buried together around 1967. Many stabbings and shootings have occurred in the area. Investigators have captured mists, orbs and EVPs of people talking. One EVP has a group of unseen people talking. Someone pipes up and asks "If we ask, do you think they'll go?" Also, some visitors have reported an apparition of a man whose grave was desecrated.

Olson Road

Rochester: On Olson Road between Old and New US 31
(aka Slaughterhouse Rd.)

The old slaughterhouse is part of what people consider to be a time warp. When you drive by, some people have claimed that this building disappears. Even if you try to walk to it, you still can't find it.

Prill School

Rochester: 500 W. Seventh St.

Sister Sarah taught at the school and died (depending on the source, it ranges from rape and murder to poison to disease). Sister Sarah haunts the school. If you visit on a night of a full moon, her ghost walks the grounds, especially next to the tree in the yard. If you put a question on a slip of paper and leave it, she will give you answers.

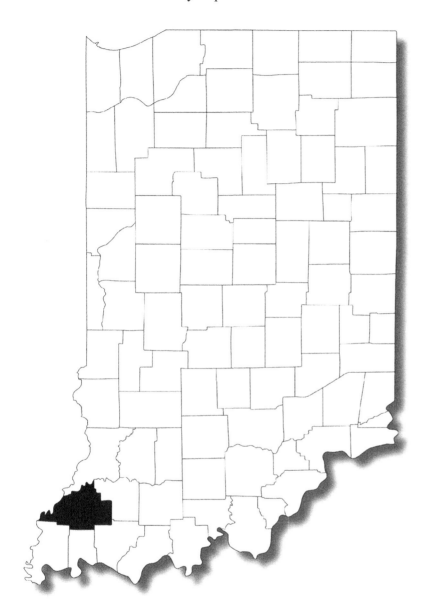

GIBSON
COUNTY

Blackfoot Cemetery
Oakland City: Off IN 61 at CR 900
(aka Old Burial Grounds)

Investigators captured orbs and the figure of a woman. One sensitive was possessed by the spirit of a man who died in a car accident. A person was thrown from a vehicle for stating disbelief in the hauntings.

Bulldog Bridge
Princeton: Head east out of Princeton on the main road

Several people hung themselves from the bridge. One man was found dead in his car, the doors were locked and windows up. Visitors feel cold spots in the summer. Some people hear growling from nearby cornfields. A woman in white lures you under the bridge. She disappears into the water.

Fairfield Inn
Princeton: 2828 Dixon St.

Guests have uneasy feelings, and experience violent shaking and convulsing, and feelings of being ill. The apparition of an evil woman seen in rooms.

Gibson County Courthouse
Princeton: 101 N. Main St.

Built in 1884, this courthouse is a great example of Romanesque Revival. A Greek cross design is made from the four towers and four entries. The building also has a widow's walk. Black walnut woodwork, oak flooring, mosaic tiles and plaster reliefs have survived for over 120 years.

Visitors hear footsteps, and yelling. They are touched by unseen hands. One visitor swears she heard a man growl "I'll get even with you!" and a felt cold breeze pass her although she was alone in the corridor.

Lyles Station
Princeton: Intersection of Lyles Station Road and CR 500 W

Founded by Joshua Lyles in the mid-1800s, this structure is part of one of the last remaining African American settlements in Indiana. Visitors can see the type of schooling children would have received in the early 1900s. Visitors and staff hear footsteps in the building. One visitor, who was intently looking at an exhibit in one of the rooms, had a conversation with a bodiless voice. When she raised her head to look at the person, no one was around her.

Oakland City University–Cochram Hall
Oakland City: 627 W. Oak St.
(aka Oakland City College)

Lucretia, the wife of Col. William Cochram (founder of the college), hung herself in the upstairs tower. Witnesses have seen the doors open and shut and have seen an orange glow from the upper windows. Pink and orange lights are also observed.

GRANT COUNTY

10th Street Bridge
Gas City: Take 10th Street north from US 35/ SR 22. It will be the bridge over Walnut Creek.
Jonesboro: Take 10th Street east. It is the bridge over the Mississinewa River. (10th St. turns into West L St.)

A worker died on the bridge. You can hear his screams asking for help.

Much controversy surrounds whether or not this bridge is actually in Gas City or Jonesboro. Both 10th Streets have a bridge. From the time the author spent in the Grant County area with family over the years, her experience has been that it is the Jonesboro Bridge. However, Readers, you be the final judge. Perhaps they both have stories to tell.

1524 Marion Avenue
Marion: 1524 Marion Ave.

An older man who owned this home likes to play pranks on people who rent the home. He hides items, and turn the television on and off. His loud booming laughter can be heard throughout the home. His wife is around as well, most often with the smell of her favorite powder emanating from the bathroom. Both of them are heard in the kitchen playing cards.

Bennett High School
Marion: 1009 Kem Rd.
(aka St. Paul Catholic School)

This now defunct high school is home to an assorted lot of ghosts.
- Gym Balcony: The ghost of a former teacher roams the hall. She was fired for getting divorced and killed herself.
- Upstairs girls' bathroom: Faucets turn on and off at random. Many times, visitors hear someone pushing a mop bucket although no one is around. One other story is about a girl in the 1980s having aborted her baby in the restroom and flushing the baby and birth material down the toilet.
- Coach's Room (West side of Gym): Rumor has it that a former coach molested a student in this location. Although the girl survived, the vibration of the past remains and her muffled sobs are heard in the late evening. A variation of this story is that a former priest molested a young male student here.
- Cafeteria: Many students report a mischievous ghost of a former student. He appears as a grey mist.. He throws cafeteria trays and trips people.

Charles Road
Marion: West of N. Bethlehem Rd. and East of SR 9/109/37

A whole pioneer family was decapitated. Today the family's screams are heard and you can hear the wagon traveling down the road. Sometimes a headless man or woman is seen walking on the road.

Converse Elementary School
Converse: 600 East Walnut St.

A 49 year old woman hung herself from the flag pole. Staff members and locals say that at night, you can see her swinging from the pole and standing on the ground crying.

The Hostess House
Marion: 723 W. 4th St.
(aka The Sleeping House)

An older woman was killed in the house. Today you can see her shadowy figure on her balcony. She also haunts the room where she slept. Sometimes she interacts with people to ask them to take care of the house. Sometimes she is seen walking in the hallway, she is also seen in an upstairs window. Some people believe it is the ghost of a housekeeper. Others believe it is Peggy "Lillian" Wilson, for whom the home was built.

Israel Jenkins Farm
Marion: 7453 E 400 S (on Club Run course)
(aka Walnut Creek Club Run; aka The Elms)

The Jenkins were Quakers who settled in Marion in 1839 and were active in the Underground Railroad. Footsteps are heard, lights turn on and off. Doors open and close, and there are shadow figures on stairs walking up to the attic and the attic door opens when no one is seen. A young man stares out of the attic window.

J.C. Knight School
Jonesboro: 12th and Main Streets

A janitor hung himself in the gym and a cheerleader was murdered in the building. You can see white lights dancing inside the school. Sometimes they are red lights or turn red.

Marion National Cemetery – VA Medical Center
Marion: 1700 East 38th Street

This cemetery and VA medical center are haunted by various apparitions of men and woman. Some are believed to be patients and other people who worked there. Some of the patients report watching deceased soldiers walk on the grounds at night and in the corridors of the hospital.

Mason's Bridge
Gas City: CR 222 to CR 400 E

In the 1940s a husband and wife got into an argument and he cut off her head at the bridge. Feeling guilty, he hung himself in the house. Two people are seen running down the hill- one with an axe. They replay the event in which you can hear screaming and crying, and the thud of the head as it hits the bridge, screams and crying. The woman is said to roam the banks looking for her head.

Old East School
Upland: S. 4th St.; south of SR 35/SR 22

The merry-go-round spins by itself and you can hear children laughing.

(Note: The merry-go-round is long gone.)

Park Cemetery
Fairmount: CR S150E south of CR E800S

In the center point of four trees, you feel that someone is touching you. Movie star, James Dean has also been seen at his grave looking down at it. There is also a spot in the cemetery with four trees surrounding it that. If you stand in the middle of them, you may feel someone touching you.

Scott Opera House
Fairmount: 45 Downtown Plaza
(aka Fairmont Opera House)

Students using the 120-year old building for band rehearsal have experienced lights turning on and off and items moving from one place to another by unseen hands. People have been locked in rooms.

Spook's Corner
Upland: West of SR 26 on CR E825S where it curves by the river.

In the 1970s a bus load of kids was supposed to have been killed in the rushing river when it careened off the road. The legend states there is a bus in a cemetery nearby, although there are no documented graveyards around. Additionally, if you go over the "iron bridge" children will try to push you off it. The bridge that is currently on this road is not iron, it is guardrails and blacktop.

Sweetser (town)
Sweetser: On SR 18 west of Marion and east of SR 13

In the late 1960s, child saw a Native American group outside at the family's old well on the property. The girl saw the Native Americans and they saw her, but when the girl told her mother, she couldn't see what her daughter saw. Others throughout the town also reported the Native Americans. They are spotted most often wearing buckskin pants and traveling in a group.

Woodcarver Building
Converse: 101 S. Jefferson St.
(aka Eastern Woodland Carvers Building; aka Odd Fellows; aka IOOF Converse; aka AJ Fisher building)

Throughout its history, the second floor used to be a doctor's office, a KKK office, and storeroom. Visitors and investigators hear a piano playing childlike songs on the second floor. People have been choked on this floor after automatic writing events. Orbs take shape on the stairway leading to this floor. People have been pushed from the stairs. A full apparition crosses from one side of this floor to the other side.

On the first floor an apparition walks through the room without interacting with visitors. In all areas of the building electronic malfunctions occur and visitors hear footsteps. Cell phones and batteries drain. People have also been locked in the building from the latch on the outside. Legend states tunnels exist under the building and throughout Converse.

On the third floor, the KKK used to meet. Investigators have reported unexplained EMF readings and shadow figures. Light fixtures swing without reason.

GREENE
COUNTY

Burcham Ford

Bloomfield: Although this is unverified, this location is supposed to be on CR 150S west of CR250S

A warrior stole a ham and the settler shot here. The Indian was buried out of fear of retribution. He was buried in the ford of Burcham Branch. Some nights he comes out of the water brandishing his tomahawk. People report feeling a breeze when he is around and hearing his war cry.

Fairview Cemetery

Linton: Take Fairview Rd. north out of Linton. It is a about a mile or two outside of town.

Polly Barnett was a derelict woman, she wandered around town trying to find her daughter, Sylvanie, who disappeared mysteriously. People of the town gave her shelter and food. People believed Sylvanie was murdered, presumably by a farmhand, although it was never proven. Her body found was never found. Polly died, without knowing the fate of her daughter. Before her death, she asked that her cat be allowed to roam to search for her daughter. The black cat is seen running through the cemetery during the day and night. It disappears when approached. The cemetery contains a memorial marker for Polly with a black cat on it.

Freeman City Hospital

Linton: 410 A St. NE

It was originally known as Freeman City Hospital after Job Freeman and his wife, who donated the land to build it. Started in June 1912, it was later renamed the Freeman Green County Hospital and later Greene County General Hospital. The hospital moved in April 1974 to its present Lone Tree Road location. Wendy's Restaurant bought part of the land and became established on the site on March 10, 1986.

Reports of footsteps and milk white, grey, and misty outlines of patients that died were seen roaming the halls prior to the hospitals relocation. One nurse reported having a conversation with a female patient who was dying- 30 minutes after she died.

After the relocation, an investigative team reported picking up visual forms and unintelligible sounds. Several pseudo-investigations of the current Wendy's and surrounding area have been done without obtaining proof of paranormal activity.

Ridgeport Cemetery

Ridgeport: SR 54 east of CR 725E

A log cabin used to sit in the woods behind the cemetery. Children who died of disease were buried in here. Today the sounds of crying and musical instruments can be heard.

White River
Newberry: White River

See Fairview Cemetery.

It's believed Sylvanie Barnett is the young girl seen walking along the river crying.

HAMILTON
COUNTY

100 North Union Street

Westfield: 100 Union St.

(aka Old Bank)

Hank West, the old night watchman haunts this building. He turns up the heat to around 90 degrees. When people try to stop him, such as putting a lock box on the thermostat, he breaks the case and turns the heat up anyway. A woman and her daughter are seen in the building as well. They may be the same people seen in a building across the street.

101-103 South Union Street

Westfield: 101-103 N. Union 102-108 South Union St.

(aka Westfield Pharmacy and flowers)

The bell between the pharmacy and florist door rings on its own occasionally.

102-108 South Union Street

Westfield: 102-108 S. Union St.

(aka Jan's Village Pizza)

Visitors and staff report whispered names, phantom touches from unseen hands and lights malfunctioning. Orbs have also been reported on the second floor.

110 South Union Street

Westfield: 110 S. Union St.

(aka Keever's Hardware; Keltie's Restaurant)

When this restaurant was a hardware store (Keever's), a friendly ghost would help the owners fill orders. Many times they would have a list of items that would need to be pulled for customers and many times those items would mysteriously appear. When Keltie's was in business, muddy boot and dog paw prints appeared during closing and early in the morning.

112 East Main Street

Westfield: 112 E. Main St.

(aka Marlow's Restaurant)

Staff at this family owned business report hearing noises and having their apron strings pulled. Additionally, the back room is a hot bed of activity including having a dark figure pacing in the back room. Photos of the area show dark figures in pictures, although they were not visible at the time the photos were taken. The family believes the activity is from family members who used to work at the establishment and have passed on.

120 North Union Street
Westfield: 120 N Union St.

Former tenants report a mean old man turning on lights, throwing bottles, and hiding items. The smell of food not served in the building is also experienced.

130 Penn Street
Westfield: 130 Penn St.

(aka Old Town Hall)

Visitors and staff see shadows in the southern meeting room. The northern offices have a floating white mist. The ghost of a firefighter, Chad Hittle, was sensed a week after his death and his spirit is seen walking up and down the west stairs. Voices call out your name when you visit, especially around the restroom area. A group of tour guests saw a Quaker man in the southern meeting room during a tour. Another tour guest had his arm scratched by unseen fingernails.

132 W Main Street
Westfield: 132 W Main St.

(Razed)

This 1844 home was reputed as haunted as far back as 1932. An elderly woman lived in the house as a child and said the ghosts of her great grandparents inhabited the house. It was accepted as part of their life. Later others believe someone became unhappy with the disrepair that befell the house and noises throughout the day and night drove tenants out.

135 North Union Street
Westfield: 135 N. Union St.

(aka the Fern; the Stalker House)

Reported to have been a boarding house and a traveler's place of rest. Visitors heard moans and people walking throughout the house and out the front door. Before the building became The Fern, an older woman lived and died in the home.

136 East Main Street
Westfield: 136 E. Main St.

A burned man is seen in the upper story bathroom/former bedroom.

141 South Peru Street

Cicero: 141 S. Peru St.

Cold spots and mists are seen in home. At least three spirits of a man and two women haunt the home from top to bottom. One woman doesn't want anyone in the home, the one in the basement loves people in the home and the man on the stairs just goes about his business as in life. Still, according to one psychic, they were all happy that kids were in the home. In the coal room, reportedly a dead body was seen.

145 South Union Street

(aka Old Fire Station; Westfield Washington Historical Society Museum)

Westfield: 145 S. Union St.

This old fire station, now museum is home to the ghost of a firefighter named Bob Mikesell. Several staff and visitors feeling breezes as if someone was rapidly walking by them. EVPs recordings include "yes" in answer to the question, "Are you Bob?" and a booming laugh.

161st and Union Streets

Westfield: 161st and Union Sts.

Joggers see a Native American in buckskins walking along the road and surrounding trees.

1139 Cherry Street

Noblesville: 1139 Cherry St.

Residents report a Franciscan monk on the second floor. Strange whispers are heard in the attic.

14921 North Meridian Street

Westfield: 14921 N Meridian St.

Pots and pans fall to the floor at night when no one is in the kitchen. The music will turn on even when the system is in the off position. One woman was chased through the building by a cold breeze. When she got into the kitchen, she grabbed her purse and went out the back, pots and pans falling after her. For many years, a sign saying "Respect the Ghost" hung in the kitchen. Many people have quit because of the paranormal activity.

15513 South Union Street

Westfield: 15513 S. Union St.

Staff at the Cool Creek Park office hear a woman and her child in the building. A dirty looking man makes an occasional appearance. He seems to have worn some sort of eye protection but the rest of his face is black as if with soot. The park itself is haunted too. A woman had an encounter with a small boy who gave her an orange ball. She tried to find his mother, but he disappeared. Local lore states that a farmhouse speakeasy and a night club were once part of the area around the park.

17272 Futch Way
Westfield: 17272 Futch Way

Once farmland, the house is part of a subdivision. The midland trail runs behind the property. In the early 2000s, the home had a portal in one of the closets. Although not as active as when the owners first moved in and had small children, it still hosts a group of ghosts from time to time. The home has had no less than 15 ghosts including a vindictive old woman who was the great grandmother of one of the children, a perverted man who enjoyed watching people in the bathroom, and a 14 year old orphaned boy who used to ride the rails from town to town.

Now, the home has spirits that drift in and out as needed. Sometimes they need something communicated so someone who is still living. Other times they are ghosts that are brought home by the owner's paranormal and tour activities.

19037 Northbrook Circle
Westfield: 19037 Northbrook Circle

Former tenants saw a woman in a long skirt and long sleeved blouse in the northern most bedroom. Personal items went missing. The grounds have several type of trees and a good energy, however, there is a deep sadness in the house.

201 North Union Street
Westfield: 201 N Union St.

Currently a dermatology office, this house was once part of the Underground Railroad. Asa Bales had a barn at this location where fugitives were hidden in a basement. Parts of the barn remain in the back of the house.

People have witnessed objects moving and levitating. One witness saw the windows blow open with a stiff wind permeating the house. When she looked outside, not a branch was moving. A former owner had issues when her son would not sleep in his room because of the noise downstairs. She had her finger slammed in a door by unseen hands. She also received second degree burns from a cold stove.

273 South 8th Street
Noblesville: 273 S. 8th St.

This former home was reputed to be William Conner's home (because of the home's description) although most people believe that it could not be a William Conner's home because of the architecture. Most people believe that the home of Conner burned (as the location was notorious for fires) and that Leonard Wild built the house on what was Mayor

R.L. Wilson's homestead. Currently under new ownership, the former Accent Shop building is said to be haunted by a woman frequently seen in the NE window sitting at a sewing machine. Lights will mysteriously turn on when no one is around. According to some local visitors, the ghost may be that of Avalin Elizabeth Keeper, a retired employee of the Accent Shop.

301 East Main Street

Westfield: 301 E. Main St.

A phantom opens doors and closes them although no one is ever seen. A dark shadow is seen pacing the floors of the basement.

311 South Union Street

Westfield: 311 South St.

Shadow figures appear to visitors. A broom once flew across the room when it was a hair salon. On one ghost tour, a person took a pictures and three figures appeared in it.

319 South Street

Westfield: 319 South St.

A mean spirit of a middle aged man creates a hateful atmosphere.

323 South Union Street

Westfield: 323 S. Union St.

A little boy was ill one day and was lying on the couch downstairs. He wished he had his balloon and it floated down the stairs to him.

417 West Main Street

Westfield: 417 W. Main St.

(Razed)

This house has been home to many businesses but none stay long. Many people believe there is something "Wrong" with the building that goes beyond paranormal activity. Several former tenants believe a demon made its way into the house and now tries to take over people who enter. Currently, this house is slated to be demolished for US 31 reconstruction. Will the demon seek a new home?

421 South Union Street

Westfield: 421 S. Union St.

(aka Barker House)

Walking is heard in the old part of the upstairs. A cupboard opens on its own.

969 Keystone Way

Carmel: 969 Keystone Way
(Note: This is now an office building)

Illusions Restaurant was one of the most haunted restaurants. Strange footsteps are heard. A cane with a clown head on it mysterious showed up after the owner killed himself in an upper office. Many of the furnishings were brought from Europe from funeral homes and castles. These items hold vibrations of the past. Shadow figures of men are seen in mirrors and several magicians' equipment failed to work. One storyteller reports her camera unable to function after a fully loaded 700 minute battery went dead in seconds. The women's restroom has a stall that will lock when the spirits are present and the water will turn off and on. The restaurant has many shadow figures that roam throughout and the alarm will go off at different times of the day and night.

Anti-Slavery Friends Cemetery

Westfield: Inside Asa Bales Park

The cemetery was attached to old Quaker meeting house of same name (no longer standing). Visitors see a wispy apparition of a woman in white, a solid color apparition of a Civil War solider, and orb masses.

145 W. Main St.

Atlanta: 145 W. Main St.

A translucent white woman with a bun and Gibson girl look watches out the window in the Spring.

Asa Bales Park

Westfield: Camilla Ct. and SR 32

Native Americans are seen walking through different areas of the park

Barley Island Brew Pub

Noblesville: 639 Conner St.

Suspected of being a former speakeasy as well as a buggy works, visitors report a little girl and a man in a hat, dusty books and work pants. Lights turn off and on. Staff and visitors have also been touched by unseen hands.

Fox Hollow Farms
Westfield: On the south side of 156th St. just west of the Monon Trail

Herbert Baumeister killed 4 known and several known victims, all men at this location. Tenants have elected to hold ghost hunts now and then. They say Herbert, who killed himself in Canada before he could be arrested, haunts the house. Herb is still aggressive, throwing items, yelling, and making threats. Residual hauntings occur in the guest house. In the woods where the bodies were dumped, visitors see a man in a hooded sweatshirt who seems to be running for his life. The pool, where much of the killing took place is also haunted. Dark figures and swimmers make appearances. Investigators see orbs, mists, and shadows.

Boys and Girls Club
Noblesville: 1448 Conner St.

Visitors and staff report children running through the old school. One visitor asked a child if she could help him and he disappeared before her eyes. At night, the lights turn off and on.

Commercial Building
Arcadia: SW corner of Main and East Streets

Bad vibes, dance hall, Victorian ceiling, people seen, radio heard, aliens seen.

East Union Cemetery
Atlanta: County Line Rd. and US 31

Cemetery has been investigated many times. Orbs and a mist that travels from north to south are experienced. Some investigators have been shoved and scratched in the cemetery.

Eck House
Cicero: 2811 Cumberland Rd.

Leonard Eck haunts this home. He built the house and has been seen by former family members who owned the home, visiting friends and by the current owners.

First Presbyterian Church
Noblesville: 1207 Conner St.

Visitors hear footsteps in the building. One boy witnessed an apparition moving from room to room. On staff member was surprised to see a woman in a long prairie skirt sitting in one of the basement rooms.

Hare House
Noblesville: 675 W. Walnut St.

This former funeral home is now home to a woman who walks up and down the stairs with a candelabra, a little boy named Charles, who runs around and plays tricks on people- and giggles. Finally, visitors report feeling sick, cold, and unhappy when in the upstairs area.

Harrell House
Noblesville: 399 N. 10th St.

The Harrell House was built by Dr. Samuel Harrell, who was a 7th son of a 7th son. He and his doctor brothers built the Harrell Hospital And Sanatorium (located at 148 N. 9th Street). Later the facility was sold and renamed Riverview. His Queen Anne home was built in 1898. The children's swings in the backyard move on their own even without wind. Other assorted ghosts roam throughout the home. Some visitors believe these ghosts are of the doctor and his patients. Others believe it is family and friends.

Heady Hollow
Fishers: 126th St. and Allisonville Rd.

A school house burned down and all the children died inside. On a foggy night, you see the children walking along the hollow. Sometimes you see them on the road and when you drive through them, they disappear like wisps of smoke.

(Note: Ron Baker's book on ghosts of Indiana mistakenly places this location on SR 13)

Hinkle Creek Church
Westfield: 21617 Hinkle Rd.

Visitors see white figures in the cemetery. Locals play midnight tag in the cemetery. One young boy spoke with the ghost children that inhabit the north side of the cemetery and said they have to wait 100 years before they can be reunited with their parents so until then, they like haunting and scaring people, especially children.

Holiday Drive Bridge
(aka Carmel Screaming Bridge)
Zionsville: Holiday Dr. off of US 421

A woman had a child outside of marriage. The father of the baby threw it in the woods. The mother went looking for the child and when she couldn't find it, she threw herself off the bridge and killed herself. Today she calls for the baby and weeps.

Klipsch Music Center
(aka Deer Creek; Verizon Wireless Music Center)
Noblesville: 12880 E. 146th St.

Formerly Deer Creek Music Center, this land used to be part of an old farm with a fieldstone house and fence. The original property had over 800 acres. The original stone house had a ghostly old woman who would click clack her tea cup and would fuss over bedding and curtains hanging strait. A black man (mentally challenged) was hung in the huge barn for supposedly raping a little white girl at the creek behind the property, but the little girl kept saying he was just her friend. When the barn still existed, you could still hear the sound of the rope in the third floor rafters of the barn.

Some visitors have suggested that Verizon might be haunted by Dave William's (musician from Drowning Pool) spirit, who died on his tour bus after playing Ozzfest in 2002.

Mill Creek Road
Westfield: Mill Creek Rd. and SR 32

The ghosts of a motorcycle wreck haunt the intersection.

Model Mill & Conference Center
Noblesville: 802 Mulberry St.

This building used to be home to the Model Mill, which showcased milling equipment and which did milling as well. Later it became Indiana Seed and now houses businesses and offices. Visitors and workers have seen apparitions and heard footsteps and voices. Investigators theorize that these occurrences could be due to the murder of a mill worker in the early 1900s.

Mount Pleasant Cemetery
Westfield: E. 236th St. and Anthony Rd.
No public access.

A dark caped figure chases people through the cemetery

Noblesville Antique Mall
Noblesville: 20 N. 9th St.

Formerly a Napa auto parts store, visitors report a woman in grey who either motions for people to follow her upstairs or motions for them to be quiet. In the south west corner of the basement, a creepy man stairs are shoppers.

Oak Road Bridge
Westfield: North of 151st St. on Oak Rd.

An unidentified white mist is frequently seen at dawn.

Oak Road Pond
Westfield: On Oak Rd., just south of South St. (171st St.)

Four children who died in the gravel pit pond try to lure you in. They appear as milk white translucent figures coming out of the pond. Some visitors say that when you're in the pond, they try to drag you under. Investigators captured a video of a rope swing (now gone) swaying during a still summer day.

Old Carmel Cemetery
Carmel: Northeast corner of Rangeline Road and Smokey Row (136th St.)
(aka Old Richland Friends Cemetery)

Visitors see a woman walking a dog and a man sitting under a tree. Mists exist in this cemetery when no other area is foggy.

Orphan's Home
Westfield: N. Union St. It is now two houses.

Ghost children still play in both locations. Giggling, toys rolling and disappearing, and small feet pattering are experienced.

Potters Bridge
Noblesville: 19401 N Allisonville Rd.

Built between 1870-1871 by Josiah Dufree, this bridge is the last of the covered bridges in Hamilton County. Closed to car traffic, it is part of a park. People hear hoof beats when no horse is around. They've also heard a man moaning when they were alone on the bridge.

Rhodes Hotel
Atlanta: 150 E Main St.
(aka Roads, Rhoades)

Information about Atlanta, Indiana is sketchy at best due to it being a small town and a firebug that destroyed much of the documentation in the 1990s. However, we do know that it was purchased in 1893 by Newton A. Rhoades for his wife, Clara. His father, Phillip was one of the earliest settlers in the area and was granted land "out west" after he fought in the Civil War.

In the early 1900s, a local newspaper touted the hotel as one of the best "east of the Mississippi". It was regarded as such because it boasted clean beds, tasty meals and a homey atmosphere. After the 1930s with bigger and better accommodations being built and the gas boom going bust, the hotel became a boarding house.

Other unsubstantiated legends peg this location as a speakeasy and a brothel. John Dillinger and Al Capone are also supposed to have visited the area.

In 2011, the house was purchased by a ghost hunting group for commercial investigations. The ghosts use flashlights to communicate to trigger questions. One ghost is supposed to be a pimp and another is supposed to be a hooker named Sarah. Dark shadows inhabit the upstairs rooms. One investigator was pushed down the attic stairs.

Riverside Cemetery
Noblesville: At the corner of Cherry and 5th Sts.

Founded in 1834, this cemetery has been somewhat neglected. After the flood of 1913, it became the "Negro cemetery", because if you put "them" in "there" no one would "bother them". Whatever.

People who visit loved ones feel a comforting hand on their shoulders. A Civil War soldier marches along the river fence line. A woman in white runs through the cemetery. On one ghost tour, the woman was seen by a group of 20 people. The author spoke to the woman and she disappeared. Despite all the pictures taken, she was not captured in a photo.

Riverwood
Riverwood (town)
Riverwood is bounded by White River, Riverwood Ave., and Riverwood Dr. (on the west side of IN 37).

Time warp experienced at this location. Rough cabins appeared and the people sitting by their cabins all looked mongoloid or inbred and would stare with vehemence at you. No one there was friendly and looked more like they would gut you and serve you up for dinner. There was one Victorian back on the river that was in good condition and it is reputed to come and go at will, as is the young long haired lass in a white dress with a green sash. The whole area around Riverwood seems disturbed and time damaged, it isn't so much a negative energy, as wrongness.

Screaming Bridge
(See Holiday Drive Bridge, Hamilton County)

Sheridan Historical Society
Sheridan: 308 S. Main St.

Grey figures seen. Items move. Footsteps heard.

Sheriff's Residence
(aka Hamilton County Historical Society)
Noblesville: Corner of Conner and 8th Streets

Staff and visitors hear footsteps downstairs and they hear doors opening and closing, yet when checked, nothing is amiss. Upstairs, a woman in turn of the 1900s clothing is seen. The jail cell on the first floor on the NE corner has a spirit that speaks or growls in your ear. The author was scratched in the guard area of the west cells after speaking with the ghost of a pimp. The apparition of a man in the juvenile cells was caught on camera after asking for any young men to show themselves. General feelings of dread are reported in the mens' cells.

Sleepy Hollow
Westfield: Grove of trees at the end of N Walnut St.

Strange shapes shift through the trees. Several people claim to have talked with and see pioneers from the town of Westfield.

Strawtown Cemetery
Strawtown: Essig Ave

The Shintapper family used to sell liquor to the Native Americans and once threw a drunken Native American on their 6ft long fire. When the other Native Americans heard of it, they plotted revenge. All the men in the area used to sharpen their weapons at the Shintappers. One day when a group of men were there, Native Americans exacted revenge, killing several white men and having several of their own men killed. Later that evening Shintapper went down the White River with his family and was never heard from again. Benjamin Fisher, was buried in Strawtown Cemetery very close to where he was killed.

Today, shadow people are seen on the ridge of the cemetery moving darkly through the property, even in daylight hours. EVP recordings include "help", "not me" and "go".

Strawtown Koteewi "Prairie" Park
Strawtown: 12308 E. Strawtown Ave.

In 1987 a set of heavy oak stairs went from the river to an old farm property near the park that a religious sect occupied and which contained a small gravesite of four adults and two children.

The park is a 750 acre home to archeological digs to learn about the ancient people who settled on the land. Footsteps are heard outside after dark. The unmarked Native American graves have mists that play over them at night. The path by the river has several translucent men running quickly down to the water.

Summit Lawn Cemetery
Westfield: On S Union across from Valley Farms Dr.

A girl in a school uniform makes people very unwelcome. Flashes of light play over the graves at night. People who live in the apartments across the street see white figures walking through the cemetery at night. Many people believe these are the people of the city still socializing.

Syd's Restaurant
Noblesville: 808 Logan St.

The longest running bar in Hamilton County, blond women have reported feeling a "cat-like" creature rubbing against their ankles. Staff report an old piano playing in the basement. The mannequin that sits in the front window changes position. Staff has taken to leaving a drink out for the ghost, called "Syd" in honor of a former owner.

Talbert House
(part of Christ United Methodist property)
Westfield: 318 N. Union St.

Harry Talbert, a former lumber baron built this house in the 1930s. Doors have open and closed on their own. Footsteps walk up and down the stairs. When they come in the next morning, the drink is gone.

Train Track Viaduct
Atlanta: North of town on E. Railroad St.

In the 1890s and later in the 1920s, men came running into town saying they saw a man waving a lantern. In the case of each occurrence, additional men went out to see for themselves and came back spouting stories of seeing the man walking toward them and disappearing when they tried to speak to him.

No known train accidents are known to have happened at this location, however, one theory is that this man died somewhere else on the line and is still on the job, making sure the train gets to its destination safely.

Union Bible College
Westfield: 434 S. Union St.

This former Quaker college (now a religious K-12 institution) houses a smaller version of the school now. Doors open and close on their own. Lights turn on in the library when no one is around. Visitors hear footsteps on the main staircase. In the adjoining hall, neighbors have the sound of music when the lights have been off and the hall closed.

Union Street
Westfield: Union St. just north of 161st St.

Native American in buckskins seen in this area and he will disappear in front of your eyes.

Vine Alley and Walnut Street
Westfield: Vine Alley between Cherry and Walnut Sts.

The town blacksmith's shop was two plats east of Walnut st. The McMullan funeral home was on the North west side of Walnut. Figures were seen traveling between the buildings. Both are gone now, but the occasional white mist persists.

The house on the south West corner of the intersection was owned by the White family who were early settlers of Hamilton County. Former owners claimed one of the White family members would help her make business decisions.

Walton House
Atlanta: 100 East Main Street

This house was built by Asher Walton in 1868 across from his mercantile store and his successful bank. It has changed hands over the years and at one time was a bed and breakfast. Visitors and staff report a persistent dark shadow that follows them down the main staircase.

HANCOCK COUNTY

11608 E Washington Street

Cumberland: 11608 E Washington St.

At Clippty Do Dawg, a pet grooming business, items fall off shelves, unseen people talk, dogs growl and bark.

During one paranormal incident, the owner was grooming a dog. She saw a bottle fly off table and land in doorway. Another bottle flew through a room when the owner was meeting with a client. Shadow people stalk and watch employees and the animals.

A dog being boarded somehow escaped from his cage. In the morning the staff found the light on and the cage he was in locked. Paranormal investigators caught orbs and a mist from the ceiling. When the owners used dowsing rods, they discovered the ghost's name was Charles, which matched the owners name from the 1800s.

Abraham Lincoln Ghost Train

Greenfield: Seen on April 30th on Greenfield on tracks that are south of US 40 between midnight and 7am

People report seeing the Lincoln ghost train which carried his body through Indiana. (Lincoln's ghost is probably the most transient spirit having been seen at several places within Indiana, at the White House, and in Springfield, IL. The legend has identified two trains. The first has several black crepe draped cars and the other is just a flatbed car with the casket lying on top.

Cry Baby Bridge

Milners Corner: Thomas Rd. between CR E950N and CR E1000N

Depending on the story, this is where a woman died with her baby or where a baby died in a car crash. In one version of the story, the baby wasn't found when the police investigated. In another version, the baby was found half eaten by dogs (sometimes still crying, but it died later). Still another version said the mother buried it alive. In any of these versions, if you go across the bridge you can hear crying.

Hays Cemetery

Milners Corner: Thomas Rd. between CR E950N and CR E900N
(aka Main Street Graveyard)

Some people believe a girl who made a pact with the devil is buried here. Other visitors have seen orbs, mysterious figures and even devilish beings. Some people have reportedly chased through the cemetery by specters ranging from an old man to a younger man with a hatchet.

McCray Cemetery
Wilkinson: Off SR 109 and CR N1000E

Residual haunters abound in this cemetery. Many apparitions have been seen at the same time.

Old Fair Grounds
Greenfield: SW corner of Market and Third Sts.

James Keener was the lamplighter of Carthage and an African-American Civil War veteran. In 1875 James' son Billy was lynched as a rapist. Billy's last words were "Men, you are doing a great wrong." People came to view "the rapists" body and he was buried in the Greenfield Potter's field. James was outraged and supposedly said "I hope I live to see all of them dead." Three of the men who were part of the lynch mob met bad ends. One became terminally ill, yelling for people to "get that man away from me". Another was killed in an explosion, and the other was killed in a car crash. Billy's innocence was never proven, although later the woman who accused him recanted.

Today, because of the great wrong done at the lynching site at the old fair grounds, people have reported feeling a sense of dread and malice.

The Plantation Club
McCordsville: CR 700W and Pendleton Pike
(aka Casio's; razed)

A speakeasy in the 1930s and a place for gangsters for longer than that, the Plantation Club saw its fair share of action. It had bulletproof panels, a foot thick steel cash door and tunnels for quick getaways. Known for gambling and women, several cabins were provided in back of the bar for extra entertainment. After one woman known for wearing blue was killed, she was seen roaming the cabins.

A woman was killed by her jealous husband in the club's cloakroom. From that time forward, that room had one area that was extremely cold. One employee would hear knocks on the door, but no one would be there.

In its last incarnation, the speakeasy was known as Casio's. The former owners Mike and Donni Nickerson couldn't save it from the wrecking ball and the establishment was razed.

Now it is a wider road and a closed driving range. Avid ghost fans still go by to take pictures. They capture many orbs. One has to wonder if the patrons of the driving range were touched by the woman in blue.

Weston Village Apartments
Greenfield: 424 Roosevelt Dr.

A woman saw a one-eyed monster in her bedroom. Others have seen the ghosts of a man in tattered clothing, and a woman with a burned face. Another ghostly woman gently blows in the ears of the males in this apartment complex.

HARRISON COUNTY

Battle of Corydon Memorial Park
Corydon: .5 miles from the center of Corydon on Old SR 135 South

On July 9, 1863, 450 members of the local home guard fought with Confederate Gen. John Hunt Morgan's Raiders on the south hill. After about thirty minutes, the men surrendered to Morgan and his 2,400 Calvary units, there were five casualties and 11 wounded. On one investigation, a psychic saw four translucent men in the woods, believed to be part of the military, surrounding the investigators. In all, there was a boy, a black man and two other men who could be farmers. Each figure was armed. They did not wear military uniforms, but wore military style hats and caps. During this display the temperature readings spiked hot and investigation equipment malfunctioned. EVPs were captured including the name Emma, who's believed to be the wife of one of the men.

Blue River
Corydon: Blue River

A woman in a canoe was decapitated when she ran into fishing line that was strung across the river. Many evenings she paddles her canoe in search of her head.

Corydon Town Square
Corydon: Town Square

Mary Bouchet was arrested and charged with murdering her child. She was hung in the town square. Her voice and cries are heard there today.

Dove's Nest
Corydon: Unknown

This location was a brothel in downtown Corydon. It is said to be haunted by several women who had either committed suicide or who had been killed by jealous customers.

Lickford Bridge and House
Harrison: Lickford Branch Rd.

The bridge was built in 1920 and rehabbed in 1989. In 2007, the bridge was closed and declared unsafe. A through truss bridge runs over Indian Creek on Lickford Branch Road.

Many stories about this area abound. The most famous is that of an evil Satan-worshiper who sacrificed his illegal slaves under the bridge. Some parts of the legend say he cut the slaves' throats himself with his long fingernails.

If you go to the bridge, he will appear from behind a tree and walk toward you. Some visitors have reported being punctured by his long nails. Other visitors said the handprints of slaves appear on your car. They say the slaves are trying to push your car off the bridge and onto the road to get you away from the man.

The Lickford house is next to the bridge. Supposedly Mr. Lickford went crazy and killed his family, burying them under the porch of the house. If you go into the house, he will throw objects at you. In pictures taken at the location, the family has appeared. Batteries have been drained and compasses refuse to work.

Ohio River

Maukport: Two miles west of Maukport on River Rd. (Maukport/New Amsterdam Rd.) where the road is very close to the river.
(aka Mauckport)

Pirates loved this area around the Ohio River. One night a boatman fell asleep and was ambushed by pirates, who severed his head. From that time, he's been seen headless, wandering the river beds west of Maukport.

HENDRICKS COUNTY

Creature from Hell

Danville: Land west of Danville

Two friends were rabbit hunting in 1883 and went into the forest to the west of Danville. They were chased by a creature resembling a horse with blue flame eyes. Other people said it had zebra-like features. Others believed it had a forked tongue and snakes for a tail.

Danville (town)
Danville

Charlie O. Williams is reported to haunt the area. Police Officer William Wright has a picture from October 18, 2002 after a car accident that occurred at Clinton and Maples Streets. Charlie is in the picture in the middle of the fog. He is also heard whistling and jingling coins- as he did in life.

Davee Home

Danville: 3527 Cartersburg Rd.

Once a popular mineral springs resort that operated into the early 1900s, this house is a home to multiple spirits. A girl in a blue dress runs around the yard. She is also known to turn lights on and unlatch a gate. Conversations from disembodied voices are heard around the pool. A ghost is seen in the laundry room of the home, apparently as surprised to see visitors as the visitors are to see them. One of the upstairs rooms is host to ghost voices. Orbs have been seen as well.

Haunted Bridge
Avon: CR 625E, just south of US 36
(aka Danville Bridge, aka White Lick Creek Bridge)

An Irishman, Dad Jones, fell into the wet cement and drowned in one of the supports when the bridge was built. He is encased in the bridge. A woman jumped off a train that was passing over the bridge. Screams, moans and whispering are heard. The apparition of a man is also seen and tapping can be heard from the bridge (supposedly the man tapping to get out).

Haunted Bridge
Danville: South of US 36 to the east of Shady Lane on East Broadway.

Although this location is often confused with the Avon Bridge and vice versa, another version of the story goes that a woman jumped with a baby off the bridge because she was unwed and felt she had no choice. Now, hauntings range from the appearance of the woman, a crying baby, a woman that will attempt to push you off the bridge.

Hummel Park
Plainfield: 1500 South Center St.

By the bridge over the river on the west side of the park, a woman holds a child and screams, terrifying visitors.

Maplewood
Around Maplewood

On November 1, 1883 the Danville Republican reported that a creature with the head of a horse "as large as a pork barrel" was seen in the area. The creature's six inch long and wide eyes shot light from them. The hair on the beast writhed like black snakes. Its zebra like body was covered in feathers all the colors of the rainbow. The wings were 12ft long and its tongue spit fire, which killed anything within six feet of it. It also has three feet long horns. When it climbs trees, the tree instantly withers and dies.

Royal Theatre
Danville: 59 S. Washington St.

A middle aged couple is seen in the theater. Noises are heard in projection booth and restrooms. Lights turn off and on. Light bulbs malfunction. Sometimes the spirits laugh at you or call your name.

HENRY COUNTY

Community Corrections
New Castle: 100 Van Nuys Rd.

Disembodied voices are heard throughout the facility.

Guyer Opera House
Lewisville: 110 W. Main St.

During a popular Wild West gun show, a little boy was killed by a ricocheting bullet. The same year, the owner OK Guyer died. His funeral was held in the opera house.

Dressing room lights mysteriously turn on, off and burn out. Sometimes the lights will turn on, one by one and turn off the same way. Odd loud noises come from the back of the auditorium and temperature changes (hot and cold) are common. The auditorium doors open and close by unseen hands. The light booth also experiences drops in temperature. Shadow and transparent figures are seen throughout the building, especially on stage and in the dressing rooms.

Monkey Jack Bridge
New Castle: S. of S. Greensboro Pike on CR S225W

A couple had car trouble. He went for help. She stayed. The wind started and the rain came. After, she hard a scratching. Thinking it was her boyfriend,, she got out and found him with a knife in his back, his throat cut and hanging from a tree. The scratching was his fingernails on the roof of the car. If lovers go there, they will hear this too.

Pest House
Knightstown: SR 109 as you enter Knightstown. It is a private home and a great example of red brick Victorian Empire style architecture with its tower and dormer windows.
(aka Morgan House)

Originally, this home was built by Charles Dayton Morgan who was a wealthy banker, lawyer and state representative. In the 1920s this building was used to quarantine victims with contagious diseases and long term issues such as TB. The death rate was very high. Even before that, Knightstown had its share of trouble with the 1902 small pox epidemic. The building is haunted by people who died in the building.
The site of the quarantine station is very active, with nurses and patients walking next to it. A lady in a black dress haunts the building. Some people have witnessed furniture moving on its own across the floor. One ghost will open the door to visitors and tell them no one is home.

Train Depot
Springport: CR E800N West of IN 3

A young man in a suit is seen walking through the building.

HOWARD
COUNTY

208 E. Mulberry Street
Kokomo: 208 E. Mulberry St.
(aka Old Jacob's Funeral Home)

This location is rumored to have been a Sears and Roebuck store and an African-American funeral home. In 1901 it was known as the Smith and Keller Funeral Parlor, later to become Smith and Hoff. In 1919 it became known as Jacob's Funeral Home. Orbs drift through the funeral home. Black shadows walk through the building and basement. Some people believe it smells of decomposing bodies. A black fog is said to seep through the building. Screams have been heard. Shadow figures are seen. Many items at the funeral home seem to hold paranormal properties. Water turns on and off, as do lights. Visitors hear footsteps throughout the building.

3510 Southlea Drive
Kokomo: 3510 Southlea Dr.

Doors open, and people hear cups moving around. Wind would move through the home like a whisper. The front door opens and closes, unlocking for no reason. Cold spots are felt even on warm days. A cold beer can was found one morning on the stove when no one had put it there. Doors would open, but with the lock set in locked position. Families seem to move out quickly.

Adams Mill
(See Benton County)

Carter Street (50 N) and County Road 400 East
Kokomo: North east corner of Carter St. and CR 400E

A man and his mother lived together. She died and haunted the house. Her son moved because he couldn't handle living with the paranormal. Transparent figures seen moving within the house. Orbs are seen and strange taps are heard on cars.

County Roads 600 East and 500 North
Kokomo: CR 600E and CR 500N
(Note: Home and barn are gone. Another house occupies the spot.)

The house contained a locked room in which an entity was released in 1972. The day it was released a young man, Bob, who was about to leave for Vietnam, rifled through the historic belongings in the room. As he went to bed that night, someone yelled, "Keep that door locked!" Bob's wife Carolyn of a woman in a long skirt was saw and heard. An apparition of a young girl looking out the front door has also been witnessed; footsteps were heard all over the house. Some of the issues are attributed to a man who hung himself in the old barn.

Ferrell House
Plevna: Razed

Crops will not grow where the house and barn used to be. A woman hung herself in the barn and her ghost was often seen swinging from a rope.

Gateway Gardens
Kokomo: 800 E. Hoffer St.
(aka Garden Square Apartments)

Rumored to have been built on an old graveyard, some people believe that not everyone was removed and relocated. Legs without bodies walk the area, and teardrops fall from the ceilings.

The C row apartments have the most activity. In apartment C-1, demons were said to influence and possess people living in the apartment. C-3 reports telephones ringing with no one on the line or voices that sound as though they are coming from a long distance and seem to come mainly from dead family and friends. C-11 reports feelings of being watched as well as seeing shadow people.

Disembodied legs and legs in boots are seen frequently. People have reported being locked in the apartment without provocation. C-13 has had apparitions of people in different time periods from mid 1800s to the early 1900s. Other children who grew up in this apartment reported having talked with spirits about their lives. Some of the spirits wanted the children to "come with them".

In F-16 instances of demons influencing children have been reported. Legend has it that a son pushed his mother down the stairs in this apartment and broke her neck.

Hopewell Cemetery
Kokomo: On Van Sickle Rd. (CR 400E) just north of Carter St. (CR E50N). Once on Van Sickle Rd., take the first left. Somewhat overgrown.

Transparent apparitions walk through the cemetery. Apparitions of a small boy are seen. Sometimes he is playing with an airplane and other times he's crying.

Jerome Cemetery
Greentown: CR150S and CR1000E

A shadow figure in a black cape is seen in the cemetery with two dogs. Fogs and mists appear at will.

Kokomo Hum
Kokomo

Almost 100 residents in Kokomo have reported feeling ill and have sought medical treatment for headaches, joint pain and other symptoms they attribute to "the Kokomo hum". Since residents have reported a hum that only can be heard in certain areas. Many people believe that it is caused by industrial equipment, mining, or factories outside Kokomo. The city of Kokomo hired a firm, Acentech Inc., to investigate and they alleviated the issue somewhat by finding an air compressor at the Hayes International plant. Still, other people still believe the noise is extraterrestrial in nature.

Satan's Church and Prairieville Cemetery
Russiaville: CR W650N between CR N1100W and SR 26

This cemetery next to church, boasts glowing red eyes, shapeless mists and whispers. Growling and mysterious voices are heard throughout. It is claimed that a cult used the church for rituals.

Seiberling Mansion
Kokomo: 1200 W. Sycamore St.
(aka Howard County Museum)

Some people see a solid figure of a woman seen in a rocking chair. The reflection of a mannequin that had been moved to a different floor was seen in a first floor mirror immediately after it has been moved. The basement seems to be a hotbed of activity filled entities and lights mysteriously going out without warning.

HUNTINGTON COUNTY

Batson Cemetery

Warren: SR 3 off of Willow Rd.

(aka 13 Graves)

The remnants of an old limestone walkway have been the source of many legends at this cemetery. Some believe the limestone is not a walkway but unnamed graves. If you count them walking one direction, they will number 13. If you count the other way, they number 12. Another legend of this place is that an old man used to be caretaker of a blind school that was torn down years ago. As the children were scared of ghosts coming out of the cemetery, he used to go into the cemetery where the children could see him. He told the kids he'd keep anything from coming to get them at night. One night while sitting in the cemetery, the man died of a heart attack. One of the children in the school said he came to her and asked her to get someone to take care of his body. He is buried in the cemetery. Today, people have seen his apparition as well as captured orbs and streaks of light.

One other story concerns the area is a house (some people say it was the blind school). Disease swept through the building and killed many people. They were all buried together and concrete was poured over them. The building was burned to the ground

Browns Corners

Markle: West of I-69 at CR S200E and CR E100S

This area is home to creatures some might be considered Bigfoot. One creature seen at the location is brown and similar in shape to a human. Some reports put this creature at about 9 ft. while others say it is more around 6 feet. Another creature that is pale in comparison has been seen is estimated at 4-7 feet in height. These creatures have been seen day and night in the area and have been seen for at least the last 50 years. Many people have attempted to speak to the creatures but when they speak to it, the creature runs away. People who have pursued it describe a wail, a scream similar to an animal that has been caught in a bear trap.

Local legends say that some of the Indiana State Police have gone missing (some say due to KKK activity, others say the creature got them) and only their uniforms were found- neatly folded in a pile. No conclusive proof of this has been discovered. A story has been circulating about a couple that went out to the area and went into the woods. When they came back to the car, one of their windows was shattered, the car was turned on (although the key was not in it) and a rather large handprint had been melted into their dashboard.

Canal House

Roanoake: E. of Roanoake on US 24. Remnants of Wabash and Erie canal 1.7 miles east

Lorenzo "Van" VanBecker had a farm here. He tried to increase his wealth in many ways- one being a lodging house. He hired Mariah Heddwick, a woman suspected of being a witch. When Van's wife fell ill, Mariah said she could help her. Instead of being helped, Van's wife died. From that point on, someone has been heard calling out for help.

Today, this area has a number of bright lights that are seen flitting through the trees.

Forks of the Wabash
Huntington: Forks of the Wabash

A house along this area of the Wabash belonged to Chief Richardsville. At one time it was remodeled adding a door that led from the Chief's quarters to the servant's rooms. In this area, cold breezes and temperatures are felt. Many people feel that the Chief or his staff are still in the home. Some believe that they've seen "wisps of the spirits" of those who still roam the area.

Horace Mann School
Huntington: 521 William St., Apt. 307

This school is now apartments but the former visitors haven't left- yet. Apparitions of children and adults have been seen. One EVP seems to have caught someone talking about homework.

Huntington College
Huntington: 2303 College Ave.

A woman shrouded in black (or white- depending on the account) is seen gliding through the PE Recreation center. More men see her, but women have seen her as well. The lights in this building turn on and off without human help and the faucets turn on by themselves. The toilets flush seemingly spontaneously.

Mt. Etna (town)
Mt. Etna (town): East of SR 9 on SR 124

Mt. Etna was settled by German immigrants and named after a Sicilian volcano. Today, it is a partial reservoir and a mecca for hunters and fishermen. The Salamonie Reservoir runs over the northern section of this town. The reservoir was originally built to control flooding in the Upper Wabash River Basin (Mt. Etna) as well as relieve flooding along the lower Wabash and Ohio rivers (southern Indiana). On the northern end of the town a sign reads, "Road ends in water." To create the reservoir, Mt. Etna cemetery was relocate. With the coming of the reservoir, residents no longer had a direct route to the county seat.

Many people believe that the unhappiness in this town caused by the coming of the reservoir and also the relocation of the cemetery is the source for the negative energy and apparitions that are seen in the area.

Monument City
Monument City remains: Take W Monument City Rd. east of CR S700W. It takes you very close to the reservoir. GPS coordinates: 40.763736, -85.592122
Monument City Memorial Cemetery: CR S800W just south of CR W250S

This town was flooded in 1965 to create the Salamonie reservoir. Some visitors report when the reservoir is low, ruins of this city can be seen, and the phantom sound of the old church bell can often be heard. The Monument City Memorial

Cemetery was moved. It houses the town's namesake monument and includes a memorial to Polk township residents who lost their lives in the Civil War. The cemetery was moved around 1965 as well to make room for the reservoir. As a result, many people including psychics believe that this area of the reservoir and the new cemetery hold negative energy from the disturbance of both the cemetery and the town.

Polk Road
Huntington: Polk Rd.

A woman died on train track that used to run through here. Today, as you drive down this road, a woman who looks as if she'd been caught in the rain will stumble down the street. When you approach, she disappears or she will get into the car and tell you how she died. Some accounts say she leaves bloody handprints on your car.

Salamonie River State Forest
Andrews: The park office address is Salamonie River State Forest, 9214 West-Lost Bridge. Its main access in Wabash County is SR 524 and CR 100S.
(aka Wabash County State Forest)

Near the Salamonie Reservoir, black shadows have been seen running through the forest. Strange lights also have been known to appear, along with a foul odor. Witnesses have even claimed to see wolf-like creatures wandering about the forest. Hikers say that time seems to stand still while hiking and the trails appear to shift, causing some unlucky people to be lost.

A phantom church bell rings and someone dies. The smell of death and long, dark shadows that seem to follow visitors along the Reservoir. Lights from unexplained sources are seen. Apparitions of wolves are frequently seen and some visitors are chased by them. Visitors sense being watched and some visitors have become lost on trails citing a sense of being lost in a space warp/time shift.

Warrick Hotel
Huntington: 511 N. Jefferson St.

Although the current building is home to a haunted house, some people believe the story behind the building. As the story goes, the original hotel burnt down on October 13, 1904 killing 302 people including members of a circus. Unexplained noises and apparitions are heard and seen. Some people believe that visitors to the area have disappeared and were found babbling incoherently at Devil's Backbone or have not been found at all. Rumors persist, despite a lack of evidence supporting this story.

JACKSON COUNTY

191 W. Harrison Drive

Seymour: 191 W. Harrison Dr.

(aka Richard's House)

When a little boy named Richard died in the home, his parents planted a rosebush to remember him. When the parents moved, the new owner tried to get rid of the bush but couldn't. Every time they dug it up, it would return even bigger. The owner was eventfully successful. From that point, the bathtub in the home would drain when the plug was in place, clothing was displaced, and the television was operated by unseen hands. A picture fell from the wall and rolled to the television. Many noises were heard at night but nothing was ever found out of place. No figures were ever seen and the events seemed to abate when the person who dug the rose bushed up moved out.

County Road 275S and Guthrie Cemetery

Medora/Guthrie: CR 275S and Guthrie Cemetery

In 1861 a Civil War soldier , Aesop Wilson, Co. B, 22nd Inf., died of typhoid fever in a camp near Boonville, Missouri. His mother refused to bury him and for 12 years, she kept his sealed, charcoal-packed coffin in the hallway at the front of the house. Often she could be seen talking to her dead son and sewing by his side. In 1873 her husband, Creed Wilson had two spiritualists from Louisville come to the house to communicate with her son. They held a seance and supposedly she heard Aesop's voice say it was time. They buried him in the cedars north of their house on CR 275 S. Creed died two years later and was buried in the Leesville Cemetery. When his wife died a couple years later. The house remained vacant. In 1905 Aesop's last letter to his mother was found in the house. Eventually, Aesop's grave was moved because US 50 was ran through the area. It was moved to a "pasture" in the southeast part of Leesville or as some versions go, to the Leesville cemetery to be next to his father. Although legend claims that when the mother died, the people who took care of her estate buried Aesop's remains when they buried hers, we know that this is not true. The legend also says her ghost comes back to her home because she's mad that her son was buried. People in the area never wanted to go by the house; because they said they see white shimmering figures of the family in the house.

600 E. Tipton Street

Seymour: 600 E. Tipton St.

A Civil War soldier walks in this Papa John's Pizza restaurant. This hazy, transparent apparition never fully materializes. The store next door is reported to have thuds, bumps and voices come from it, even when no one is renting it.

Azalia Bridge

Seymour: US 31 north out of Seymour turn right at Azalia. It's the first bridge.

Several legends surround this bridge. First, a couple who went to a dance were killed on the bridge. If you drive to the bridge and honk your horn, the couple will appear and ask for a ride. When you give them a ride, they will get out before you can get them to their location. Screams have also been associated with this bridge.

Another legend involves a woman who was run out of town because she was pregnant. She stayed at the bridge and eventually threw her baby off the bridge and killed herself. Some people say you can hear the baby crying or see it crawling on the bridge. Other visitors claim if you visit the bridge after midnight, that the woman will possess your body and try to drive you off the bridge. Yet another story involves a little girl who was walking home being hit by a car. If you stop on the bridge at midnight she will get in the car, but as you leave the bridge she disappears.

A final story involves a farmer who caught his wife cheating on him, so he cut off her head. She roams around the bridge looking for her head. It's said if you see this white transparent woman that you too will die without your head.

The Coffins
Bobtown: CR 500 E
(aka The Flats, The Bottoms)

The legend states that in the late 1950s or early 1960s a policeman was called to a party at the Coffins. The kids killed him and put him in a tree. He wasn't found and he tree grew around him. Some people claim at night you can see his ghost roaming around, and see him peer down at you from the tree.

Another dubious legend claims that the poorhouses and insane asylums would bury their dead in shallow graves rather than pay for a funeral (and because experiments were conducted on the individuals (see Central State). The coffins would pop up during times of high water and they would float down the creek.

Babies are heard crying. Sometimes the cry of a wolf is heard. The ghosts of Native Americans are seen in the trees surrounding the area. Other apparitions include a boy, a moaning woman, and three white spirits that travelled in a pack around the coffins area.

Cortland Bridge
Cortland: On IN 258 between N CR 425E and Vehslage Rd. Some accounts state it is the pool to the north of IN 258 closer to Cortland and others believe it is the one to the south of IN 258 at the same location. Still others believe it is a single pool on the south side of IN 258 farther to the east and closer to Vehslage Rd.

On one side of the road is a stream. On the other is a large lake. Allegedly this lake is bottomless. Many people have gone into the lake and have never resurfaced. Some people believe the lake's bottom is full of quicksand. Geological surveys show another lake under the current lake.

Crothersville City Cemetery
Seymour: Take Main St. past S. Bethany Rd. Take first right road. Cemetery on left.

A statue in the cemetery is said to shake your hand. Other visitors say that it isn't the statue, but the ghost of a banker who died in the late 1800s after he bankrupted the bank he worked for.

Earl D. Prout Auditorium

Seymour: 1350 W. 2nd St.

In one of the homes that used to be at the site, a woman killed her daughter. Visitors, staff, and students hear a girl playing. Strange voices are heard in the auditorium. Some of the voices have been captured on recordings but cannot be made out. A little girl in blue skips through the room.

Freeman Field

Seymour: Includes the Freeman Field Airport and industrial park. (Near "A" Ave)

Part of the legend is that a Horten (German fighter plane) is buried at the field. Two Hortens flew in one day, but only one left. Supposedly it was buried, although no one can prove that conclusively. Today, ghosts of the workers at the field are seen. Sometimes they will talk to you as if you are part of their time period. Other times, they pass you without saying a word or acknowledging you.

Haunted Railroad Tracks

Seymour: From Seymour you take IN 11 south to 100 S. Wischmeier. Turn right on to 100 S. Wischmeier and take that road all the way till you see a dead end sign. Keep going straight it turns into a gravel road. Keep going then you'll see the rail road tracks.

The legend states that a carload of people were killed by an oncoming train. Several suicides have occurred in this location. If you use your cell phones or radios, strange noises come over them like old radio frequencies.

Interstate 65

Crothersville

A phantom Ford is seeing driving on I-65 for at least 40 years. It is sometimes seen on main roads. It always outruns the police and has no driver. One woman was unlucky enough to be stopped at a light with the vehicle and became very unnerved when the car's radio switched from commercials to hard rock. Additionally, motorists have reported being tailed by this vehicle.

Old Weddleville High School

Weddleville: SR 235 runs through Medora. The school is on old US 50 east of Medora. This school is currently undergoing preservation and will be available for rental through the Weddleville Cemetery Association.

This structure is over 150 years old and is believed to be the oldest remaining pre-Civil War school in Indiana. In more recent times visitors to the old school have heard children talking inside the building. They've heard writing as if on a slate or chalk board. Presumably teachers have asked students questions, and the unseen children have answered.

JASPER
COUNTY

Asphaltum

Asphaltum: Between CR N250E and CR N300E on CR 600N.

At one time, this town was home to American Lubricating and Refining Company. Many oil wells scattered the countryside, and unfortunately the wells were shallow. During its heyday, according to some sources, Asphaltum was filled with many saloons and brothels. Railroaders were said to have come to Asphaltum to party then leave on the same train that brought them. Little evidence of that decadent life exists today. All that remains are a couple homes, possibly some oil tanks, and a few abandoned oil wells.

The wooded areas to the south of the former town are said to hold its remains, including its many spirits. A solid apparition of woman in a dark blue gown is said to run through the trees as if pursued by someone. A look of extreme terror covers her face. Some visitors have reported hearing the sound of two sets of footfalls, presumably the woman's and her pursuer's. Some investigators have speculated that she is a prostitute trying to escape from one of her customers, or perhaps even her employer.

Memory Gardens

Rensselaer: 250 N. McKinley Ave.

Reportedly a statue at back of cemetery moves, follows and stares at you.

Moody's Light

Rensselaer: CR 230E to Meridian Rd.

A phantom light is seen making its way through the farm fields and is said to change color and size.

(See also Moody's Light, Francesville, Pulaski Co.)

St. Joseph's College

Rensselaer: St. Joseph has a map of the campus on its website.

- Aquinas Hall: This is the supposed site of exorcism. No one at the school wants to speak of it.
- Drexel Hall: Now restricted and on the list of Indiana's most Endangered Landmarks. Voices are heard when no one is around.
- Dwenger Hall: Demons roam the halls. Lights are seen by people outside.
- Hallas Hall: A young woman delivered a baby in this building and it died. You can hear the baby cry.
- Theater: A priest hung himself in the theater after an unsuccessful exorcism gone badly. People see shadows on the catwalk. When the lights are off, they see the outline of a white figure dangling from it. Doors open and close without reason and the stage is full of cold spots.

Smith Cemetery

Rensselaer: Corner of Surrey Rd. and CR 100

(aka Twin Cemeteries)

A Romeo and Juliet scene plays out here. The couple killed themselves, and wanted to be buried side-by-side. Instead the families buried them apart. Now they reappear to attempt to reunite. If you park in front of the two cemeteries, you will see a dark haired woman and a man in a suit walk across the road. Also, your car may die. People who are profanity have been attacked.

JAY
COUNTY

Adams House
Portland: 520 E. High St.

(aka Coldren's House)

This home was built in 1894 by David L. Adams. Today, the owners report paranormal activity. Investigators report feeling welcomed by the home.

Blood Road
Dunkirk: CR 700 just off Eaton Pike

Driving down this road, you'll feel a bump and see a trail of blood. The legend goes that a man killed his wife and put her body in his car. When he hit the bump in the road, her body fell out and it was dragged down the road. Another story is that a farmer and his son frequently traveled the road. The boy would jump out of the truck while it was moving so one day his dad chained him to the truck. When he jumped again, he was dragged over two miles. Heading west you will see nothing on the road, but if you go east, you will see blood on the road. Supposedly the home where they lived (unknown location) is very haunted; the boy is buried in the basement.

Crybaby Bridge
Redkey: On IN 1 at CR W825N

Supposedly a school bus full of Girl Scouts went over the bridge, and now you can hear them crying down there. If you stop on the bridge and turn off your car, it might not start again.

Gray Hotel
Redkey: 10 High St.

Many entities of men and women are in this former hotel. From the basement to the top floor, items are manipulated; lights turn on and off, footsteps are heard. Visitors are touched by cold, moist hands. People are plagued with physical symptoms as well. Dizziness, upset stomachs and feeling hot and cold have been reported. A barber shop was once located in the hotel. Its owner was killed near the railroad tracks next to the building. Fairies, pixies and other mythological creatures have also been reported.

Laughing Scarecrow
New Corydon: SR 116 west of CR N750E

From September to November, an apparition of a scarecrow appears in the woods to the west of SR 116. It laughs and screams at people.

Little Salamonia Cemetery

Portland: Boundary Pike Road and CR 300S.

(aka Boundary Pike Road)

A boy and his mom died on this road. They are buried in the cemetery. They come out at night and stand in front of your car. If you keep driving towards them,they disappear at the last minute.

New Corydon

New Corydon: SR 116 west of CR N750E. The devil creature is seen west of CR N700E along the banks of the Wabash River.

Strange lights dance on the country roads around this area. Additionally, a feeling of dread pervades the area. Investigators report a creature described as a hump-backed devil with hoofed feet.

Old Portland High School

Portland: It was turned into a middle school and torn down in 2002.

A janitor fell off a ladder killing himself and the person holding the ladder. Cold spots and apparitions of the janitor are experienced.

Pringley Cemetery

Portland: West of US 27 on CR 500N, go north on N. Liberty Rd. After the sharp left turn, you'll see a bridge. Cross the bridge and go north to the cemetery.

Shadow figures carrying lights go up to the cemetery and disappear. They will also follow you back down the hill. Investigators report these lights as guiding lights. Some investigators believe they are more sinister in nature.

Shoestring Tree

Redkey: Unknown

(aka Shoetree)

A man was killed and his shoes thrown into a tree. He haunts the area because his killer was never found. According to the legend, he tries to kill you and throw your shoes in the tree.
Another part of the story goes that a man was walking through the woods and found the oak tree, when he looked up, something slit his throat. If you touch the tree, the same fate will happen to you.

Wentz Cemetery
Portland: CR W650S

(aka Cinderella's Grave)

To the south of the Jay County Conservation Club is a cemetery. Several stories circulate about this place. There is a grave with "Cinderella" written on it. This name supposedly goes with a boy who is buried there. Another version states it is a girl who was abused by her family and died. The people around the area put the stone there with the name Cinderella because they didn't know her name but wanted to give her dignity. Supposedly, when you count the stones going right there are 13 and when you recount left, there are only 11.

JEFFERSON COUNTY

American Legion Post 9
Madison: 707 Jefferson Street

(aka American Legion Home)

An old woman in black and a man in dress pants with suspenders haunt the basement. People report strange feelings, being touched and cold spots.

Big Creek, Fairmount, Baxter, Monroe, and St. Patrick's Cemeteries
Madison: State St. and Michigan Rd.

These cemeteries are at the same crossroads. Visitors have reported feeling ill, feelings of dread and feeling very sad in these connected cemeteries. Additionally, a little girl with long dark hair and black eyes walks through these cemeteries and sometimes follows visitors.

Clifty Falls State Park
Madison: 950 Cross Ave.

People hear moaning and see a woman near the walkway to the falls.

Clifty Village Mobile Home Park
Madison: Clifty Dr. (SR 62) & Chauncy Ln.

Items disappear. Pets in the residence seem sensitive to unseen spirits. Shadows shift through the wooded area to the south. Voices are heard calling names of residents and visitors.

East Splinter Ridge Road
Madison: East Splinter Ridge Rd.

Three small children, with a milk-white ghost dog are seen at various spots on this road.

Hanover Beach
Hanover: Off S. Riverbottom Rd.

A riverboat full of people sunk. A minister drowned while going for help. He appears on foggy nights at 2 a.m. No word on the fate of the others.

Hanover Cemetery
Hanover: Off W. First St. on Lowrey Ln.

Visitors have felt nauseous and cold. The legend is that Benjamin Bennett who was a student at Hanover College, drowned in the Ohio River. While his body was never found, but a tombstone was put in place for him.

Hanover College
Hanover: 359 E. LaGrange Rd.

Donner Residence Hall: A student committed suicide in the residence hall. Items move and moans and crying are heard.

Parker Auditorium: Dr. A.G. Parker, former President of the college haunts the auditorium. Visitors have seen him as a transparent and solid form. He is heard talking and he is also attributed to many odd sounds and missing items.

Hanover Nursing Center
Hanover: 410 W. LaGrange Rd.

A photo with a green mist has been reported as paranormal activity. Balloons mysteriously move about the nursing center. A piano plays on its own although no one is around. Activity increases before a resident dies.

Jefferson County Library
Madison: 420 W. Main St.

A ghost nicknamed Charlie rides the elevator in his wheelchair and strokes women's arms and legs. He lived at the location before it was a library and loved women.

King's Daughters' Hospital
Madison: 1 King's Daughters' Dr.

A lady in white haunts the second, third and fourth floors. She's been seen in the early morning from 2am-6am. On the fourth floor, a little boy rolls a ball down the hallways at night. Workers have seen the ball and have rolled it back to him.

Lanier Mansion
Madison: 601 W. 1st St.

The youngest Lanier son, who drowned in the Ohio River, is seen walking through town, from the river to the house and on the grounds. A ghost cat is seen and heard. In the children's room, the bed creaks as if someone is sitting on it and footsteps are heard running in the upper floor. The first and third floors are home to a lady in red who makes appearances toward the late afternoon. The third floor beds seem to be slept in as well; staff must remake them often. A puzzle that is kept there always looks as if someone has played with it. Voices are heard throughout the mansion. Doors that are bolted from the inside open on their own.

Little Doe Run Road Cemetery
Madison: E. Little Doe Run Rd.

Little Doe Run is allegedly haunted by a person named Flavius Bellamy.

Madison Country Club
Madison: Country Club Rd.

In 1842, this home was called the Hunter House. In the mid 1850s, the site was used as a fairground. During the Civil War, the home was used as a hospital, and after the war, it became Madison General Hospital. At one time, it served as the Indiana State Fairgrounds. Civil War soldiers walk the course. Chains rattle and Confederate soldiers are seen.

(Note: Country Club is closed but the grounds and building are used for private events)

Madison State Hospital
Madison: 711 Green Rd.
(aka Muskatatuck)

Orbs and noises are heard on the site.

(Note: This facility is still in operation, although many buildings have been closed/remodeled. Be respectful.)

Ohio Theater
Madison: 105 E. Main St.

The balcony is a hotbed of activity; orbs are seen and cold spots are felt. Two ghosts are said to haunt the building- a stagehand that fell from the balcony and a heartbroken chorus girl who killed herself by jumping from the balcony.

Springdale Cemetery
Madison: 5th St. and Suggett Dr.
(aka Cemetery at Hanging Rock Hill)

On Easter morning a statue of an angel cries blood.

Windrift Motel
Madison: Private residence. On Clifty Drive .5 miles before the entrance to Clifty Falls State Park

Shadow people and apparitions may be seen in the former hotel.

JENNINGS COUNTY

Baldwin Cemetery

Vernon: IN 25 to lane on left side that disappears into trees. Cemetery at end of lane.

Mary Smith sits by her grave crying. She was accused of being a witch. A man attacked and raped her. To cover his crime, he stabbed her to death. She's been seen at her grave in a bloody dress. Drops in temperature are reported in the old part of the cemetery, and voices are heard in the newer part. EVPs are frequently gathered. In one men's voices were captured saying "nothing" and "it wasn't my fault".

Commiskey (town)

Commiskey: South of Vernon on SR 3

Commiskey has gray mists, cold spots. Items will disappear and are returned elsewhere. Gray figures of a man and woman move about in the home. People have reported hearing their names spoken when no one is around.

Downtown Bed and Breakfast

North Vernon: 51 N Madison Ave

Once used as temporary housing for railroad men, this bed and breakfast now features several ghosts. Visitors have witnessed game of chess played by unseen hands. Footsteps walk down the hall and stairs day and night. Investigators have great success speaking with the spirits. At last count, 12 spirits inhabit the building. A couple of men said they died on the railroad, one in an explosion.

Jennings County Historical Society Museum

North Vernon: 134 E. Brown St.

In 1838, this former stage coach stop was home to Matthew Phillips, who drowned. Beds in the museum seem to be slept in. A child's footsteps are heard.

Muscatatuck Urban Training Center

Butlerville: CR 350 N and CR 475 E
(aka Muscatatuck State Developmental Center)

The Indiana Farm Colony was originally a working farm for disabled adult men. In 1925, the structure changed and more education was added to the residents' lives. When the institution became the Muscatatuck State School in 1941, the facility allowed women as well. At present the facility is used for Homeland Security Training.

Visitors report a bigfoot-esque creature at least seven feet tall.

Six Mile Cemetery
Hayden: South of W. Base Rd. on CR 610

A smallpox epidemic over 150 years ago killed the parents of the children, leaving many orphans. The town nurse tried to do her best but the disease spread to the children as well.

Ghostly figure of a woman nurse walks or runs across graveyard and stands at a fence near the road. Hear children crying and giggling. A gravestone in the shape of a chair moves on All Hallows Eve.

JOHNSON COUNTY

Atterbury Job Corps Center
Edinburgh: Hospital Rd.

Footsteps are heard frequently on the campus when no one is around. Yellow glowing eyes are seen in the woods. A woman holding her head in her hands walks around. By the field house, a scarred man walks and talks to himself. WWII soldiers walk through the building. In one dorm a clock flew off the wall. In the Rosa Parks dorm, three women from the Civil War era walk through the dorm. The cemetery on the property is a hotbed for orbs. The apparition of a small boy talks with you about his red truck. A discussion between a woman and a man can be heard, although it is unclear what they are saying. Legend also places the area as a Native American burial ground and Native Americans have also been seen as well. In the theater, a man in black sits in a chair. He is believed to be the same man in the woods. Sometimes he whistles. People describe feelings of sickness in different areas.

First Christian Church
Edinburgh: 306 S. Walnut St.

Orbs and a grey mist have been captured at this location. A transparent stooped old man who shuffles slowly is seen entering the building.

Franklin College
Franklin: 101 Branigin Boulevard

- Bryan Hall: In the early 1980s, a fire destroyed much of this building, a student burned to death. Today students and staff smell burning flesh and fire to the point that classes have been cancelled. Screams are also heard. Legend has it that an older girl killed a younger one, dismembered her, and put her in a wall. She was found in the wall of the second floor during summer break. She is heard beating against the wall and crying. A professor hung himself in the attic and the rope is supposed to still be in place. The door to the 4th floor opens even if it's locked.
- Old Main Theatre: It is haunted by Charlie. Supposedly a French student hung himself in the theater. One student had a person appear on the piano. Another student playing the piano heard someone scream, "GET OUT!" People have been touched by unseen hands in this building.

Greenwood Cemetery and US 31
Greenwood: West of US 31 north of Main St.

A girl in white walking by the road will get in and ask to be taken home. Before she can tell you, she disappears. Other times, they say she runs through Greenwood Cemetery.

Henderson Cemetery
Greenwood: CR W200N and CR N575W

(no public access)

Locals believe the Grim Reaper himself haunts this cemetery in hopes to find new victims. People hear footsteps when no one is around and a shadow figure wearing a tattered cape is seen gliding through the cemetery during both night and day. Strange figures that dance at the corner of visitors' eyes are reported

Historic Artcraft Theatre
Franklin: 57 N. Main St.

This 600 seat theater opened in 1922 as a vaudeville and silent movie theater. Below the stage are the original dressing rooms. Perfume is smelled and shadow figures are seen in the third and eighth rows of the theatre. Seats lower and rise at will. EVPs have also been captured.

Main Cemetery
Franklin: On South St. across from Tearman Hotel

Many experience feeling of discomfort are felt. Recently EVPs of a woman with static over her voice said that she wanted to get out. Another EVP caught a woman asking "what am I supposed to do?"

Nicholson Home
Greenwood: Moved from Mills and Mann Roads to Southport and Mann Roads in 1997.
(aka Rand Home)

David Nicholson, a contractor for the Marion County Courthouse, built this home from 1870 to 1876. The Rand family owned the home from the early 1900s until the mid 1960s. Part of the home's legend states that it was once used as a boarding house and someone committed suicide by hanging in the middle upstairs bedroom. In 1997 it was moved by the Indiana Historic Landmarks Foundation to its current location. The day it was scheduled to move, one of the trucks carrying half the home wouldn't start. In retrospect, some people speculate that the home didn't want to be moved after all. Locals, who were quite interested in the move told stories of a child accidently shot by hunters nearby. Her spirit and those of a nearby cemetery haunted the home. Another story is that a little girl broke her neck after falling from the home's second-story balcony. An Indianapolis Star photographer took a picture of the home in which a little girl was peering out from an upper window. The photo is now all over the Internet.

Investigators have reported odd EMF readings in the building, which is now a private home.

Podunk
Bargersville: Go south on SR 135 and turn right on Division Rd, which becomes a narrow road, eventually turns into a twisting narrow road. Eventually the road will become Podock. When you reach Podock and Dillman Road, you've reached Podunk.
(See also Nashville, Brown Co.)

A baby crawls on the road and sometimes laughs and cries. Visitors feel emotional outburts. Some have been pushed and scratched. A story claims a phantom truck follows motorists. One version of the stories at this location includes a phantom truck that will follow you. Many people have reportedly seen this truck and lights that appear and disappear just as quickly. Investigators have seen strange mists and half apparitions.

Toner Maley House
Edinburgh: 606 E. Main Cross St.

This bed and breakfast is full of elegance and the royal treatment. From pillow-top mattresses, candlelight breakfasts and plush sheets, this location is not only a pleasure to stay in but a wonderful place for a haunting.

Spirits like to spend time in the library. A woman and a man have both been seen reading and looking at books. As you approach them, they smile and disappear. The woman is in an elegant Victorian dress with upswept hair. The man, who has mutton chop sideburns, sits in a chair, smoking a pipe. A young woman in early 1900 clothing and a suffragette hat walks down the stairs and slams the front door.

Willard Restaurant
Franklin: 99 N. Main St.

Built in 1860 as a hotel it was later sold to a prohibitionist, Eliza Willard. Many visitors believe that she haunts the establishment in an effort prevent drinking and other vices. Several people report having tried to light cigarettes only to have their matches and lighters extinguished with a puff of wind. People felt as if they were watched. The scent of lavender and gardenias lingers in the air. Other visitors report a presence in the woman's restroom. Several unexplained photos have been taken and apparitions have been seen. EVPs of a woman's voice have also been caught by investigators.

KNOX COUNTY

Fort Knox II
Vincennes: 3500 N. Lower Fort Knox Road

This fort was actually called Fort Knox and the locals nicknamed it Fort Knox II. In 1803 it was built for $200. Many duels were fought here, most notably for desertion. In 1811, William Henry Harrison gathered his troops here before the Battle of Tippecanoe, where Native American's were heinously slaughtered. Karma, being the woman she is, saw to it that. Many of the troops died of their wounds upon their return to the fort.

The fort was disassembled a year later and it is now a state historic site. The ghosts of the dead soldiers and other slaughtered Native Americans haunt the grounds.

George Rogers Clark Memorial
Vincennes: South 2nd St.

As Indiana's oldest city, it is no wonder this area has its share of ghosts. Vortices and orbs have been reported in this beautiful structure dedicated to George Rodgers Clark, known for a brigadier general on the northwestern frontier during the Revolutionary War.

Otter Pond
Vincennes: Enter from Witterreid Ave.
(aka Otter Lake)

Donna Mariana Gonzales settled by the lake and fell in love with a local boy named Duffee. Her father wanted her to marry an older man in Mississippi. Instead, she took her life in Otter Lake where her beloved found her. Still, her cries can be heard. Sometimes her face peers at you from the water.

Purple Head Bridge
Vincennes: At the end of W Ferry Rd.
(aka Stangle's Bridge)

Many hangings occurred on this one lane bridge. One poor man tried to hang himself. His head was torn off, shooting blood onto the bridge. Visitors claim to have seen his purple head levitate toward, them and heard a scream as if someone is jumping off the bridge. One investigator was witness to this phenomenon and saw a spray of blood covering another investigator. When a picture was taken, the blood was not seen. A woman said goodbye to her lover here as he went off to war. They were to marry when he returned, but he was killed. Upon hearing the news of his death, she put her wedding dress on. At 11pm when she heard the train coming she stood on the track and was run over. Some believe they see James Jonston, a Revolutionary War hero, because he is unhappy people are on his land. Other stories indicate a battle between Native Americans and soldiers was fought here and several of them were killed in the water. Visitors say the head is also seen below the bridge through the planks.

Sigma Pi Fraternity
Vincennes: Old Wheatland Rd.

(aka Sigma Pi House; aka Shadowwood)

The national headquarters of the Sigma Pi Fraternity is haunted by ghost children. They are believed to be the children of the original owner, Col. Eugene Wharf. The Wharf makes an appearance from time to time.

Col. Wharf supported the Confederacy; and the area around his home was named Rebel Hill. Doors banging and footsteps have been heard. Cold spots manifest before people see the ghosts. Fogs and mists have also been reported in the home, usually accompanied by changes in temperature. A host of apparitions have been seen, ranging from men in Civil War uniforms to workmen and women.

Some of the oddest happenings have centered around objects being manipulated. People have poured hot coffee, only to have it go ice cold. Objects have moved across rooms and levitated. Lights turn on and off.

Ghost Hollow
Wheatland: 1 mile NE of Wheatland.

Now used for coal mining.

Lucy was a redhead who was born on a farm. When she got into arguments with her parents, she would take off on her horse. Once she and her father cooled down, the arguments would be forgotten the arguments would be forgotten. One day she said she'd been invited to a gathering of friends and she'd ride there. Her dad had a fit because she would be out late alone and he forbade her to go. She said she'd leave anyway they would never see her again and then she took off. When a storm started brewing she decided to go home. No one knows what really happened, but the next day her headless body was found on the path leading home. She is said to reenact her ride nightly, scaring people with her headless figure.

KOSKIUSKO
COUNTY

Barbee Hotel
Warsaw: 3620 N. Barbee Rd.

Once a high class hiding spot and retreat for Al Capone and his cronies, this lakeside hotel is now host to a variety of ghosts. Capone stayed in room 301. Visitors and staff have smelled his cigar smoke. In the bar/restaurant, bartenders and visitors have seen several misty figures sitting at booths. When they approach the figures, they simply disappear. In the Gable/Lombard suite, one guest woke up to cigarette smoke and the apparition of Clark Gable sitting at a table smoking a cigarette. As the guest woke his wife, Gable disappeared from sight. Guests and staff hear footsteps on the stairs and several orbs and mists have been captured in pictures.

Berst House
Leesburg: 5677 N. CR 150W
(aka Green-Stone House)

Built in 1868 by Titus and Matilda Berst, the building is now home to several ghosts. Two girls have been seen playing, and scared former owners enough that they moved out. A man and a woman are seen in one of the downstairs rooms. A musty odor in the back of the home is often smelled, although no reason for the odor exists.

Buffalo Street
Warsaw; North end of Buffalo St.

George Ininger used to run a hamburger joint in the early 1900s. Today, his spirit is seen at work in his sanitary uniform, walking home.

Devil's Back Bone
Warsaw: SR 25 south of Warsaw

A family in a horse and wagon lost control of the rig. They ended up in the swamp and were sucked under. Visitors hear the wagon, the impact and their screams. Others say they've seen the reenactment of the accident.

Leesburg Lights
Leesburg: Leesburg between North Webster

Mysterious lights follow people. Visitors speculate these lights are no more than house lights or car lights. Others believe they are lights from a UFO or pixie lights.

Little/Big Barbee Lake
Warsaw: Little/Big Barbee Lake

A Native American maiden walks the shores of the lake. At times, she's also seen floating above the water in the full moon light. She seems to be a residual haunting of unknown events in the past.

Merbrink

Winona Lake: 410 Administration Blvd.

Once used for many learning events like the Chautauqua Conference and Bible conferences, Miss Phoebe appears in a white gown on the porch. Dolls and other items move from room to room. Cold spots and breezes are felt. The scent of flowers and incense is detected. Miss Phoebe was also seen napping on a couch by a former resident.

North Webster Elementary School

North Webster: 5475 N. CR 750E

A playful young boy spirit named Daniel (in tan pants and a blue sweater) turns the lights off and on and sits in the library. On the first and second floor, footsteps of a woman in heels walks across the floors. The lockers in hallways open at random times.

Pennsylvania Railroad tracks

Warsaw: Zimmer Rd.

In December 1882, William Hull's axed and beaten body was found by the railroad tracks. Hull was a big man with gorgeous long black hair, which made him a very striking figure. He owned a butcher shop and was generally liked, but had a penchant for drink and became a bully. John Shaffer, who was accused of fighting him, was charged with murder and convicted. Shaffer appealed and the second trial ended when Hull having was hit by a train. Once the second trial ended in 1883, Hull started his haunting of the railroad. Several people, including railroad engineers, have seen a ghost with an axe and a ghost that flagged down the train.

Sacred Heart Church and School

Warsaw: 135 N. Harrison St.

Visitors to the school gym feel light-headed when entering. In the center of the gym, people feel the hands of many people pushing them. Footprints appear in dust on the floors and a scraping of metal on metal is heard.

Sawmill Lake

Leesburg: Sawmill Rd.

Mists and apparitions are seen. A ghost dubbed "Whitey" by the locals is very noisy. Loud thumps can be heard at random times. A man can be heard yelling. Legend states that a drunk driver crashed into a home over 30 years ago and died.

Syracuse Creek
North Webster: CR N650E south of CR E1120N

In 1903 a small bridge crossed this section of road. A headless woman appeared when people came to cross the bridge. She is still seen today, waiting for the next person to cross the stream.

Train Tracks
Winona Lake: Train tracks east of Winona Lake

Mike Fitzgerald was struck by a passenger train on New Year's Eve 1868. His ghost carries a lantern and continues to walk the tracks. Visitors, investigators, and train men have seen him flagging down the train.

Tumbleweed Inn
North Webster: North Webster

A ghost named Uncle Earl opens and closes the Inn's refrigerator, presumably looking for beer. Another uncle showed up in a WWI uniform to tell his family he was leaving and they wouldn't see him again. The family received a telegram that day saying the uncle had been killed a week earlier. The family also reported the sound of a moving suitcase at night and a mysterious unseen person swinging on the porch swing.

Warsaw Public Library
Warsaw 310 E. Main St.

The building was once used as a checkpoint for the Underground Railroad during pre-Civil War days when slavery was legal. The basement still harbors spirits. Late at night employees have reported hearing children crying and seeing mysterious figures moving about the bookshelves.

LA GRANGE COUNTY

Brushy Prairie
Brushy Prairie: US 20 between CR N1150E and CR N1000W

A Lady in White haunts this road. Her final destination is a cemetery. Similar to Resurrection Mary (seen in Chicago, IL), she wears a beautiful dress and disappears when picked up by motorists.

Riverside Cemetery
Lima: East of SR 9 on CR E500N and 3rd St.

Crissy (aka Christina Hahn; aka Crissy Hand; aka Skunk Girl; aka Skunk Lady; aka Skunk Woman) was born somewhere between 1838 and 1847. The 1870 census has her born in 1847. Her father and mother, Mason and Clarissa Hand died, in a boating accident while she was young, her brother Royal. Her younger sister Henrietta's fate is unknown.

What is known is that she fended for herself. Supposedly marrying four times, Crissy had to fend for herself. was very robust in nature and possibly helped build the railroad tracks around her home. She lived in what most people considered squalor. Animals, mostly skunks, were her friends.

For years, she lived in a house on the northern side of Riverside Cemetery. Later in her life, the people of Howe built her a home on Twin Lake and took care of her. She was a very friendly soul who would converse or share her home with anyone. Although she owned a lot of land, she never sold it and it went to her estate after her death.

She is allegedly buried on the east side of Riverside Cemetery. A plaque commemorates her life. The only person who knew where she was truly buried died before her gravestone was set.

LA PORTE
COUNTY

1800 Elston Street
Michigan City: 1800 Elston St.

Voices are heard, footsteps, and ghost figures can sometimes be seen. People see a shadowy man in the basement.

415 Virginia Avenue
LaPorte: 415 Virginia Ave.

The original house was built in 1856 and burnt in 1885. A young teenager died in the fire. In the 1950s the house that was built in the same place was turned into apartments. The people who have died in the area of the apartments still haunt the building. A young woman has been seen warning people of fires. Items in the apartments move on their own. Doors open and close without the aid of human hands.

County Road 50 North
Michigan City: CR 50N off US 421

This area is home to a time warp. The white house that sits at the corner of this location is sometimes not there. At other times, however, people will be able to see it.

Barker Mansion and Civic Center
Michigan City: 631 Washington St.

For years this location has been considered haunted. Built in 1857 by John H. Barker, who built the Haskell & Barker Railroad Car Company, this house embodies gentility.

A handsome apparition of a beautiful young man appears to teenage girls. A woman in Victorian clothing enjoys interacting with tour groups. Visitors and staff see a couple dancing in the home. A small girl bounces a ball down the stairway.

Belle Gunness House
LaPorte: McClung Rd. There are now many houses on the property where the house once stood.

Belle Gunness was a widow with children. People felt sorry for her children, especially when bodies were found in the house. When the search was over, 14 whole people were found with several unclaimed bones and teeth. Apparently Belle had killed her husbands when she tired of them.

In 1908 the Bell Gunness house burned. A burned, decapitated body of a woman was found. The body was possibly Belles, or perhaps one of her victims.

When Belle died, Ray Lamphere was tried and convicted of her death and died of TB in prison. He had been in love with her, and had helped her bury the bodies and he also ground some up for her hogs to eat before slaughter. He also confessed the body in the fire was a homeless woman from Chicago. Belle was supposed to contact him after the incident died down, but she never did.

People hear people screaming, feel cold spots and hear heavy labored breathing as if someone is running.

Blue Chip Casino
Michigan City: 777 Blue Chip Dr.

A woman in a blue sundress and long red hair haunts the casino. She shows herself in guest rooms and in the restroom. The room gets cold. If any water is around, faucets turn on or glasses spill.

Briar Leaf Golf Course
LaPorte: 3233 N Old State Road 39

A spirit likes to pull pranks on visitors. It moves personal items. A member caught the voice of a man saying "Rodney". The former owner was named Rodney Morozowski.

Fountainview Terrace Nursing & Rehabilitation
LaPorte: 1900 Andrew Ave.

The building is rumored to be on top of a Native American burial ground. A female patient was found out of bed, and dead on the floor. She couldn't have gotten out because her bedrails were still up. Today she haunts the buildings.

Hangman's Road
LaPorte: Orr Lake Rd. (the dead end part that goes south)
(aka Orr Lake Rd.)

In an old tale of a broken down car, a man goes for help and comes back. He can't find his companion. Seeing a drop of blood on the windshield, he looks and finds her hanging from a tree. Legend states many people have been killed here. People have seen a person hanging in the trees and white figures running through the trees.

Hesston Steam Museum
LaPorte: 1201 CR E1000N

A ghostly Native American man accompanied by a coal black horse walks by visitors.

Kingsbury Ordnance Plant
Kingsford Heights/Kingsbury (near LaPorte): East of US 35 on US 6
(aka Old Military Base)

This former ammunitions plant served in WWII and employed over 20,000 people. The plant was a manufacturing facility and housing for workers of the plant. By 1959 the plant had closed and part of the land was sold for the Kingsbury State Fish and Wildlife Area. Visitors see soldiers and civilians walking around the area and report smelling gas. Legend has it that gas explosions occurred during production. Which killed several workers. A hanged man can be seen hanging on a rope, and motioning to visitors.

LaPorte Cinema
LaPorte: 608 Colfax Ave.

A young teenage girl haunts the Cinema. She appears in the tile of the floor and appears in the bathroom. She's also been seen in the office and the theater. Her death is unknown; according to legend, she drowned in a near by pond, fell off a Ferris wheel, or died inn a fire in her family's home.

Laporte High School
LaPorte: 602 F St.

A young Native American girl died and her ghost still wanders where she faltered on a small hill across the street from what would be come La Porte High School's baseball field. The restrooms in the school flush without reason and the faucets turn themselves on. Cold spots are felt in the school and on the grounds. Lights turn off and on and loud noises are heard when no one is nearby.

Lambs Chapel Cemetery
Rolling Prairie: E 600 N and N. Fall Rd.

A beautiful woman runs through the cemetery. She is most frequently seen at night, but she is also seen during the day as well, walking amongst the stones. History states that her car broke down and when she got out to see if she could fix it, a man jumped out and chased her through the cemetery, where he caught and killed her.

LaPorte Medical Building
LaPorte:'I' and 10th Streets
(aka 'I' and 10th Street Clinic, aka the Andrews Mansion)

Part of the trail of tears, this area was a resting place for the Native Americans as they were pushed west. A young girl died during the winter they stopped at this area. The building is currently a medical clinic The elevators erratically move from floor to floor and the bathroom doors often lock, trapping occupants. Chairs also skid across the floor, pushed by unseen hands. A woman is also seen in the attic and her footsteps are heard. A woman walks along the back balcony. A man in a suit walks along the porch. The old crank handle doorbell has long been disconnected, but is said to crank on its own. Once, when this happened, there was no one at the door, but footprints were in front of the door (no where else) where someone would have stood. Some believe a little Cherokee girl is haunting the building. Others believe a woman who fell in love with a man who went to the California gold rush is waiting for him to come for her. After he left, she died in a train accident.

Le Mans Academy
Rolling Prairie: 5901 N 500 E
(aka Le Monds Academy)

The area around Rolling Prairie was settled in 1831 as Nauvoo. It was later called Portland and Plum Grove, because of the wild plum trees. Native Americans were marched through the area on the Trail of Death/Trail of Courage. In 1857 it was named Rolling Prairie. One hundred years later LeMans was established. Although in 2003 the school closed its doors, feelings of uneasiness are sensed here. Investigators have seen orbs, shadow figures and have been touched by unseen hands. Today, the property is owned by the Legionaries of Christ and houses the Sacred Heart Apostolic School.

Light House Premium Outlet Stores
Michigan City: 601 Lighthouse Place

Staff and shoppers have had multiple interactions with the ghosts here. A boy looks out the windows. A woman in a long coat walks through the stores.

Lincoln Elementary School
LaPorte: 402 Harrison St.

Lights and water turn on and off for no reason.

Michigan City Prison
Michigan City 201 Woodlawn Ave.

Shadows and flickering lights are seen within the prison walls. In one cell on cellblock x, an inmate had recently lost his cellmate and he heard someone whisper in his ear, "You're next." The next night, the inmate woke up with someone clawing him. The guards couldn't explain it.

Old Chicago Road
Michigan City: Off County Line Rd, on Porter County side.

The Mafia used to use Devil's Bridge as a "family" burial plot. – Apparitions of 1930s era men have been seen. Orbs and mists have been captured on film.

Old Lighthouse Museum
Michigan City: 1 Washington Park Marina

For 150 years, the lighthouse has graced the Lake Michigan coastline. Harriet Colfax, a lighthouse keeper from 1861 to 1904 haunts the museum. Footsteps are heard on the stairs and at times, a translucent figure is seen climbing the stairs. Many people believe it is Ms. Colfax on the stairs.

Old U.S. 30
Union Mills: US 30 between Hanna and CR 600 W

A blue figure has been seen at the railroad for over 20 years. In 1987 a man was hit by a train at 3 am. Today around the same time, he can be seen carrying a lantern.

Orr Lake Road
LaPorte: N.Orr Lake Rd south of W 150 N

A doctor's wife and daughter died. He was so distraught he preserved them in pickle brine. Today the doctor is long dead but you can see him and his servant (the Hookman) reenact the pickling every full moon in the woods.

(See also Hangman's Road)

Patton Cemetery
LaPorte: North of SR 4 entrance off Clement St.
(aka Patten Cemetery)

Belle Gunness is buried in this cemetery. She and others are said to walk through the cemetery as if they don't know they are dead.

(See Belle Gunness House, LaPorte, LaPorte Co.)

Posey Chapel Cemetery
LaPorte: Corner of E1000N and N400E

A preacher hung himself from a tree next to the gate. Visitors see the residual haunting of this event. Orbs, EVPs and moans have been captured. One EVP features a woman singing and a guitar playing. A transparent nun is said to cross the street at this location and disappear. Also, a white mist is seen at the top of the hill.

Range Road Pond
LaPorte: Range Rd. and E 700 N

On March 26, 1993 Rayna Rison went missing. A month later her body was found in this pond. Many visitors report feeling a heaviness, even without knowing the unfortunate story. Several visitors report seeing a swirling mist around the pond, and hearing footsteps.

Saugany Lake

LaPorte: Saugana Trail and N 600 E

Chief Suagany protects this lake from any negative energy and events.

Soldiers Memorial Park

LaPorte: Grangemouth and Waverly Rds.

In 1930 a small boy drowned in Stone Lake near the bridge. He haunts the walking trails and can be seen walking down them or near the bridge. When people have tried to talk to him, he laughs and disappears. Sometimes, he will say "hello" or tell "he can't stay" and walks back to the woods.

LAKE
COUNTY

173 Avenue and Holtz Road

Lowell: Intersection 173 Ave. and Holtz Rd.

Driving east on 173rd St, at the top of the first hill, you can see Holtz Rd. Many people have reported seeing accident scene lights on the second hill. When getting to the second hill, the lights and vehicles are gone.

36 Detroit Street

Hammond: 36 Detroit St.

In this home and on the entire block, strange occurrences happen. Visitors and residents feel cold spots, feel icy unseen hands touch them and witness levitating items. Several visitors have had books, magazines and a vase thrown at them. Many residents say that someone unseen watches in many of the homes.

501 Indiana Street

Hobart: 501 Indiana St.

The Spencer family was well-to- do. The oldest child killed his sister, Mary and while in jail, he committed suicide. The murder is reenacted in the home. Investigators have heard a child running through the house and have heard piercing screams.

Bishop Noll Institute

Hammond: 1519 E. Hoffman St.

This organization has many spirits. In A-Wing's second floor, visitors, staff and students hear footsteps and talking. In the classrooms, chairs tip over without provocation.
Several deaths have occurred on site including one in front of the library, and the now unused pool, and in A-Wing on the second floor where a janitor hung himself. Additionally a girl who was turned down for a part in a playkilled herself in the auditorium. Now, anyone who auditions for the lead gets hurt, has mishaps or becomes ill. The library has permanent cold spots and visitors to the empty pool area hear laughter at all hours of the day- and night.

Black Oak Neighborhood

Gary: The Black Oak Neighborhood is located in the SW part of Gary. It is bounded by (roughly) Cline Ave., US80, Chase St., and W. Ridge Rd. Exact location of the school is unknown.

An old schoolhouse which was once a speakeasy and home to prostitution now houses many leftover spirits. Visitors used to hear voices of men going into the basement. A woman in red walks inside the building and outside on the grounds. Often she is crying. Even though the school house has been razed, people still experience the phenomenon associated with this location.

Circus Train accident

Ivanhoe (near Hammond): Ivanhoe is east of Cline St. on W 9th Ave. near Hammond. The tracks that the circus train took run north from W. 9th St. and curve east and go past Kennedy Ave.

On June 23, 1918, the Hagenbeck Wallis circus train crashed and killed over 100 people and animals. Locals believe that it is the animals, and not the people who haunt the nearby woods, although some investigators have picked up EVPs of human voices.

(Note: Most of the people who died are buried in Woodlawn Cemetery (Forest Park, Illinois) in the area known as Showman's Rest)

Cline Avenue

East Chicago: Cline Ave. between East Chicago and Griffith, Indiana

Sophia, a Polish immigrant fell in love with someone who wasn't Polish. They decided to get married secretly; she waited in the church. He never showed. Distraught, she threw herself into the Calumet River. She still walks along Cline Ave and the river.

Crown Point High School

Crown Point: 1500 S. Main St.

The school was built on a cemetery. Unearthed several graves in order to build the school. The site was once Luther's Grove, which was owned by an early Crown Point family with same name. Lights throughout the building turn off and on, especially in the gymnasium. Sports equipment moves by unseen hands. Voices are heard in different classrooms and to stop when doors open. The auditorium catwalk is haunted by spirits who are seen walking high above the stage.

East Chicago Marina

East Chicago: 3301 Aldis St.

A handsome gentleman ghost assists visitors. One woman had a conversation with him. He told her he normally doesn't show himself but she reminded him of his daughter. Then he disappeared.

East Chicago Public Library

East Chicago: 2401 E Columbus Dr.

Patrons hear voices. Staff see books removed from shelves when no one is present.

Fairchild House
DeMotte: 212 Ninth St. SW

Orbs were captured on film and whispers are heard throughout the house.

Forrest Hill Neighborhood
Merrillville: One block east of Broadway St.
The Potawatomi lived here. Animals react to unseen things by barking, growling, hissing and running

Gavit High School
Hammond: 1670 175th St.

People report hearing footsteps on the roof as well as seeing a ghost who likes to open windows. Students hear screams at odd hours at evening events. White figures walk the halls.

Grand Boulevard Lake
Lake Station: West side of Grand Boulevard Lake

A man is seen as a residual haunting and a gun shot is heard. Interestingly enough, Andy Figueroa was found dead here one June morning inside his car.

Grand Kankakee Marsh
Lowell: 21690 Clay St.

Although the house that used to sit on this property is long gone, the whole area is believed to have been part of a Native American burial ground. Visitors and investigators report seeing Native American figures, and capturing orbs on pictures. Strange mists are seen throughout the property. A female Native American walks the property and seems very "thoughtful".

Griffith High School
Griffith: 600 N. Wiggs St.

A girl appears in the mirrors in the bathroom next to the auditorium. The legend states that a girl hung herself in the bathroom with an oversized belt. In the school library, chairs tip over and books fly from shelves. The occurrences are believed to be from a ghost of a young man who died of a heart attack in the library.
cars, gives directions to her home and disappears at the cemetery—usually with the driver's jacket on. Drivers who venture into the cemetery find their jackets on her tombstone.

Hedgewisch Baptist Church of Highland
Highland: 8711 Cottage Grove Rd.

This church is said to use exorcism rituals on a regular basis. In 1992, Pastor Win Worley held an open house for anyone needing an exorcism. Over 500 people from a number of states and countries attended. Today, some of the exorcised spirits are said to haunt this church.

Highland High School
Highland: 9135 Erie St.

Bobby Haymaker walks through the hall and does laps in the gym. Basketballs also bounce by unseen hands in the gym. Bobby died during gym class.

Hobart Cemetery
Hobart: At Front St. and E. Cleveland Ave.
(aka Crybaby Woods)

A baby cries in the cemetery. Visitors have photographed orbs and mists.

Indiana Bridge
Lowell: Two miles east of I65 on Clay St.

Three people were murdered and thrown off the bridge here. Their spirits are seen falling from the bridge. Mysterious fogs are also reported in the area.

The John Dillinger Museum
Hammond: 7770 Corine Dr.

John Dillinger was a notorious gangster/bank robber in the early 1930s. Aside from a few minor crimes, he was thrown in jail, after a bank robbery. In 1933 he was paroled and then went on the robbing sprees he is most famous for. His short-lived reign as a wanted man came to an end on July 22, 1934 at the Biograph Theater in Chicago when he was gunned down in an FBI trap.

Dillinger is said to haunt many places in Indiana- the location of his boyhood home, Crown Hill Cemetery, where he is buried, the Slippery Noodle in Indianapolis. He also haunts this museum.

Visitors and staff hear his voice (and possibly the voices of his gang) in a possible residual energy type interaction. Additionally, he speaks to visitors. One notable incident involved a small child. An unseen person informed his mother that the boy put something in his mouth. The mother checked and he had indeed put money in his mouth. The boy later said, pointing to a photo of Dillinger, that he tried to take money from the boy.

Kahler School
Dyer: 600 Joliet St.
Cemetery is St Joseph Cemetery to the east of the school.

Agnes Kahler haunts the school because she couldn't stop teaching even after 50 years! Books fly from library shelves and toilets flush when no one is around. One student reports going down a hallway in which several lockers opened, slamming the doors back on their hinges. In Agnes Kahler's classroom, boards fall from walls and the door swings open. Additionally, the door has been seen opening and closing as if someone is entering or exiting. Maps hanging on the wall unroll in the room. Alarms go off without reason on a regular basis Kahler is buried at the cemetery next door. Even the assistant principal, Tim Doyle, has a story. A few years ago, the motion detector on the exit nearest the cemetery was tripped. On the surveillance video, a grey blur was seen exiting toward the cemetery. When the old part of the school was torn down, a memorial plaque for Miss Kahler disappeared out of a locked classroom when it had been taken down for cleaning. A boarded up window fell out of its frame.

Kaske Home Historical Museum
Munster: 1005 Ridge Rd.
(aka Munster Historical Society, Stallbohm-Kaske House Historical Museum; Bieker House)

Built as a private home in 1837, legend has it that the original home burnt down on Halloween 1949. Now it is a historical society. The attached barn was (which was destroyed by arson) haunted by dark shifting shadows and a figure of Wilhelmina Kaske (Shallbohm) who would lean out the window and sometimes wave. The upstairs of the historical society is haunted by a figure that once threw a can of open paint at a painter. Visitors and staff feel cold spots throughout the building, most notably in the upstairs rooms, and hear footsteps. A child runs around the home and you can hear its footsteps and giggles. A piano plays with no one around. Faces appear in pictures.

The Kaske home is part of Heritage park and rumors abound that the Kaske family was buried in the park. Indeed in the twilight hours and late into the evening, misty figures roam the grounds.

La Llorna
Hammond: Between Cline and 5th Avenues

A female ghost in a white blood-stained dress roams the area. This story is told in many cultures. In Indiana, she is said to have had children outside marriage. Because the father wouldn't marry her, she killed them all. When she told him what she'd done, he threw her out. She felt very bad and searched for the kids. When the police finally found out, she'd either killed herself or been killed by or at the river. Today, people still see her searching and crying.

Lake County Historical Museum
Crown Point: Old Lake Courthouse, Courthouse Square, Suite 202

A seal impresser was missing for months and later found on a windowsill. When they picked it up, dust was under as though the seal had just been placed in the location. They believe it is Avis Brown, a previous historian playing a prank.

Lake Prairie Cemetery
Lowell: Wicker Blvd. and W. 181st Ave.

Investigators have captured orbs and mists on film. Many of the investigators believe that the mists are the same spirits as the apparitions seen in the cemetery.

Lillian Holly House
Crown Point: 205 E. South St.

This Queen Anne home was built in 1890 for Flora Norta Biggs (widow of James H Biggs). Lillian Holley lived in this home probably longer than anyone and died in it at the age of 102 in 1994. Today, she's seen rocking on the front porch.

Little Red Schoolhouse
Hammond: 7205 Kennedy Ave.

Colored lights dart about the place. A small ghost boy hangs out in the school and walks along the road with his books.

Lowell Police Department
Lowell: 428 E. Commercial Ave.

Jail keys are heard in locks and on chains. Staff heard footsteps going upstairs. It is now occupied by the Chamber of Commerce.

Lowell Public Library
Lowell: 1505 E. Commercial Ave.

Flanked by Lowell Memorial Cemetery on one side, and a tombstone manufacturer on the other, it is no wonder this library has paranormal issues. Employees, both current and former, have noticed doors opening and closing by themselves, music playing from an empty storage room, books falling in succession from different parts of the building, and interesting odors.

Michael Jackson's Boyhood Home
Gary: 2300 Jackson St.

Michael Jackson, 80s iconic popstar, surprises visitors by appearing to them. Orbs of light also permeate the property. The cries of children scare visitors. Some people believe all of this is residual energy from when the Jackson family lived in the home.

Old Botanical Gardens
Hammond: 626 177th St.

(aka Reaper's Realm; aka Jayme House)

Joseph E. Meyer founded a packager herb company in 1910 and constructed the Botanical Gardens building in 1926. At one point the second floor was damaged by fire.

The former owners died and now haunt the location. People hear walking upstairs when they are alone. In the woods behind the gardens, white, misty figures walk through the trees. When Reaper's Realm takes place, two women are reported as helping, although they are unknown to the people on site. Lights turn on even though the batteries aren't in the lights. Automated mannequins for the haunted house functioned, although their power source wasn't active. One ghost, referred to as Mary is blamed for many of the incidents. One woman is heard crying in an upper floor.

The bedrooms are haunted. The one to the left of the stairs on the second floor has a small closet- the door is often found open. In the bedroom to the right, smells, noises and glowing eyes are reported. Children laughing and playing surprise visitors.

(Note: Some folks believe this location is also the site of the Jayme House, which is attributed to being an old saloon, although no proof of this history is evident.)

Old Homestead
Crown Point: 227 S. Court St.

The oldest home Lake County was built in 1847 by Wellington A Clark. Visitors hear children playing in the home as well as footsteps when no one is around. Items go missing in the home, which is in the process of restoration.

Old Lake County Jail
Crown Point: 232 S. Main St.

This jail's claim to fame is John Dillinger's escape from it using a soap gun. In use until 1960, visitors see mists and orbs as well as hear footsteps. Jail doors slam and staff and visitors hear harsh words from men. Investigators saw a transparent woman on the main stairs. Sounds of stones skipping across the floor are often heard- which was a way that inmates communicated. One investigation team caught an EVP that said, "Shut that damn thing off." A man answering as Everett Daniels, US Army, also identified himself. Later it was discovered his family donated items to the museum. Visitors feel fingers in their hair and touches on their arms and legs. Many visitors have had "things" brush past them. Orbs are captured in pictures. Screams come from the catacomb area. Shadow figures are seen walking through the entire structure and even a typewriter has functioned on its own.

Phantom of the Open Hearth at U.S. Steel
Gary: One North Broadway

A worker who fell into a vat of hot steel appears when the steel is poured.

Reder Road

Griffith: S. Colfax St to Reder Rd (Ct.). Reder Road has been partially closed down and is quite overgrown. The railroad tracks are still accessible.
(aka Reeder Road; see Ross Cemetery, Griffith, Lake Co.)

This location has many stories. Elizabeth Wilson drowned in a nearby swamp in a car accident. She haunts the side of the road waiting for a ride home. When you reach Ross Cemetery she disappears. Many people speculate this disappearance is because she was buried in Ross Cemetery.

Also associated with this location is the classic boyfriend hanging above the car story. A boy and girl are cuddling and hear a scraping sound outside the car. He goes to investigate. After a while the girl still hears scraping and is worried that her boyfriend hasn't returned. When she gets out, he's hanging from a tree by his neck/feet with a belt, a rope, etc. and his class ring and/or feet are scraping on the top of the car.

The solstices and equinoxes are equally busy times for the area. Some people claim satanic rituals occur in the cemetery and nearby fields. Additionally, a path that leads down the road is said to take you to a church. There you can hear the screams of a parishoner driven to insanity and death by a mentally disturbed pastor. On your way there, you pass railroad tracks that host a dark shadow man who will follow you down the tracks and down the path.

This area has long been associated with mafia connections, not only from the bodies found in the area but also the bootleg and other business deals made in the area in serene privacy.

Ridge Road

Gary: Ridge Rd., most often seen between Kennedy Ave and Broadway.

A woman in a wedding gown walks this road. She killed herself in Calumet River on Halloween night.

River Forrest Jr. Sr High Schools
Hobart: 3300 Indiana St.

These two schools were at one time separate. The tennis courts used to house the pool for PE. A child drowned at the school, so they demolished the pool. The boy is seen in the high school gym, and in the jr school multipurpose rooms and the high school cafeteria.

He only comes out at night, especially for school sponsored events. Not seen during school hours- late night for events. Janitors don't like being in the school after 9pm because of all the noise- including chairs and desks moving.

Ross Cemetery

Griffith: Whitcomb St and W. 50th Ave.

Elizabeth Wilson died in a car accident off of Reeder Rd (see entry) and is buried in the cemetery. Her boyfriend was pinned in the car. She gets into

Sacred Heart Elementary

Whiting: 1731 Laporte Ave

Closed in 1999 due to financial issues, this school hosted several priests and nuns who came to the area to retire. Chairs are pushed and moved throughout the school. Teacher and students voices scared the janitorial staff and early arrivers at the school.

Saint Casimir's School

Hammond: 4329 Cameron Ave.

(aka Resurrection)

A janitor and a girl who died in the 1953 fire haunt the school. The girl roams the halls near the restrooms. The janitor is often seen at the opposite end of the hallway. He will look at you, then moves his mop bucket down the hallway or into a classroom and disappears.

Sherwood Lake Apartments

Schererville: 801 E. Sherwood Lake Dr.

A woman pushed her son in the lake while they were feeding ducks because she got mad at him. Her son drowned. The boy is seen in the pond and people have heard his screams.

Southeast Grove Cemetery

Crown Point: From 153rd Ave. turn right onto Southgrove Rd. Look for entrance on left (if you get to 157th Ave, you've missed the turn off.)

(aka Gypsy Graveyard)

Glowing figures, mists and orbs are seen at the cemetery. The ghosts are attributed to the many gypsies who were sick and died on the spot. Behind the cemetery, the ghost of a wolf/dog chases visitors but never quite catches them.

Whihala Beach

Whiting: In Whihala Beach County Park (near Lake Shore Dr. on Lake Michigan)

In the woods by the beach, visitors see ghostly outlines of sailboats and bathers. Laughiterand water splashing is also heard.

LAWRENCE
COUNTY

818 14th Street
Bedford: 818 14th St.

Sylvan Moore had an affair with Atlee Osborn's wife. One night in 1928, Atlee, a stone carver, came home to find the two together. As Moore fled, Osborn followed, eventually beating him to death near 15th and H Street.

This scene is sometimes reenacted by a residual haunting.

Bedford
Bedford: Downtown Bedford

The night watchman patrolled the city streets, especially after a rash of break-ins were reported. In 1875 George Carney, a young Irishman, performed his duties with pride. One night he caught two men robbing the J.W. Mitchell drug store on the south side of the town square. Arthur Bissot and George Bachtel shot and killed Carney over postage stamps and less than one dollar in change. Green Hill Cemetery has a monument dedicated to Carney.

This scene is still reenacted by a residual haunting. Investigators have picked up unclear EVPs and have seen the members of the events and have heard the panting of someone running.

"I" Street
Bedford: The house is no longer standing, but it was near the current location of the Bedford Office Supply (1634 I St.)

In 1903, Susanna Ireland lived on I Street, earning her living as a dressmaker. On Labor Day 1903, her daughter ran to the Rippey Hotel and said her mother had shot herself. Investigators found Susanna neatly placed on the floor as though no struggle or evidence of the shooting had taken place. Cora Weeks, Susanna's daughter, and Cora's husband were charged with murder. According to the Lawrence County Historical Society, no court or newspapers exist that explain the outcome of Cora's charges. This was largely due to another murder that occurred- that of Sara Schafer.

Building owners in the area have reported seeing a woman from the early part of the 1900s looking as though she's working. One woman saw a white figure in a light colored dress with a pin cushion on her arm.

Lawrence County
Lawrence County: Johnson, Monroe, Lawrence and Brown County borders

A headless horseman is seen roaming the area riding on his horse.

Lawrence County Courthouse
Bedford: 916 15th St.

On the third floor of the courthouse, a woman watched her husband hanged on the north lawn. Her face froze in horror and is imprinted in the window.

Lawrence County Jail
Bedford: 1002 17th St.

In 1893 John Turley was in jail for shooting Lew Price, a train conductor. Drunk Turley had argued with Price over the train fare. As Price left the car, Turley shot him. A crew of 44 men stormed the jail and took Turley to an apple tree in front of the jail where they hung him.

Today, this jail is the Old Jail Art Center, where a host of different artistic media are taught and encouraged. Doors close without reason. Lights flicker off and on. Agonized wailing is also heard. Psychics say that there are many more spirits than Turley's in the building. A woman who was put in the cells for drunkenness and prostitution is said to have been taken advantage of by jail staff while in their care. Another man named Tinkey communicated that he was a long-time resident of the jail and he just didn't know where else to go after death.

Oscar Medaris Home
Bedford: Near 13th and "J" Streets

In 1918, Jack Taylor, a railroad foreman, was shot on the porch of the home where he boarded. Apparently Mr. Medaris was jealous of the attention he perceived Jack paid Mrs. Medaris. Jack pleaded not guilty by reason of insanity.

Investigators have captured the sound of two gunshots, the number fired in the killing. Others have reported seeing a man strolling up the walks of several homes in the area. Witnesses describe him as medium height and build, with a slouch cap and a weathered appearance.

Sheeks House
Mitchell: Where the New Albany and Salem Railroad crosses the Ohio at the MS Railroad.

Sheeks house was built in 1853. Doors would be found open when they had been securely latched. When nailed shut, doors would be found open with the nails rolling on the floor.

Spring Mill State Park
Mitchell: SR 60 three miles east of Mitchell

A female voice greets visitors as they enter the park. Other conversations with disembodied female voices occur within the park. The grist mill has had reports of several shape shifting entities. Photos of these entities have been captured by visitors and investigators. Investigators see a shadow figure in the mill at odd hours.

Stack Rock (in Wilson Park)
Bedford: 2107 Denson Ave. (you'll have to walk in the woods to see the rock.)

Limestone blocks make up this tall structure. Many paranormal investigators consider this location a portal to the other side. Investigators have recorded many EVPs and several instances of automatic writing exist.

Whispers Estates
Mitchell: 714 Warren St.

Legend has it that Dr. John and Jessie Gibbons had a foster daughter, and took care of other children. One child, Rachel, is said to have died in a fire in the home during Christmas 1912, although no proof of her existence has been found in local history. Five graves, although not confirmed by any reliable history, are said to be in the back yard. EVPs of Rachel and ghost children have been recorded. Apparitions of white, grey and black figures have been seen especially in the front parlor. EVP saying owners name when played backwards. Doors shake as though someone wanted entry into the building, yet no one was seen.

One story goes that a group a women spent the night in the house and after a few hours they were ready to leave. When one woman went home and told her husband that she didn't experience anything, he asked to listen to the EVP recordings she made. One one recording, as the women were talking about going up to the attic, her husband heard, "I'm waiting for you." on the recording.

Tunnelton Tunnel
Tunnelton: Between Tunnelton Rd. and Tunnelhill Rd.

A watchman fell asleep and didn't flag a train, to warn them of the sharp turn in the tunnel. The train crashed, killing everyone, including the night watchman. Since then, he's been swinging his lantern at midnight, trying to warn the train. The light is small at first, then it gets bigger as it swings from one end of the tunnel to the other. Some people have also witnessed seeing the train and the sound of a train in the tunnel, when there was no train present.

A man who was decapitated during its construction is seen in the tunnel carrying a lantern and his head. A legend that states a graveyard sits on top of the tunnel. During construction, the bodies fell into the tunnel. A family was killed when their wagon fell into the water. Now you can hear their screams.

Two guards would meet in the middle of the tunnel to switch sides during their shift. Once, one guard didn't see the other and went to tell him it was time to switch, he walked back to see if the other man was already on the other side. The missing guard was swinging from a noose. At night, you can see the hanged guard swinging in the tunnel.

Finally, a legend states if you write your name in the tunnel, when it is erased, you'll be dead-which seems to have happened to a number of folks. Countless stories of friends writing names only to see one disappear and that person dying have been told. It has even happened to people who move away. It seems once your name is in the tunnel, it will be erased when you die- no matter where or when that will be!

MADISON COUNTY

107 E. Pierce Street
Alexandria: 107 E Pierce St

A girl in overalls is seen in the house. She pulls pranks on people such as pulling their arms or touching their hands in the kitchen. She has also been seen in the early morning in the living room, sitting in a rocking chair. The girl visited one person in a dream and indicated there was a diamond under the floor boards of one of the bedrooms.

1118 Meridian Street
Anderson: 1118 Meridian Street

This building has the ghost of a crying woman in early 1900s clothing. Nothing more is known about the woman.

1412 Main Street
Elwood: 1412 Main St

This 1880s building has been home to many businesses. In the 1940s the front was remodeled for a nightclub. iIt is believed during this time that a fight broke out and two men killed each other over a woman named Lottie, who was one of several taxi dancers at the night club. A former owner remembers doing some renovations between tenants and witnessed a man chasing another through the back hallway and down the stairs. Lights are still seen in the building today and over the last few years, the building has stood more empty than used.

206 Vineyard Street
Anderson: 206 Vineyard Street

Formerly a boarding house, religious publishing house, this home is full of playful spirits who never make a physical appearance. One that rushes out the front door, and another likes to visit folks in the bathroom. Another likes to walks down the stairs. It is believed these spirits are those of people who stayed at the home while it was a boarding house.

709-711 Meridian Street
Anderson: 709-711 Meridian St.

Chief Anderson has been sighted on the rooftop of buildings in the area. It used to be the Meridian Hotel, across from the old police station.

6451 W. 300 South
Anderson: 6451 W 300 S (53rd St.)

Cory Clark and her daughter Jenna were killed here a few years ago. They were killed by Frederick Baer who randomly picked them. He first slit Cory's throat and then chasing 4 year old Jenna down and slitting her throat as well. He returned to Cory to rape her but was unable to complete the act.

Today, the duplex is haunted by the sound of running footsteps and piercing screams. The neighboring duplexes along the road are put on the real estate market often.

1218 W. 6th Street
Anderson: 1218 W. 6th Street

A variety of ghosts have been seen and felt in the house. Once home to sufferagettes, the building has several ghosts. A woman is seen in the upper hallway, seemingly upset that her view to the oval window (now covered by vinyl siding) is blocked. Additionally, an older woman who used to live in the west side (when it was apartments) can be heard talking. Phantom steps walk up stairs that no longer exist.

700 W and 300S
Anderson: SW corner

One could never guess from the outside that this bungalo-eque house was once in part a one room school house. Throughout the house ghosts have been seen, felt and heard. In the upstairs bathroom, the apparition of a child is seen. In the schoolroom, a bodiless pair of boots pace in front of the fireplace. Phantom footsteps are heard up and down the stairs. A caped man was seen throughout the 1970s and 1980s in the house. 30 years after these events, he was seen in the barn. A demonic entity scuttles about the downstairs late at night and an incubus took advantage of a young woman in one of the upstairs bedrooms.

Airport Rd. Bridge
Elwood: W 1000 N and SR 37

In 1965, Joseph Lila killed himself at 8pm on this bridge by shooting himself in the mouth. He reenacts this event on the anniversary of his death- May 24.

Anderson High School
Anderson: 4610 Madison Ave.

A teenage girl from the 1960s killed herself when she found that a boy she liked wasn't going to take her to a dance as promised. She is seen hanging in the old auditorium (now classrooms) and she walks through the new part of the school (formerly part of the outdoor area).

(Note: Anderson High School was originally located by the WigWam on Lincoln St. In the 1990s, Anderson High School was relocated in the Madison Heights High School on the south side of Anderson. Long live the MHHS Pirates- You may have jackhammered our beloved mascot but Pirates never die!)

Arby's Restaurant

Anderson: 2820 Broadway St.

A big man sits in the lobby and frequents the men's restroom, opening the door with unseen hands. Employees report seeing him walking through the kitchen after hours.

Aqua Gardens

Anderson: Aqua Gardens (now an activity center for Shadyside park). The area in which a girl died is now owned by Aqua Marine of Anderson located at 1115 Alexandria Pike. *(aka Activity Center for Shadyside Park)*

Aqua Gardens was purchased by the city of Anderson in 1970 and renamed Shadyside Recreation Center. In the 1960's some teenagers coupled up and decided to have an evening party at the swim beach. They had a small fire, a few beers, and marshmallows to roast. Things turned for the worst when everyone decided to go skinny dipping. Amy Chapman couldn't swim, but got in the water with everyone else. It was dark and no one could see very well. Amy must have stepped in a hole or into deeper water and drowned while everyone else was splashing and yelling. No one heard her cries for help. At daybreak, her body was found floating.

For years afterwards Aqua Gardens was closed except for a trail that bordered the former swim beach. Locals knew the unfortunate girl roamed the area. Children were cautioned about going back to Aqua Gardens.

If anyone is there after dark, she is seen on the shore, wet and wearing mossy seaweed. She warns other swimmers to not venture out very far. Sometimes she is seen floating on top of the water late at night to keep others from skinny dipping and drowning.

Bethel Pike Bridge

Alexandria: W 1100 N east of Orestes Rd

On June 13, 1955, five men on this bridge died after it collapsed. Two cars hit head on and were thrown into the water. The people in the car were between the ages of 18 and 23. You can sometimes hear the reenactment of the event, and can hear the men groaning and calling for help.

Bickels Cafe

Anderson: 21 W 8th St.

This location suffered an all-day fire on August 30, 1878 during a fireman's strike. Some non-striking fighters attempted to gain control, but it was insufficient. Other firefighters were called in. The strikers refused to help and tried to prevent anyone from fighting the fire. The blaze destroyed over 10 businesses. A man was found dead in this building's stairwell after the fire was out. Immediately a parking lot was made over this artificial grave.

Since the fire, visitors have smelled smoke in the building. Footsteps are heard. The apparition of a man, believed to be the man who perished in the fire, is seen walking though the building at night.

Bocco Cemetery

Anderson: West side of CR100E, between CR350S and CR400S

It is named after Issac Bucco (aka Bocco), who donated the land for the cemetery. Orbs and an apparition of a woman are reported in the south west corner of the cemetery.

Bronnenberg Home

Anderson: SR32 to Rangeline Rd. onto E 100 N (Lindberg Rd). *Razed.*

The Lindberg home was originally a family home, which later turned into an orphanage Today it has all but disappeared. The home reverted to its former grandeur when visitors entered the home. When the wind blew, the dust swirled around unseen figures.

Note: This home has since been razed and the land where the house once stood is now the Bronnenberg Youth Center.

Buck Creek Bridge

Anderson: East of Rangeline Rd on E CR450N Access it east of N CR1000W on E450N.
(aka Activity Center for Shadyside Park)

Built in 1910 and restored in 1984. Visitors report seeing a noose with a body swinging from the bridge.

Camp Chesterfield

Chesterfield: North of SR32 on Washington St.
(aka Spook Camp)

In this peaceful place, ghostly figures are said to walk freely on the grounds. Many voices are heard when no one is around. In the past, Harry Houdini proved some of the spiritualist techniques used in the early 1900s were fake. Today, this serene area is home to a retreat-type atmosphere, public events and a religious shrine. A small child haunts the woods. Both the Western and Sunflower Hotels have reported activity. People hear footsteps and conversation when no one is present.

One group of people who decided to plan a trip had a terrifying dream the night before. All of them dreamed that spirits from the camp were hovering over them and wanted to take them with them. Needless to say, they never went.

(Note: The Sunflower Hotel is not open for overnight stays.)

Chesterfield Christian Church
Chesterfield: 207 E. Plum St.

A man was found dead in the boiler room in the 1940s. His death was never solved. Today lights flicker off and on. Doors open and close by unseen hands. Mysterious handprints on windows and mirrors appear without cause.

Destroyed Cemetery
Alexandria: Southeast corner of Harrison and 4th Streets (next to Alexandria School of Scientific Theraputics)

This destroyed graveyard is now a parking lot. with a small marker commemorating the location. History doesn't indicate if the bodies were actually moved when the area was paved. From earliest times, this spot has been home to ghost stories. Originally a graveyard, then a church were built upon it. However, when girls were kidnapped, never to be found again, it was decided it was too far out and the Native Americans were too much of a threat. The girls were said to haunt the area.

Eventually, the land reclaimed the burial ground. One account states that when the storms rolled in and the wheat was high, the graveyard looked like spirits were rising from their graves (although one ghost was proven to be crows). The ghost travels through town often visiting Chaplain Cemetery, Beulah Park and has also been seen on Berry, Black and Monroe Streets.

Dicky Road
Anderson: Dickey Road, just west of Dr. Martin Luther King Blvd.

(aka W 57th Street)

The railroad tracks on this road have long been a source of legend. Even before Anderson Memorial Park Cemetery was established, a misty, dark apparition of a funeral procession was seen near the railroad tracks heading south to north.

Elder House
Alexandria: Right side of Park Ave, just north of E 1000 N

Strange lights can be seen at night, but no one or nothing is found.

Elwood Opera House
Elwood: 202 South Anderson Street

Constructed in 1887, this opera house was an all-purpose. After it discontinued opera in 1905, the Masons used the building and it had several professional offices. The "blue room" was used by the Masons and seems to be a hotbed of paranormal activity. Shadow figures race from place to place in the building. Doors open and close randomly. Several investigators have been pushed on the second to third floor stairway.

Falls Creek Park
Pendleton: Falls Park Dr.

This historic park is home to two residual hauntings. Rachel Harris fell into the creek while being chased by her lover John. She was most likely killed instantly from a blow to the head by the rocks around the falls. John dove in after her only to be pulled down by her lifeless body. The residual haunting of this event is reenacted in the early mornings, usually around 7:15-8:00 am.

In 1824, John Harper and four others were hanged on the north east side for the murder of nine men, women and children. Harper escaped but his friends became the first white men in Indiana hanged for murdering Native Americans. Today, eyewitnesses claim that they hear the men swinging in the wind. EVPs of distressed men crying "No, No!" have also been captured.

Florida (Station)
Anderson: Between CR 375 N at the railroad tracks and CR 200 W (Cross St).

A Native American burial ground sits between CR 375 N at the railroad tracks and CR 200 W (Cross St). Although no official records exist, this area is old and the homes built at this location seem to only have yards (versus buildings) in the area where they burial site would be.

Investigators have taken readings in the area. and orbs and shape-shifting shadows have been spotted. Several investigators have reported shadows shifting into wolves, birds and other animals. Residents of the area find arrowheads in their yards.

French Cemetery
Frankton: NE Corner of Washington and Clyde Streets

In 1917 a Madison County woman, May Berry, a Red Cross nurse, was the first American woman to die on foreign soil during the war. She is seen walking through the cemetery and sitting under a number of trees within the cemetery. She is wearing a dress with a white apron over it. Today, the Frankton May Berry Post 469 remains a tribute to her.

Grand Ave
Anderson: At the curve of Grand And Indiana Avenue.

Anderson natives know the curve on Indiana Avenue used to extend across an old iron bridge. At one time it was known as "The Singing Bridge" or "The Humming Bridge" for the noise that tires made as they went across the ironroad of the bridge. Many people wrecked cars, motorcycles, and other vehicles on this road. Although the bridge is no longer there, legend states that there used to be a residual haunting of a man who threw himself from the bridge after his fiancee jilted him. Two other incidents are attributed to hauntings. A woman with her children plunged off the bridge in bad weather.

Also, four boys ended up falling off he bridge and into the river below. The cries of all these people are heard at various times of the day and night in the area.

Additionally, just a little south west of the bridge was the Brown Street dump. Two twin boys by the last name of Salley were trapped in an old refrigerator there. They are seen playing in the area to this day.

A little further down Grand Avenue, before Broadway Street, is a train trestle. Once a gathering place for picnics, the overgrown area is now host to less savory affairs. A woman was killed when she fell from the trestle and is now said to haunt the area, showing herself as a filmy apparition screaming like a banshee at those she meets.

Grand Avenue and Huffman Court
Anderson: Grand Ave. at curve

These three roads seem to be a hotbed of activity. Huffman Court is next to a backwater swamp just off White River. An empty field had to be crossed before reaching the backwater, which was home to many frog species, a very large golden carp, and several kinds of water birds. If you follow the edge of the backwater you will come to an old abandoned train trestle. Near the trestle are the ruins of a small house and tiny barn. An old woman used to live here with her pony. She used the pony to haul firewood in a small cart and to go to and from a local store. The pony eventually died and was buried in the yard of the house. The old woman put a granite marker. Today you can hear the ghost train clacking down the trestle as well as hear the locomotive's sharp whistle. The old lady is said to be roaming the property sometimes crying and grieving the loss of her pony. Occasionally she will throw pebbles at intruders when she wants to be left alone.

Gruenwald Historic House
Anderson: 626 Main St.

Native America burial grounds are located on this property. Although the official story is that they are under the parking lot to the south of the house, early maps show this to be untrue. The burial ground extends to the house and north of it to the apartment buildings that stand there.

The two story log home (now covered in brick) was built in 1860 by John Berry. The rest of the home was remodeled in the Second Empire style by Moses Cherry in 1873. Martin Gruenwald owned the house shortly after and lived there until 1933. The house has had its share of heartache. Gruenwalds' wife, Wilhelmina Christine (Dick) died at 49 of a lung disease. He resided there alone after her death until 1933.

On a full moon there is a lot of ghost activity here. Volunteers feel ghostly presences. Some don't want the living to leave at closing time. The ghosts will position themselves in front of the doors, trapping workers. They believe one of the ghosts is Wilhelmina Gruenwald. She did not want the home changed and now parts of the land have been changed. The electric typewriter seems to have a mind of its own. An attic window is said to be home to an old lady peering out at the mission across the street.

Volunteer tour guides, working alone in the home, have felt they are being followed, and report that it's not unusual to enter the home and find the electric typewriter typing by itself. An internet rumor states that two people must now be on duty in the house because of the hauntings.

Highland High School
Anderson: 2108 E 200 N

A boy is in seen in the old gym (auditorium), usually running or breathless. Sometimes he's seen in the locker room. Legend has it he died of asthma at a sports practice.

Inness Mansion
Alexandria: 601 S Indiana Ave.

The home was built by John Inness, who didn't live to enjoy it. Shortly after the home was finished, he died, and left a pregnant wife, Mary and a daughter named Blanche. When the baby was born, he was named Robert, because the couple had originally wanted to name the child so if it were a boy. As time went by Robert was finally left alone in the home with a caretaker. Robert died in 1977 and the caretaker died in1983.

People have been tapped on the shoulder Cold chills, footsteps, and feelings of uneasiness have been reported. Furniture moves on its own, sometimes coming precariously close to dumping the contents on hapless onlookers. Shadow figures have been seen, including that of a little boy. Hot and cold spots have been detected. EVPs of children and an older man have been recorded.

Lick Creek
Markleville: E 800 S, S500 E and N 975 W

Five white traders killed some Native Americans for their furs to earn an easy buck. Other white settlers found the bodies on their way to church. The men were caught and jailed, except for one, Thomas Harper, who went to Ohio. The other four men were hanged from a tree in the area.

Although it cannot be definitively proven, there is a grove of trees south of E 800 S at this crossroads. It is said the tree from which these men were hung at is in the woods. Investigators report hearing the cracking of necks and seeing bodies swinging from trees.

Markleville (Town)
Markleville: Woods off SR 38 between Lick and Chadwick Creek

In these woods, 10 foot tall man is said to morph into a beautiful woman with black hair and a white gown. She first appeared to two men on January 26, 1896 and has been seen periodically since.

Memorial Circle Wesleyn Church

Anderson: Park and Raible Ave

The church is supposed be haunted- looked like people just picked up and left.

Monroe Street

Anderson: Monroe St. exact location unknown

On Monroe Street, a house that has since been razed was rented by a young woman and her friend. One evening a few friends decided to visit them as well as another tenant in the building. While talking about the Falls in Pendleton and other haunted locations, a copper ashtray scooted across the table. The young woman and her friend said that the spirits were just wanting them to know they were there.

(See Falls Park, Pendleton, Madison Co.)

Moss Island

Anderson: Moss Island Rd. and Anderson Frankton Rd.
(aka Moss Island Mills)

Moss Island Mills used to be directly on the river. For many years because of the mills the Moss Cemetery was called Moss Island Cemetery. The mills provided meal and lumber for the inhabitants. Built in 1836 by Joseph Mullanix, it was preserved long after it was out of use.

Moss Island Mills (razed) is a very dark and foreboding area. The area around Moss Island Road and the Anderson Frankton Rd. is especially interesting. Strange creatures, too large to be native birds, have swooped down on people. Apparitions of men in work clothes and women in prairie skirts are seen on the curve of the road.

Mounds State Park

Anderson: 4306 Mounds Rd.

Dwarfs in blue gowns are seen here. Some people have reported encountering blue-gowned dwarves in the park and nearby along the White River at Noblesville. According to Delaware Indian legend, they are the Puk-wud-ies, a tribe of little people that still inhabit the forest. Many investigators have entered the park only to find that they've entered a time warp and instead of spending a couple of hours investigating, six or more hours have elapsed. Additionally, visitors have been out after dark and have seen various transparent spirits of Native Americans and white men. Two eyewitnesses were hiking in 1975 past on of the serpent mounds. The birds got quiet and there was a group of native men in the woods close to them. They gestured the couple over and one of them gave the woman an old bead, which she still has today. The men walked off and disappeared.

N CR550 W
Alexandria: N CR550 W

Three girls were killed on this short stretch of road. They had a cat with them. One of the girls died six months after the murders. She would never talk about what happened. Today, the ghosts of the girls are seen in the car on the road.

Nicholson File
Anderson: Broadway Street North of Grand Avenue *(razed)*

Many of the people who used to work in this old plant swear that it was haunted by other employees who died. Various apparitions of dark shadows, transparent partial entities and solid full color ghosts were seen.

Old Anderson High School
Anderson: 1301 Lincoln St.

A young teenager was raped and killed- her screams are still heard. The old part of the school on the second floor has a ghost that will throw things at you. This ghost seems to have moved to the Wig Wam area. At a recent event where Hillary Clinton spoke at the building, several women in the WigWam's restroom reported many rolls of paper towels being thrown, and crashing into the wall.

(See also Anderson High School, Anderson, Madison Co.)

Paramount Theatre
Anderson: 1124 Meridian St.

Originally opened August 20, 1929, this glorious theater is one of the two "atmospheric" theaters remaining in the United States. AS the lights dim, the ceiling is a veritable panorama of twinkling stars and clouds. In full light, visitors are treated to a Moorish courtyard effect. This majestic theater contains one of only three Grand Page Theater Pipe organs left in the United States. Throughout the 1970-80s, this theater deteriorated and after a lengthy restoration, it reopened in 1995.

Today, brilliant art work and decorations aren't the only items gracing the theater. In the dressing rooms, a woman wearing in heavy stage makeup is seen primping, dressed in a corset. A man with a broom walks on the stage and appears in the orchestra pit. The upper balcony is haunted by two mischievous boys who have been caught throwing items into the seats below.

Old Maplewood Cemetery
Anderson: High St. and W. Grand Ave.

The statue of the Hilligoss children bleeds. In the older part of the cemetery, neighbors have seen white shadows moving, drifting from place to place at night.

Old Train Trestle
Frankton: West of Short Street across the river.

In 1947 a young lady was on the bridge contemplating suicide. She had come home to find her husband cheating on her. She went to the train trestle, and waited for a train, then ran out in front of it. On foggy nights you can hear her screaming, and see her walking across the bridge.

Quick City (Town)
Quick City: North of Frankton, on CR 550 W, on the east side of the road.

Once a city for a glass company and its employees, the company was owned by a man named Quick. By giving natural gas away for free, Quick enticed other companies to come to the area. Once the gas boom went bust, so did Quick and all the companies, they left and took the citizens of the area with them.

St. Mary's School and Church
Anderson: 1115 Pearl Street

Built in the late 1800s, the site was used as a meeting center for the Indiana tribes and white men in the early part of Anderson's history.

For years, students, teachers and other staff have seen whispy white and black mists and shadows in the northwest showers and bathrooms. The boiler room has had phantom footsteps since the 1970s and footsteps echo in the hallway. The ghosts are believed to be departed staff and church members.

Sigler Cemetery
Frankton: South side of CR 850N (Cemetery Road), west of CR 575W (Washington Ave.)

The cemetery sits at the end of the road across from some abandoned homes. The Sigler family built the cemetery. Jacob Sigler owned the land where Frankton is now. Frankton was named for Francis "Frank" Sigler who designed and developed it.

Strange orbs fly through the cemetery during the day and evening. Mysterious "strands" of lights are also seen by visitors.

These lights seem to be shimmering strands of ectoplasm in various colors (blue, red and orange have been reported).

State Theatre
Anderson:1303-1316 Meridian St.

Sadly unused, this former theater was built in the 1920s and was home to stage and screen stars. In the 1960s Anderson's downtown went downhill and took this theater with it. For a time in the late 1990s, it operated as a live venue, but seems to have gone belly up with the rest of the town.

From at least the 1960s, the balcony of the movie theater was haunted by a man in a suit. He was known to sit down next to movie goers and scare them by disappearing into thin air. Later, when the balcony was closed due to safety issues, the man moved to the main seating area. After the theater closed, many patrons during the '90s claimed to have seen him in the upper restroom areas. Workers also saw the man backstage.

Swamp Light
Alexandria: CR 400 W and SR28

"The Light" as it was known, came out of the swampy area where this intersection once was. The light started very bright and stayed all night, but returned to the water at dawn. During its time ashore, it would be in the trees, along the ground and in the air. People generally believe it is hunting something. Voices whisper but one can't make out the words. One man was chased home by the light and investigators report the same happening at least a mile away from the place.

Union Building
Anderson: 1106 Meridian Street

Originally built as a department store, it was later refurbished to house offices. In one of the early law offices, a secretary who stayed late on Friday to work on some letters was killed by an irate client, who cut her throat. She was not found until Monday morning by one of the attorneys.

People have seen this woman, dressed in 1940s clothing walking though the offices and spaces that now occupy the building. Additionally, a residual haunting of the act occurs. Many visitors have claimed to have heard her scream and drop to the ground in the early evening.

MARION COUNTY

Acton Miracle
Acton: Acton and Southport Rds. (NW corner)

On I-74 a man named Bob stopped to put on his rain coat and was struck by lightning. Paramedics were called but no one could revive him. A woman in a black dress appeared with a bible and put it on his chest. He began breathing again, although he was in a coma for many weeks.

The area around Acton used to be part of a spiritualist campground which dated from the 1850s. Now, the Franklin Township Historical Museum owns a dress that may have been worn by the remarkable woman.

Broadripple Park
Broadripple: 1550 Broad Ripple Avenue

Established in 1846, this park is in the heart of the oldest part of Broadripple and was used as an amusement park in which one child was killed in a roller coaster collapse. Today the swings move when no wind is apparent. Phantom Native Americans run through the park and several Victorian women are seen walking through the park.

The Falls at Broadripple
Broadripple: College Avenue

From strife between German and Irish immigrants in its early history to numerous train collisions to fires and murder/suicides along the Falls, and amusement park accidents Broadripple has had a bloody past.

One of the earliest ghost stories attached to this location is about a Native American who stayed after the majority of his people left. He stayed, as he had gotten along well with the people in the area and he was content to live from the waters and woods around Indianapolis. Apparently he had an enemy or two and he was found with his throat cut along the falls. No one was ever charged in his murder but his figure has been seen in Broadripple at the falls and the park for almost 100 years.

Cumberland Cemetery
Cumberland: Muessing Rd.

Many graves here are from very young people. Investigators have seen orbs and have had mists appear in their photos. Who or what the spirits are is yet unknown although many investigators believe the mists and orbs represent people who are buried in the cemetery.

Action and Atomic Duckpin Bowling
Fountain Square: 1103 Shelby St.
aka Play Action Duckpin

The fourth floor is still home to parties that end when the living enter the room. Footsteps are heard throughout the empty building and the elevator runs up and down the floors carrying unseen passengers. Several patrons have been greeted in the elevator with a cheery "Hello there!" A ghost woman who is attributed to the footsteps also makes occasional appearances.

Holy Trinity Catholic Church
Haughville: 901 N. Holmes St.

Haughville is a gem of forgotten history in Indianapolis. Settled by German, Irish, and later Slovene immigrants, Haughville was named for the Haugh, Ketcham, and Co. Iron works. It has always been an industrial area and a working class neighborhood and it is currently experiencing a slow but progressive rebirth.
Priests indicate visitors "feel people" as if they are happy that they are not forgotten in the history that is Haughville. Some parishioners believe it is the builders of the church.

2910 North Delaware Street
Indianapolis: 2910 North Delaware Street

The Beck family used to have their vases and china thrown around. When the police were called for disturbances they found all in order, then police heard a crash resulting in a shattered mirror. For weeks this type of event occurred. A priest was called to perform an exorcism (most likely a blessing). Now this address is a vacant lot.

Alley
Indianapolis: North of 119 S. Meridian St.

David "Buck" Burkhart killed a man over whiskey at the site in the mid-1800s. The man who was killed is seen gasping for break and a rowdy group of cheers is sometimes heard in the alley. Investigators have captured mists on pictures believed to be the man.

Athletic Club
Indianapolis: 350 N. Meridian St.

Private John Lorenzano who died in 1992 in the building fire, is said to haunt the former Athletic club. Now the building is a set of condos, but at one time, when guests stayed in the building, he would wake people up at night or would be seen walking down the hall. One current resident reports still seeing a firefighter in the building on occasion. During the same fire, an older gentleman died. He is seen walking in the lobby.

Alverna Retreat House
Indianapolis: 8140 Spring Mill Rd.

This structure is a Franciscan retreat. A man with white hair and a dark suit roams the halls. It is believed to be Hugh McKenna Landon in a sailing outfit. Now the area is a private housing development

Athenaeum Foundation
Indianapolis: 401 E. Michigan St.

Built from 1896-98, this building was the hub of the German community. Home of the oldest restaurant in Indianapolis, it also houses many spirits. Strange bumps and thumps are heard throughout the building. Staff hear whispers, fined papers missing and have seen tables that have been readied for customers "unset". Grey misty figures roam the second and third floors and shadow people inhabit the theatre. Jolly Werner, a man who died by drinking too much and falling into a fireplace, is seen in the old part of the restaurant. Dr. Helene Knabe, a doctor who spent much time at the location teaching for the North American Gymnasts Union and the Medical College of Indiana has been seen in the east section on the first and second floors. Peter Lieber, of Lieber Beer and the Indianapolis Brewing Company is often seen in the Damenverein Rooms and the Ballroom.

Barton House
Indianapolis: Corner of Michigan and Delaware Streets
aka Delaware Flats

The ghost of Dr. Knabe, a woman who was killed in the building, haunts her apartment. In other parts of the building, lights turn off and on, items move from one place to the other and many people have reported hearing footsteps in their apartments when no one is there.

Benjamin Harrison Home
Indianapolis: 1230 N. Delaware St.

.

Former home of the president for whom the home is named, the Harrison family bought the lot in 1867 and lived in the home (with exceptions to Harrison's jobs) until 1913 when the children moved to New York. Staff and volunteers report hearing footsteps up and down the stairs as well as seeing a woman in a grey dress wearing a black brooch in the third floor ballroom.

(Note: the home is now a vibrant museum dedicated to President Benjamin Harrison and history.)

Boggstown Cabaret
Indianapolis: 6895 W. Boggstown Rd.

Shadow figures are seen throughout the building. Apparitions of a man and woman appear in the old dressing rooms, lights flicker on and off and visitors report being locked in the bathroom, unable to leave. Visitors hear many strange noises in the downstairs when the crowds go home at night.

Brookside Park
Indianapolis: 3500 Brookside Pkwy S. Dr.

Brookside park was founded in 1903 with a rustic look and feel. The idea was that visitors would find minimal intrusion by the drives that wind their way through the park.

Several spectre figures are witnessed by visitors, including a woman who roams the banks of Pogue's Run. She is seen walking along the bank, a shimmering woman with plain features. On October 19, 1903, Myrtle Wright, a grocery clerk was found dead by Pogue's run. In her possession was a quantity of laudanum, yet none was found in her system. Her cause of death remains a mystery.

Butler University
Indianapolis: 4600 Sunset Ave.
(The university has a great map on its website)

- A ghost named Lydia that hung herself at the Zeta Tau Alpha house (now the Tau Kappa Epsilon house) makes herself known by haunting room #1 and the attic of the home. She moves keys and knocks things off shelves. Electrical difficulties and televisions turning on and off are also part of Lydia's doings.
- A dark, dank tunnel from Atherton Union to Schwitzer Hall used to be a dining hall. The dining hall was closed and the entrances sealed for mysterious reasons. Speculation is that a woman was raped and murdered in the tunnel.
- Jordan Hall is said to be haunted by a frail thin girl with large dark rimmed eyes.

Henry F. Campell Mansion
Indianapolis: 2250 Cold Spring Rd.

A ghostly man is seen in this home.

Cathedral High School
Indianapolis: 5225 E. 56th St.
(aka former site of Ladywood High School)

The current incarnation of Cathedral High School sits on the former Ladywood school for girls run by the Sisters of Providence. Loretto Hall, which used to be the main building of Ladywood reported that lights would turn on and off and a nun would be seen walking the halls and lighting candles in the attic. Today the building is used for classrooms, administration, athletics and storage facilities. Students, faculty and visitors still report mysterious footsteps in the halls and several staff members have reported a glowing light going from room to room after late night events.

Central State Hospital
Indianapolis: Bounded by Tibbs Ave, Warman Ave, Washington St. and Vermont St.
(Central State Insane Asylum; Indianapolis Asylum for the Insane; Central Greens)

Opened in 1848, this hospital started on a bad note and stayed that way (as did most institutions of this sort). From the beginning overcrowding and undertrained/overworked staff made the care of these patients trying. Unscrupulous employees and vendors alike routinely served spoiled meat, dairy and vegetables to inmates. In later years, the institution became outdated and rundown, in addition to lack of training dollars spent on staff and almost every year from its inception, the question was asked "do we close it down". Finally in 1994, after uncovering severe patient abuses and a general feeling that large institutions did more harm than good, Central State closed its doors for good. Since then, the buildings have been vandalized by gangs, misused by ghost hunters and pseudo film makers.

Some of the more famous ghost stories around Central State include a man reporting hand prints on his throat from an attempted choking. A ghost nurse appears in the tunnels. Screams and cries heard at all hours of the day and night and shadow figures move in buildings and power house. People feel dread and sickness on the campus.

Today phantom lights shine near sundown in the windows of the Bolton and Evans building as possibly a sense of things to come in the evening. (Note: These buildings are now gone, but people still experience the feeling of people and investigators capture orbs.) People smell smoke where Seven Steeples burned and people report seeing the reenactment of one inmate stoning another inmate to death.

(Note: The location is slated for renovation and some demolition According to the Indianapolis-Marion County police Department, no one is allowed on site day or night due to too many vandals. No trespassing signs are posted.)

City County Building
Indianapolis: 200 E. Washington St.

In the 1960s a witness was shot in the elevator. Although access to this elevator was curtailed for a time, people reported the elevator as functioning although no power was running to it. The shooting victim has also been seen in the area around the elevator.

Court Street
Indianapolis: Court Street and Pennsylvania Avenue

The figure of H.H. Holmes has been seen in this garage. He was reported to have frequented a seedy hotel that was on the street during his killing years.

(See H. H. Holmes House, Irvington (Indianapolis), Marion County)

Crown Hill Cemetery
Indianapolis: Bounded by Boulevard Place, 38th Street and Michigan Rd. Waiting Station is off Boulevard Place

Similar to Resurrection Mary in Chicago and the dead prom girl asking for a ride, Crown Hill legend tells us about a girl that approaches visitors at the corner of Michigan Rd and 38th Street. She will climb in the back seat and instruct you to her house. When you approach, she disappears. Inside the cemetery a little girl giggles and talks about her horse at the grave of James Whitcomb Riley. Voices of the confederate dead buzz in the area of the Confederate grave site moved from Greenlawn cemetery. The waiting station offers us a glimpse into the paranormal with phantom footsteps, slamming doors, and rustling papers. The filing cabinets that house the immaculate records of the cemetery open and close on their own.

Crown Hill has a lush history that began in 1864 and is the permanent home for President Benjamin Harrison, James Whitcomb Riley, John Dillinger, and lesser known people such as Dr. Helene Knabe (see Barton House entry), a hill that houses over 700 orphans and others. At over 550 acres people come from many different places to enjoy the scenery and reflect.

(Note: This cemetery offers public tours. Due to inaccurate and unauthorized filming, before considering photography or videography for public consumption, not for profit or not, must be cleared through Crown Hill. The cemetery is privately owned and operated and has very strict guidelines of usage of its name, logo and of its interments.)

Davidson and New York Streets
Indianapolis: Davidson and New York Streets

In the few homes in the area many tenants and families report hearing gunshots and the tortured groans of a man. Knowing this area is next to an interstate and not the best of places many scoff and say that it is more human than paranormal. However, at one home in the middle of a winter snow, the tenant heard the shot and the groan and heard a knock at her door with someone saying "Please help me." Grabbing a gun of his own, the tenant walked to the back door and found no one there- no footprints either. The tenant checked the front door and around the house. No footprints but his own were there.

Interestingly, in April 1902, a man named August Hoffman was shot by police at this intersection. On January 5, 1903 Paul Marks, who was a machinist, was found shot through the heart on the railroad tracks that cross New York between Pine St and Dickson St.

Delaware Flats (aka The Barton Center of Hope)
Indianapolis: northeast corner of Delaware and Michigan Streets

Dr. Helene Elise Hermine Knabe was slain in this building on Oct 23-24, 1911. Her spirit has appeared in the kimono which was said to contain her blood splattered by the killer. While the building was under renovation, she moved items that were stored in what was her office. She did not like the clutter. Other people living in the building said she walks up and down stairs and levitates many items throughout the building. An EVP was captured of her saying "It's terrible."

Decatur Central High School
Indianapolis: 5251 Kentucky Ave.

In October of every school year, the school cultivates the smell of burnt rubber and the lights malfunction. The manifestation of a girl is also seen and heard crying in the auditorium. The legend behind these events is a drunk driver that killed a girl named Angie in the vehicle as it drove into the school auditorium in October 1979.

Embassy Suites
Indianapolis: Corner of Washington and Illinois Streets

Once the Hotel Bates was where Abraham Lincoln spent a few evenings, eventually it was made over and rebuilt as the Claypool Hotel, which was one of the very best hotels in Indianapolis. After it was razed, Embassy Suites was built in its place. Throughout the history of these hotels, the makings for ghost stories have been present. Abraham Lincoln's ghost is seen all over the US. In the Claypool two famous murders took place Dorothea Poole was killed in 1954 and stuffed in a dresser and Corporal Naomi Ridings was killed in 1943. Her killer was never caught.

Lights mysteriously turn on and off. A female military officer is seen in a lower level restroom. One woman checked in, went out for dinner and when she came back to her room, found all her belongings repacked on her bed.

English Hotel/English Opera House
Indianapolis: Razed. English Hotel (SW Quadrant of the Circle)/ English Opera House (NW Quadrant of the Circle)

Razed. English Hotel (SW Quadrant of the Circle)/ English Opera House (NW Quadrant of the Circle)

Purported to be one of the best hotels and opera houses in the United States, both were razed in favor of more modern buildings. In the opera house, a former actress practiced her lines and a man fitting Mr. English's description encouraged her. He disappeared before her eyes. In the hotel the ghost of an African American waiter walked the halls. Today, people still report seeing both spirits in these buildings.

Gas Light Inn
Indianapolis: 2280 S. Meridian St.

At one time, this bar was home to a candy store and legend has it that John Dillinger frequented the building during his heyday. Investigators and staff hear phantom footsteps and glass breaking in the basement and in the attic. Visitors have seen apparitions throughout the building including the back room. Once, an earring floated to the bar. One investigator was held in the basement by an entity which would not let her leave. Every time she tried to move toward the door, she was physically pushed back. After a paranormal magician did a few nights of magic in the building staff believed he stirred up something even more terrifying and refused to let him return to complete his engagements.

Green Lawn Cemetery *(now part of Diamond Chain Company)*
Indianapolis: 302 Kentucky Ave.

The cemetery has long since gone but occasionally, a body makes its way to the top of the dirt. Bordered by Kentucky Avenue, White River and West Street, this location has more to offer than fencing. Civil War soldiers were the last to be removed and reinterred at Crown Hill Cemetery in 1933. Because of this deliberate oversight, several soldiers haunt the employee parking to the back of the building. Inside the building, machinery turns off and on at will and the light dim and flicker with no explanation. Many times, security is called only to find no earthly person has disturbed the building or grounds.

Hannah House
Indianapolis: 3801 Madison Ave.

Alexander Hannah, a former state legislator, built the home in 1858 and bought his bride Elizabeth to the home. Hannah was anti-slavery minded and opened his home to shelter fugitives. Tragedy struck when a lantern tipped over in the basement with the fugitives trapped inside. Instead of opening himself up to the measure of the law, it is suspected Hannah buried the fugitives on his land- or in the basement (although no conclusive proof of either has been found).

Many reports of paranormal happenings have been documented. Strange noises, smells and apparitions are observed here. Alexander Hannah makes an appearance now and then. Once he told a visitor to go back downstairs and mind his own business. Even Elizabeth was seen wearing a dark dress one day and a peach colored dress another time. She is also suspected to be the woman who peeks out an upper floor window. Cold spots move from room to room. The smell of death is attributed to Hannah's stillborn child. Chandeliers, pictures and curtains move by an unseen (and sometimes felt) breeze. Old canning jars stood along the wall in the basement at one time and it sounded as if they were being smashed. When visitors went to look, nothing was amiss. Electrical equipment malfunctions- everything from investigation equipment to CD players. Visitors smell burning wood and see the shadows of fugitives in the basement. People have also been touched in virtually all areas of the house. Other visitors have smelled the cloying scent of roses and lavender.

Hawkeye
Indianapolis: 3200 Cold Spring Rd.
(aka Wheeler-Stokely Mansion; aka Stokely Mansion Conference Center)

A member of the Millionaire's Row, Frank Wheeler (who was part owner in the Wheeler—Schebler Carburetor Company and co-founder of the Indianapolis Motor Speedway) built the home as a summer house. This Arts and Crafts home was completed in 1911. Later William Stokely of the Stokely-Van Camp Packing Company bought the home. Features of the house include a porte-cochere for the automobiles and a Japanese tea garden. Additionally, a roofed walking path for pets remains.

This building has a host of spirits. First, a woman runs out the west doors and into a phantom carriage. On the dog walk to the north of the home, visitors have been pushed to the side by unseen hands. A man walking a dog is often seen on the dog walk. In the foyer, a man without a head is seen. The doorbell rings when no one is there. A light in the library turns on and off for no reason. Frank Wheeler, who killed himself in the master bathroom, is still seen reenacting the tragedy- including the gun shot. Features of the house include a porte-cochere for the automobiles and a Japanese tea garden. Additionally, a roofed walking path for pets remains.

Hedback Community Theater
Indianapolis: 1847 N. Alabama St.
(aka Footlight Musicals)

Once part of Camp Morton, a military camp renowned for mistreating its prisoners, now this theater experiences the ghosts of these mistreated soldiers. Lights turn off and on. Some lights seem to be banging out Morse code. Civil War soldiers for both sides are seen throughout the building, but especially in the basement where a headless soldier delights in scaring people. In the upper part of the theater footsteps are heard, the rattle of swords being unsheathed have been heard and a woman without a head is frequently seen.

House of Blue Lights
Indianapolis: 6828 Fall Creek Rd.

Skiles Test, inventor of the underwater swimming pool light, had a great tragedy in his life. His wife died mysteriously and the legend states he kept her in the house surrounded by blue lights. Many visitors and trespassers stated that they used to see him eating and talking to his wife in the coffin. Test died in 1964 and although people who knew him tried to keep the house as a remembrance, it was razed in 1978. The property is now Test Park. Many people who remember the times state that Test used to hang blue lights all year long because he loved the lights. Other people remember he was eccentric but good man who kept train cars of ketchup. Even more people say that Mr. Test was aware of the rumor and delighted in obliging curious onlookers with his blue lights. Others believe the folklore is untrue. Still, the rumors persist.

People claim to see the blue lights still and the figure of a woman and man walking hand and hand through the area where the house stood. Orbs and mysterious mists are also reported.

Indianapolis Firefighters Museum & Historical Society and Firestation Union Hall Theatre
Indianapolis: 748 Massachusetts Ave.

Located in Fire Station 2 which was in use from 1871 to 1929, the museum provides a great look into firefighter history in Marion County. It is the oldest surviving firestation in Indianapolis and the last survivor of four identical firehouses. Today it hosts fire safety events in addition to historic interpretation. Running footsteps have been heard in and a mysterious fire fighter figure has been seen in the museum area where old equipment is on display.

Indiana Repertory Theatre
Indianapolis: 140 W. Washington St.

The artistic director, Howard, used to jog around the mezzanine. One day he jogged outside in the fog and his nephew is said to have hit him with the car. Today, Howard is heard jogging in the IRT.

Indiana School for the Blind
Indianapolis: 7725 N. College Ave.

As with any institution with a history, the Indiana School for the Blind has had its share of growing and education pains. Suicides, murders in the area and natural death has followed the institution over the years. Many visitors and staff members believe these people are still present. A young, skinny girl is seen walking the grounds. Electrical problems plague the area- lights turn on and off, televisions change channels without reason. Closet doors creak open and closed. Toilets flush although no one is occupying them.

Indianapolis Public School #18
Indianapolis: 1001 E. Palmer
(aka Abraham Lincoln 18)

Legend states the school is on an Indian burial ground and that the upper floor caved in killing children and a teacher. Visitors report hearing balls bouncing in the school and seeing the class assembled in a line in the gym as if waiting on instructions.

Indianapolis Public School #50
Indianapolis: Miley Ave at W. Market St., next to Indianola Park

Cold spots and mysterious noises are reported inside the school. Outside in the large grassy area, children are heard playing and the squeak of a merry-go-round is heard.

Indiana State Fair Grounds
Indianapolis: 1202 E. 38th St.

In 1862 the state fair began humbly at what is now Military Park. Over time, it moved progressively farther north until it reached its current location by 38th street in 1892. Throughout its life, the State Fair had quite a few tragedies, including a boiler that exploded killing onlookers, race car drivers killed in crashes on the track, murders nearby, and the Halloween disaster of 1963 during an ice show in which a propane tank exploded, killing dozens of employees and spectators.

Visitors and investigators report smelling exhaust near the track. Cold spots are felt and thick mists are reported in the Pepsi Coliseum as well as phantom figures of people from former times walking the halls and sitting in the seats.

Lights flicker on and off and now and then the scent of smoke is detected. While attending an event, one visitor had a conversation with a woman in the coliseum. The woman was waiting till the crowd thinned and a woman started talking with her. The visitor talked to the investigator "with great sadness" about the 1963 event. The visitor had a child with her and turned away momentarily to attend her child. When she turned back, the woman was gone. Another ghost of Greyhound, a race horse is heard and seen on the race track as well as in his former stall in the Palin Barn. Elvis Presley is also reported seen on occasion.

Inlow Hall
Indianapolis (IUPUI): 316 N. West St.
(now part of the Inlow Hall on IUPUI's campus)

The West Street and Indiana Avenue area has seen better days. No longer a residential area, it has grown into a concrete monster. Not many remnants of the neighborhoods exist until you reach Ransom Place.

A man has been seen in the building gasping for breath. He is seen in work clothes, unshaven and seems to be backing away from someone. In our research, we found that at 316 N. West St. John Emerson, a lumber dealer, was shot in the right temple by a man who ran away and was never caught. Emerson died February 16, 1910.

James A. Allison Mansion
Indianapolis: 3200 Cold Spring Rd.

Built between 1909-1911 this home was James and Sarah Allison's summer home. James co-founded the Prest-O-Lite company which produced superior car headlights. Additionally he helped design Speedway and a partner in the Indianapolis Motor Speedway. He was also famous for starting the Allison Transmission Company. Now it is part of Marian College's campus.

It is used for a conference center and people can rent it for special occasions. Keys and other objects go missing. Objects move from place to place. And the library is continually rearranged. Legend states that the pool was where James' love child was drowned and a baby's cry is frequently heard here.

Janus Building/Janus Lofts
Indianapolis: 255 McCrea St.

This building has seen much unrest. Situated in the Wholesale District where jobbers filled wholesale orders for stores and other customers, the building was built in 1905 and rehabbed in 2003. Since that time, people have reported strange happenings in these pricy but beautiful lofts. Strange footsteps are heard. In one apartment, lights turn on and water runs. When one tenant asked the entity to stop turning the water and lights on, he was greeted with a chilling laugh as the water and lights turned off and on.

Kessler Blvd and 19th Street
Indianapolis: Kessler Blvd and 19th St.
(seen right and left for 1 block of the intersection)

Eight foot tall beast described as a dog walking on two legs with glowing red eyes. Some witnesses describe the legs of the creature as turned backward; other witnesses describe them as muscular, hairy and turned in at the knee. Best time to see is between 8pm-12am.

LS Ayers Tea Room
Indianapolis: 650 W. Washington St.

Legend has it that a former manager and worker got into a knife fight over a woman and one man was killed. This residual haunting is said to replay itself, even today, despite the tea room being moved to the Indiana State Museum.

Larue Carter Hospital
Indianapolis: Union Dr. on IUPUI Campus (razed)
(Note: The new Larue Cater hospital is in the old VA Hospital on Cold Springs Rd.)

Several employees reported seeing apparitions of early nurses and nuns on the property. The third floor bathrooms had issues as patience and staff frequently heard workmen in the bathrooms but when they would investigate, no one was there.

Lockerbie Glove Factory Lofts
Indianapolis: 430 Park Ave.
(aka Indianapolis Glove Company)

Built in the early 1900s and expanded in the 1920s and 1930s, this buildiing is truly a historic gem. The glove company stayed in business until the recession of 1982 and then moved out of the building. That same year, the building was renovated for home use. People remember the factory and on a warm summer day they remanence that the whir of dozens of sewing machines echoed through the neighborhood. Today, the ghost of one employee haunts the building. She is seen on the elevator and sometimes chats about how the building and business used to be.

Madam Walker Building/Theater
Indianapolis: 617 Indiana Ave.

As the first female African-American millionaire, Madam C.J. Walker ran her beauty product business from this Egyptian and African inspired building. As a theater, the building was once a focal point of the jazz movement on the near west side of Indianapolis.

Although the theater is somewhat mum on what it believes in the paranormal, visitors experience cold spots and see shadow figures in the theater.

Magic Moments Restaurant
Indianapolis: 1 Pennsylvania St.
(Note: No longer in business.)

This former restaurant boasted several paranormal events- tables set for guests that would mysteriously "unset" and cold spots penetrated all areas of the establishment. Legend states that illegal boxing matches were held in which some of the participants died.

231 S. College Ave.
Indianapolis: 231 S. College Ave.

The ghost of one of the former owners of the Milano Inn or possibly a former tenant named Mary plays with visitors in the upstairs room of the restaurant. She touches people on the shoulder, face and she even blows in their ears and their hair! EVPs of various qualities have also been collected.

Mill No. 9 Lofts
Indianapolis: 624 E. Walnut St.

Located in the historic Real Silk factory and later the Printing Harts Center, Inc., there is more than beautiful urban living happening in the buildings. During renovation, the entire mornings work for one construction worker was undone while he was at lunch. Bolts and studs were removed from ceilings and floors. No one connected with the work could be blamed because they were all at lunch together. Footsteps echo through halls and several tenants have reported strange rappings in the wall. One tenant said she played a yes/no game with the rapper and found that it was one of the people who used to work for Real Silk.

Millersville Bridge/ 39th Street Bridge
Indianapolis: 39th Street across from the Indiana State Fairgrounds

Although this bridge is now largely used for foot traffic for the fair, occasionally the sounds of someone splashing into the water and cries of help are heard. In the early 1900s two brothers were fishing. One fell in and as the creek was high and rushing, was carried away. The other brother was never the same. Additionally, the large figure of something described as everything from Bigfoot to a Wampus Cat has been reported under the bridge as well.

Monument Circle
Indianapolis: At the intersection of Meridian and Market Streets

Reports of a small boy are reported. The child has interacted with many people. The ghost of a man who killed himself is said to put people against the glass on the observation deck. Staff report elevator malfunctions and the sound of footsteps on the many stairs when no one is in the area.

Morris Butler House
Indianapolis: 1204 N. Park Ave.

Built in 1864 by John Morris, the area was devoid of other homes until later in the 1870s. The Noble Butler family occupied the house next and resided there in some form until 1957, when the family held an estate auction and left the declining neighborhood. In 1964 the Historic Landmarks Foundation occupied and restored the building over time opening it as a museum.

The sounds of children running though the second floor and a much unused upper turret room is also home to footsteps. Through the magnificent tower of the home, footsteps are heard walking down the tower stairs. One recent visitor reported seeing a hazy figure of a child walk into one of the upstairs rooms and heard the child giggle as if playing a game.

Morton Place
Indianapolis: bordered by 19th and 22nd Streets and Delaware Street and Central Avenue.

This land hosted the State Fair and later became Camp Morton during the Civil War. It was named after Governor Oliver Perry Morton. By 1862 it was a prisoner of war camp which housed over 15,000 soldiers. On the south side of the camp was Camp Burnside which housed the volunteers, invalids and the reserve corps. After the war, the State Fair was brought back to the grounds until 1891. Today it is on the National Register of Historic Places. Many of the homes in this area still date from the late 1800s when it was turned into a neighborhood. Owners report seeing many Confederate and Union soldiers. One woman was in her backyard planting a garden when three Union soldiers in formation walked through her background. She described them as milky white and transparent. Another home owner was surprised to see a Confederate soldier with crutches walk down her main staircase. Yet more people have heard cries of men in pain and heard military calls and cadence during all hours of the day and night.

Murat Shrine Temple
Indianapolis: 510 N. New Jersey St.
(aka Murat Theater; Old National Centre)

Elias Jacoby, a potentate of the Murat died in 1935 and has been haunting the building ever since. He's seen in the Egyptian room in person and as a light emanating from different places in the room. A shadow of a figure in an X position is seen on the Egyptian room stage where a worker fell to his death. People have also reported seeing this figure by the electrical panel of the stage and they report feeling very cold in his presence. Jacoby has also been seen in his box seat in the Egyptian room. and a blue light has moved from his box seat into his painting. Drinks unattended by workmen have been emptied by unseen people. Lights turn on and off by themselves, the elevator runs with no one in it and a portrait of Jacoby changes from young to old depending on the time of year. The portrait has also been seen crying.

Old City Cemetery
Indianapolis: Corner of West and South Streets
aka Greenlawn Cemetery

Now a fence manufacturer, this building is full of unrest. The building itself reports electrical problems although electricians find nothing out of order. Heavy footsteps are heard at all hours of the night throughout the building. Outside in the parking lot, a group of Civil War Soldiers wait for employees to come out and follow them to their cars. Supposedly all the bodies from this cemetery have been reinterred at other places but many people have their doubts.

Old Spaghetti Factory
Indianapolis: 210 S. Meridian St.

Formerly home to several dry good distributors, The Old Spaghetti Factory now hosts more than food! The Banquet room is home to strange noises and light bulbs popping. The locked door in the basement that leads to the city tunnels as well as the women's bathroom is where people hear a baby's cry. Staff and visitors hear kids talking and laughing on a back stairway and in the banquet room. Some people have speculated that these noises come from children who were employed before child labor laws. No proof of this has been found, however it is interesting to note that in addition to dry goods, one of the companies manufactured work shirts and overalls.

Paul Rüster Park
Indianapolis: 11300 E. Prospect St.
(Cemetery next to entrance)
(Paul Ruster Park Cemetery)

Paul Rüster was killed by a train and was buried in the foundation of an old house (near park entrance). Some people have heard him playing a harmonica or have seen him walking on the road and in the park.

Phoenix Theatre
Indianapolis: 749 N. Park Ave.

The theater makes its home in a renovated 1907 church in the historic Chatham Arch neighborhood. Props have been moved, footsteps have been heard and shadowy figures have been seen during rehearsals and performances. Most people believe these spirits are people who have been connected with the church and the theater.

Riverdale
Indianapolis: 3200 Cold Spring Rd.
(aka The Allison Mansion; aka Allison Conference Center)

On the edge of the Marian College campus, the Allison Mansion, built and known as Riverdale in 1909 to 1911, was the summer home to the James A. and Sarah Allison. The home has been used as administrative offices and housing for the college as well as a home for the Sisters of St. Francis. Now, the home is used for special events.

People have reported odd happenings in the building. Items are missing, most notably keys (which a former nun used to collect) furniture and books are rearranged from one place to another. A baby's crying is heard near the indoor pool. Part of the legend is that the Allison's had a baby that drowned in the pool. Depending on the source, sometimes the baby is described as a servant's baby that drowned or was killed because it was either Allison's child or the mother couldn't bear to be a single mother. People have been pushed down the grand stairway and have heard their names called. One of the most compelling pieces of evidence for paranormal activity is the number of people who have held special events in the former home only to have their faces in pictures covered by a mist. The former master bedroom is haunted by Sarah and the billiards room by James. The basement door is known to close and lock when you enter the area. Feelings of dread follow. Candles blow out at events for no reason.

Rivoli Theatre
Indianapolis: 3155 East 10th St.

Built as a Universal Studios theater in 1927, this theater treasure still as some of the original gum woodwork, leaded class and terrazzo. The auditorium accommodated up to 1,500 people which was large for the time. Later the theater was used for live jazz, swing and rock bands.

Many owners state that the building was haunted. Mysterious people would sit in the seats and laugh and talk as if enjoying a show, although none was playing. When asked why they were there, the intruders disappeared. One man walks through a row of seats as though trying to go through a full row only to disappear in a wall. A woman in a white dress is accompanied by a man in a tux and they sit in the theater as well. The bathrooms seem to have activity as the water turns on and off, toilets flush and conversations with people who are nowhere to be found take place. Cold spots are felt in the projection booth. Lights turn on and off and a light appears in the auditorium that grows dimmer and stronger, eventually to disappear altogether. Other ghost includes "Lady Rivoli" who appears in the projection booth. Electrical problems believed to be caused by the paranormal are also reported. Other noises include muted conversations and glass breaking.

Rock Bottom Brewery
Indianapolis: 10 W. Washington St.

This building was the scene of the Bowen-Merrill fire that killed 13 firefighters in 1890. Today, a burned smell is detected, firefighters from another time have had conversations with customers, staff and bartenders, and cold spots are felt throughout the building.

James Whitcomb Riley House
Indianapolis: 528 Lockerbie St.

James Whitcomb Riley is seen on the stairs and in the sitting room. Sometimes he laughs or smiles at people who witness his apparition.

Old City Prison
Indianapolis: Razed. This jail was the fourth city jail located south of Washington St. at Alabama and Maryland Streets

This old city prison was built in the 1890s and was made of Indiana limestone. One ghost that was widely reported was that of Robert Munson. On August 29, 1906, he was seen by inmates as being thrown against the bars of his cell and later died. But he was the only person in his cell. His death remained a mystery and inmates reported seeing him in the cell. Inmates put into his old cell reported being woken up by Munson reenacting his death as well as being visited by his spectre looking down at them.

St. Joseph's Cemetery/ Calvary Cemetery/Holy Cross Cemetery
Indianapolis: West Troy Ave. and Bluff Rd.

A conglomerate of Catholic cemeteries, this area is home to small children who dart behind tombstones throughout the cemetery and giggle with delight when you can't find them. One investigator visited in winter and heard the children giggling and heard them "step through the crunchy snow". When she looked back, she found small footprints following her. The footprints ended behind a large stone.

St. Joseph's Catholic Church
Indianapolis: College Ave. and Park St.

The legends state that the stigmata occurred simultaneously to 92 witnesses in the church. The church was built in 1871 and left abandoned in the mid 1949 for a more spacious area closer to the congregation.

Footsteps and banging have been heard in this historic building and one group of visitors witnessed the stigmata on the hands of one person after visiting the basement and seeing colored orbs. Another visitor came face to face with the ghost of a priest that walked through him. Current staff at the restaurant in the building have heard footsteps and seen glasses come off of the bar and drop.

Schoolhouse Square Apartments
Indianapolis: 953 Prospect Street

Originally constructed around 1870 it was started as the St. Joseph Institute and used by the brothers of the Sacred Heart. Many people have heard footsteps throughout the building. One day, several of the tenants heard a measured footstep walk down the hallway and pause at each door. Then the footsteps came back the same way pausing at each door- but this time each tenant heard a knock. When they looked in the hall, no one was there. The brothers seem to still be around as they are seen from time to time walking into various doors and walls.

Sheffield Avenue and Howard Street
Indianapolis: Sheffield Ave and Howard Sts.

The sound of children playing and gunshots are heard at this location around the December holidays. Oddly enough, Claude Baker, who was 12 was shot by Earl Foster, 13, when they were playing holdup- on December 18, 1911.

Spiritualist Psychic Church
Indianapolis: 1415 N. Central Ave.

This former mansion is now a church. The ghosts of many former residents haunt the mansion and several orbs and mists have been captured on film.

Stutz Business Center
Indianapolis: 212 W. 10th St.

Harry Stutz, a player in the Indianapolis automobile industry, built the buildings as part of his factory. Today mysterious thumps and bumps are heard, including footsteps. Cold spots are reported by various tenants and one man reports having seen Harry Stutz himself in a second floor office.

Sylvia Likens House
Indianapolis: 3850 E. New York St.
(Note: Razed in April 2009.)

Sylvia Likens was in the care of Gertrude Baniszewski in the summer of 1965. For three months she endured abuse by Baniszewski, her family and the children of the neighborhood. They burnt her with cigarettes and tattooed "I'm a prostitute and proud of it!" on her stomach. The end came when she was tossed in the basement for days. Trying vainly to scratch herself out of the basement, eventually she passed out. The members of the home threw her into a cold bath and pitched her body on a stinking mattress in the upper front north east side room, where she died of malnutrition and shock from her skin wounds.

Since that time, the home has never kept tenants well and has largely stood empty. In 2003 an organization tried unsuccessfully to form a woman's shelter/education center. From the time Sylvia died, she was seen not only looking out the window but also in the cemetery in which she is buried (see Oak Hill, Boone County entry).

Tuckaway House
Indianapolis: 3128 N. Pennsylvania Ave.

In the Meridian Park neighborhood, this 1906 bungalow was purchased in 1910 by George and Nellie Meier. George was a famous clothing designer and Nellie read the palms of the stars. President Roosevelt, family members and other presidents also had their palms read by her. Nellie even predicted the ultimate demise of Carol Lombard (Clark Gable's wife) before her fateful plane trip from Indiana.

The home has had spirits since the time of Nellie and her spiritualism, but today, guests appear and disappear at will, random screams are heard and a woman dressed in early 1900s clothing appears as well. George Meier and his wife are seen from time to time. Mists and orbs have been captured in pictures as well. One woman staying at the home reported that she dreamed of her room being disheveled by someone and when she woke up, her dream had taken place. Pictures swing and fall from the wall. Additionally visitors have smelled the scent of perfume and roses. Some visitors have picked up EVPs including a woman saying, "it's here" and "not tonight". Other guests have felt a cloying dizziness in different areas of the home. Cold spots are also common.

Union Station
Indianapolis: 123 W. Louisiana St.

This 1880s structure was put on the National Register of Historic Places in 1974. Once a bustling train station, it now houses a few bars, restaurants and is rented in part for events.

A mysterious man believed to be John W Daughterty replays his death on the stairs to the tracks. Security guards are plagued by phantom Civil War soldiers playing hide and seek with them.

In the hotel section in the Pullman cars, people report feeling as if the cars are in motion, heard train whistles and have heard the spirits of conductors asking them to board the train. They have also been jarred awake by unseen hands. Ghosts have been seen entering the train cars, by staff although no one had booked the cars for a stay. Several staff have also heard animal noises coming from different areas of the station and have speculated they could have been stock brought through the station.

Waterbury Neighborhood
Indianapolis: 2901 W. 96th St.

Contains a condominium in which an older woman passed away. Now object are moved, disappear and noises are heard.

West Merrill Street near White River
Indianapolis: West Merrill St. near White River

Visitors report mists and orbs and laughter and singing from men. All sounds stop as visitors approach. In many of the homes across from the area, people see spirits in their home. These spirits have been known to be unhappy and wail. One visitor reports hearing the men, and hearing a woman with them. Shortly after that, a woman's body was found. She had been dead less than an hour.

Wyndam Apartments
Indianapolis: 1040 N. Delaware Street

One apartment has the ghost of an old woman in the kitchen that goes through the motions of making tea. When the woman is present, the smell of freshly brewed tea is also smelled. The apartment bathroom also inspires fear and dread, there a young woman is seen, naked in the bathtub with her wrists slashed.

Zion Evangelical Church of Christ
Indianapolis: 603 N. New Jersey St.

The church and its offices have several visitors. In the bell tower of the church, a women cries as if looking for a lost love. The bell rings when no one is around. Inside the offices, a man paces back and forth at all hours of the night as if trying to memorize a sermon. Doors also slam shut in the offices with no provocation.

1310 North Olney Street
Irvington: 1310 N. Olney St.

Visitors and former tenants report orbs, wispy figures and whispers. Lights would turn off and on at will.

Applegate House
Irvington: 5339 University Ave.

A dark figure of a young boy haunts the house. Sometimes he speaks to visitors.

Benton House
Irvington: 312 S. Downey St.

An old woman sometimes comes out of the house to yell at the children and a woman in a wheelchair is seen and heard on the second floor. One visitor also remembers talking to the woman in the wheelchair who told her about the "noisy children" in the neighborhood.

Bona Thompson Library
Irvington: 5330 University Ave.

Visitors have witnessed Bona Thompson walking through the facility which is now home to the Irvington Historical Society.

Briggs/Johnston House
Irvington: 5631 University Ave.

Owners report footfalls on the stairway and on the upper floor of the home. Some investigators believe a small boy named Joe Johnston (the son of a former owner) and his mother Mrs. Johnston inhabits the home. Visitors have also reported orbs.

Children's Guardian Home
Irvington: 5751 University Ave.

The ghost of a maintenance worker is seen working throughout the building and grounds. A child haunts the building sometimes as a misty shape and other times just as the sound of severe coughing.

John Gruelle House
Irvington: 5738 Oak Ave.
(aka Raggedy Ann House)

John Gruelle was a cartoonist for the Indianapolis Star as well as the creator of Raggedy Ann (based on the works of James Whitcomb Riley. A battery operated doll came to life in this house although it had no batteries. Lights and flashlights turned on for no apparent reason.

Haag's Drug Store
Irvington: Audubon Rd. and Washington St.
(now part of Irvington's commercial district)
(Note: The drug store is no longer a tenant but the district remains.)

Visitors and workers claim spirits of people who passed through the building are still present and guide them to help their businesses.

H.H. Homes Home
Irvington: 5811 Julian Ave.

H. H. Holmes, famous serial killer killed a young boy, Howard Pitezel in the home. A dark presence is reported as well as figures walking through the home. Cupboards open and close at their own whim and voices are heard by the owners. The heat is turned up or off as well.

Thomas Carr Howe House
Irvington: 325 S. Audubon Rd.

Visitors report odd odors.

Irvington Office Center
Irvington: 338 Arlington Ave.
(aka Irvington School #85; aka Loomis School)

Locals know School 85 as the Loomis School, so named for a favored music teacher, George Loomis. He is said to haunt the school slamming doors, opening windows and even tapping doors and walls. Some locals have also seen him from the windows.

Irvington Presbyterian Church/ Johnson House
Irvington: 55 Johnson Ave.

A ghostly choir is seen in the building and the strains of melody heard. The Sylvester Johnson house was part of this same land and razed, yet Johnson seems to continue to visit the church in his ghostly form.

Irvington Theatre
Irvington: 5505 E. Washington St.

In the apartments above the theater, tenants report strange phone calls from people who later were confirmed not at home at the time of the call. Children's voices, crying and the sounds of them playing have also been reported. One investigator was pinched. An EVP of a child's voice was captured. In what was the theater now sits a coffee house. The owner reports chess pieces moving when no one was in the shop and the restroom is haunted by spirits who like to taunt the occupants.

Jesse's Place
Irvington: Building at NE corner of Washington and Ritter Streets
(aka Buffalo Bills)

A man and his pregnant wife were shot and killed here in 1976. Several musicians report feeling an oppressive feeling in the place when they played there after the murders. Additionally one musician who used to carry a gun was punched in the back. He believes it was from the family who died.

Johnson House
Irvington: 263 Audubon Rd.

A music teacher who lived in the home and played the harp is seen from time to time sitting in the turret and her harp music is heard.

Julian Mansion
Irvington: 115 S. Audubon Rd.

Lights are reported as turning off and on, even during the years that the house was left empty after George Julian's death. A man, presumably Julian paces downstairs and workers in hospital garb are seen in upstairs windows. Ghost children have been heard playing.

Julian School #57
Irvington: 5435 E. Washington St.

A ghost named "Agnes" roams the halls in an old dress. People report seeing her during the day and evening as well as hearing her footsteps. Teachers report doors slamming for no reason, hearing music when no one should be playing and lights mysteriously flickering.

Kingsbury Medical Hostel
Irvington: 20 S. Johnson St.

The doctor who treated Madge Oberholtzer lived in this home. When visitors spoke about the doctor, they heard a crash but could find no source for it.

(See Oberholtzer House and D.C. Stephenson Mansion, Irvington (Indianapolis), Marion County)

Lincoln Ghost Train
Irvington: Bonna Ave. parallels the tracks.
(Note: As of April 2009, much of the tracks have been taken away in favor or paved trails. In Irvington town, the track is still present.)

In April of each year, visitors and residents claim to see the Lincoln Funeral train that passed through the area in 1865. Some witnesses report seeing full color and black and white apparitions on the train; other witnesses report skeletal figures. A small boy is also seen from time to time waving from the train. Some investigators theorize this was a boy who tried to cross the tracks in front of the train and died for his effort. A man who killed himself at the same location is seen by visitors as well.

Masonic Lodge #666
Irvington: 5515 E. Washington St.

Construction workers reported dark shadow figures walking in front of bright lights. Other workers felt someone touch their hands, arms or even tap their shoulders. Doors open and close on their own, sometimes accompanied by shadow figures walking through them. A film production company reported a brand new refrigerator not working and called in a repairman to fix it. Determining it was not working but had no mechanical reason it shouldn't work, it was determined to move the film stored in it to a different place, they did so. When they returned to the refrigerator it was working properly and at the proper temperature.

Oberholtzer House
Irvington: 5802 E. University Ave.

Home to Madge Oberholtzer, who was killed by D.C. Stevenson. She is seen in her home and throughout the town of Irvington. She is especially seen on stormy nights in the upstairs windows in the room she was laid out in after her death. Occasionally, when Madge is seen on the streets, she will speak with passerbys.

(See D.C. Stevenson entry, Irvington (Indianapolis), Marion Co.)

Roof House
Irvington: 5980 University Ave.

Visitors report seeing a ghost kitten. Former owners report doors and windows opening and closing with no reason. A translucent woman is seen near the attic.

Southeastern Irvington
Irvington: Bounded by Ritter St., Brookville Rd., Arlington Ave. and Beachwood Ave.

The sound of horses are heard, presumably looking for John Brown, a farmer who was killed by John Wade and Brown's wife "Bloody" Mary Brown. The motive was John's love and Mary was implicated with him in the trial. Both served life prison sentences.

South Irvington Circle
Irvington: Audubon Rd and University Ave.

Visitors have seen a milk white figure of a woman. Visitors also hear a phantom gunshot, presumably attached to a man that killed himself at the circle. A mysterious old man dressed in late 1800s clothing and sporting a beard walks through the area. Additionally, there was a fire at a school that sat on the site and although there is no official record of any deaths, visitors have reported ghostly boys playing leapfrog and some people report having had their hats removed by unseen hands.

D.C. Stevenson Mansion
Irvington: 5432 University Ave.

Former home to D.C. Stevenson, an active Klansman who thought he was above the law. He was convicted of the rape and death of Madge Oberholtzer, a state employee. During her kidnap and abuse, Stevenson kept her in the carriage house of his home. In 1986 two men were found dead in the same carriage house. Today lights turn on and off in the carriage house. Visitors report the sounds of merriment and shadows are seen in the main house. Investigators report smoke rings and the smell of cigar smoke throughout the home. (Stevenson loved cigars.)

Old Firestation
Oaklandon: NW corner of Oaklandon Rd and Broadway St

At last count, this was now a church youth center. The old firehouse has been remodeled over time The doors in the building frequently open and close. The bay doors open and close without anyone around. In the old part of the station, it is often very cold. Lights turn off and on. Bangs, knocks and other noises happen often.

Nicholson- Rand House
Southport: 5010 W. Southport Rd.

This home has several legends. The owner's daughter was killed by a car and decapitated. The girl was shot by hunters. The girl fell from the second story balcony. In any event, the story continues that the family sold it and the family who bought it cut it in half and moved it. When it was being moved, a photographer captured a photo that appears to have a little girl in the upper window. It's been widely reported that other people have captured this same image and that if you go into the room, it is very cold and breezy in the room, even with the window closed. When the house was moved, many people felt the presence of the girl and the spirits from the cemetery behind the house. Some investigators reported odd EMF readings in the house while the power was disconnect (although no mention of other sources outside of the house were investigated).

Train Tracks
Southport: Between Southport Rd and Stop 11 Rd.

A woman's baby was killed by a train when it toddled across the tracks. In grief, she threw herself in front of another oncoming train. You can hear her screams and see her run to her death.

MARSHALL COUNTY

118 South Center Street
Plymouth: 118 S. Center St.

This house is over 100 years old. Various tenants have reported cabinets opening, cold chills and lights turning off and on. One person was shoved and reportedly had a slight head injury. Apparitions that interact with residents are seen on stairs. One room in particular seems to have quite a bit of activity. Tenants tell of blankets being flung off them, and of having their faces pushed down in pillows.

8th Road Haunted House
Bourbon: 8th Rd.

The daughter and wife of a farmer were raped and killed, their bodies thrown in the woods. The husband and son were hung in the barn. At midnight you see the ropes in the barn, and you see the wife and daughter running toward the woods and hear their screams.

Ancilla College and Convent
Donaldson: 9601 S. Union Rd.

Nuns walk the tunnels of the convent and college disappearing into walls or before your eyes. Visitors have been pinched, pushed and scratched in the tunnels. Doors and windows open and close on their own. Items move around the kitchen at will.

Ewald Cemetery
Bremen: 5th Rd. east of Hawthorn
(aka Little Egypt Cemetery)

Apparitions are seen in the cemetery. Handprints appear on your car. If you walk by a baby's tombstone you hear it cry. A phantom farmer will chase you out of the cemetery- he died in a field nearby. Headlights follow you through the cemetery. In the woods down the street, a teenage girl was raped and killed. You hear her screams in the woods.

The Granary
Inwood: Next to the old post office

An old farmer in white overalls haunts the town granary. He tells you to leave because he is protecting the area. One person who visited the area in the early morning saw him standing on top the granary and watched him fall, but never hit the ground. Others have seen him in the window of the office. He has a black/white striped hat and just stares at you.

Hayloft Restaurant
Plymouth: SR30 and SR31
(Note: The restaurant burned to the ground and is being rebuilt.)

The Hayloft was originally a barn from the 1800s, in the 1970s this building was turned into a restaurant. The spirits here move items in the restaurant- glasses, table cloths, tables, and pots and pans. One of the spirits appears as a farmer preceded by the smell of burning wood. People have named the ghost of a farmer, Homer. He spends a lot of time in the Silo Room and in the kitchen. He's seen from about the waist or knees up. The staff blame Homer for items disappearing altogether or for making noises by dropping things. Patrons report a Native American who stands in various parts of the restaurant. He's blamed for displacing chairs and banging the pots and pans in the kitchen. Since this building has burnt down, some investigators speculate the ghosts were warning the owners about the fire.

Muckshaw Road
Plymouth: Muckshaw Rd.

An old truck full of ghost teenagers is seen. The teens died in an accident. On full moons, the truck will chase you.

Nighthart Cemetery
Plymouth: 7th Rd. near Jarrah Rd.

A seven foot tall shadow figure swoops around the cemetery. A loud, high pitched cry is heard.

Old Fire Station
Oaklandon: Northeast corner of Broadway St. and Oaklandon Rd.

Mysterious shadows wind through the building and the bay doors open and close at random times.

State Road 117 and State Road 110
Plymouth: SR117 and SR110

Paukooshuck, son of Potawatomi Chief Aubbeenaubbee is said to walk the road. He spent his life in the area. Paukooshuck walked the trail of tears although he was unsuccessful. Eventually he entered Chief Winamac's village and died after being in a fight.

Troll Bridge
Bremen: On 5th Rd., between Filbert Trail and N Grape Rd.
Near Little Egypt (see entry for Little Egypt)

The area is very quiet and when the paranormal happens, it is as silent as the grave. Strange lights are seen around the bridge and in the trees. A snake that transforms into a wolf is seen uncoiling from the trees to the right of the bridge. A tall dark shadow figure chases you. Investigators have reported batteries draining immediately and even fresh batteries from a brand new, never opened, package have gone dead. Once they've left the cemetery, the batteries remain dead. No sign of a troll, though!

Uptown Cinema

Culver: 612 E. Lake Shore Dr.

(aka Uptown Theater)

In the 1920s Culver had several theaters on its main streets. Vaudeville was on the bill at Uptown as well as movies. The theater was changed to El Rancho in the 1930s as it looked like a fort. It has gone through many ups and downs, and the current owner is hard at work making this landmark a viable entertainments spot in Culver. Spirits of former patrons and performers are seen still moving about the theater.

MARTIN COUNTY

409 Wood Street
Loogootee: 409 Wood St.

Reports of strange footsteps and loud, evil laughter have been reported for years at this location. Shadow figures are seen moving through the home when no one is home.

Brooks Bridge
Shoals: CR6 Brooks Bridge Rd. (east of CR31)

One fine June night, a woman jumped from the bridge. Investigators claim if you visit the bridge, you'll hear her running down the bridge and you'll feel cold air whoosh by. Another story claims a teenager killed herself by jumping off the bridge. The 17-year old was mad at her boyfriend and committed suicide. On the fifth of every month, if you visit the bridge, you will hear her run, jump and scream. Another version places the victim at middle age.

Clarke Cemetery
Martin State Forest / Loogootee: NW of US50 on Harvey Sutton Rd. just east of where Harvey Sutton Rd and Williams Rd. meet.
(aka Clark Cemetery)

Mists and orbs have been captured at this cemetery. One visitor reported visiting the site during the day and speaking with an old man who was repairing a stone. The visitor bade the man goodbye and turned to leave. She thought of another question and as she turned to ask him, she found the man had disappeared.

John F.Kennedy Gym
Loogootee: JFK Ave. between Vincennes and Riley Streets.

The basketball team used to run laps and practice here. One member tripped, fell, and died. At night you can hear the team running in the gym and you can hear the sound of someone walking and falling. On certain nights, you can see the blood stain where the boy died.

Haunted House
Alfordsville: Sugar Creek
A man strangled his family in this house. Rain, believed to be the tears of his family which fall throughout the house. The room the bodies were found in is always cold even if it is hot outside.

Hindostan Falls/ Hindostan Cemetery/ Sholts Cemetery
Hindostan Falls: South from Shoals on US50/150 to SR550, turn west and follow the signs. "The Rock" is the limestone ledge under the falls. Sholts Cemetery is between Brooks Bridge Rd. and Hindostan Falls on SR550. Hindostan Cemetery is on the SW corner of the town off SR550

This is a state fishing area, but once, it was a thriving town. In 1821 disease began sweeping the community and by 1828 the town was abandoned. Although it is unclear what type of disease took the lives of the population, speculation is that it was anything from smallpox (contracted from rats in cornmeal), yellow fever, or cholera. Many of the dead were buried in areas cemeteries; however, eventually an unknown mass grave was dug because of the tremendous amount of bodies accumulating. The majority of the townspeople eventually settled near Mount Pleasant. A local legend states that a woman who was driven out of town for being a witch cursed the town with a plague and that's why the town was destroyed. Today you can still see remnants of the old town, foundations can be found in the woods. Forgotten streets are also half covered in brush. According to locals, when the town moved to Mt. Pleasant, which was the county seat, and legend has it that the Hindostan Falls treasury, full of gold and silver was transferred to the town, but never actually made it there. This area is worth the trip with or without the ghosts because of its unique whirlpools. If you go to "The Rock" in Hindostan, you'll be able to see where the mill once stood. If the river is full, the falls are exquisite. Many visitors to the area have reported white outlines of men, women and children in the area, especially around Shoals Cemetery.

Loogootee Elementary East
Loogootee: 510 Church St.

When you look at the school, a red spot appears near the top of it. Some staff and students believe this spot appears because of a janitor that killed himself by hanging in the boy's bathroom. If you go into the bathrooms at night, you hear him pushing a mop bucked around the bathroom and hear his keys jangling. Some people also believe that the janitor used to bring his dog to work and on the second floor, sightings of a dog have been reported.

Peggy Holler
Shoals: Unknown

Peggy's husband cut her head off, and her headless ghost is often seen. Her husband is also heard calling "Peggy".

Pleasant Grove Cemetery
(aka Crane Cemetery)

Crane: On the grounds of Crane Naval Weapons Support Center. Visitors should enter through the Bloomington Gate (IN 45 and IN 58) or through the Crane Gate (IN 558,1 mile east of US 231).

This cemetery contains a glowing headstone. Enter the cemetery and turn your lights off and drive to the back. Once you are there look directly ahead of your car and you will see the headstone glowing. The glow will fade the longer you stay, but will cycle like a light house while you remain in the cemetery.

West Boggs Park
Loogootee: South of SR645E (1300E North) on US231 N

A phantom woman runs through the park at 10pm. She is the mother of a child who drowned. Late at night this woman screams while she tries to find her son. Investigators report having seen her in the lake at midnight with her son.

School House Hill
Pleasant Valley: School House Hill is off SR550 at the first western road south of SR550.

'Investigators have heard yells for help. One investigator was pushed down the hill on her way back from an investigation. She broke her wrist.

Shoals Community Junior-Senior High School
Shoals: 7900 US50

The school was constructed on a burial ground. Visitors hear unexplained tapping and rapping. Sports equipment has been known to become displaced. A strange watermark is seen to the south end of the gym. Doors close eerily on their own.

MIAMI
COUNTY

101 W. Ottawa Street
Miami: 101 W. Ottawa St.

During a renovation this home began to experience ghostly activity. Pictures fly off walls and hit the occupants. Items are flung off tables though no one touches them. A helpful spirit unplugs electric appliances that are left on. Perfumed air wafts frequently through the location. Animals react to unseen spirits by making noise, running away, and cowering. People are jerked by unseen hands that don't want to let go.

63 W. 6th Street
Peru: 63 W 6th St.

A ghost woman opens the upstairs curtains and moves things kept in storage there. Sometimes she is heard walking down the stairs.

Converse *(see Grant County)*

Five Corners Cemetery
Macy: On W 12150 N east of Old US 31

Unexplained lights and apparitions are reported. Moving orbs have been captured on film

Grissom Air Force Base
(aka Bunker Hill)
Peru: 1000 W. Hoosier Blvd.

In 1968 a B-58 Hustler pilot was killed as the landing gear collapsed. Once the fire that killed the pilot was out and the plane was safe to move, a man named Tom wanted to make sure that the fire was indeed out and no smoldering remained. As he stood near the aircraft, he noticed new footprints going from the aircraft to where it would have been a safe spot for the pilot, had he had a chance. The only other prints were his own. Following the other prints, he noticed they became lighter and lighter and disappeared.

Leonda Cemetery
Peru: 1539 W 600 S (no public access)
(aka Kings Court; aka Kings Court Mobile Home Park)

Cemetery behind the park is haunted by woodland fairies and pixies.

Mississinawa Battle Grounds
Peru: 7 miles north of Marion. Take I-69 to SR 18 East. In Marion, follow SR 15 north, following the signs to Mississinawa 1812.

Battles are still reenacted by invisible people. Guns and cries for help are heard. Many apparitions of men, women and children walk the lake. The caves around the area also contain shadow people.

Okie Pinokie

Peru: Take IN 124 east from Peru. Turn right onto 150 S (Fire Lane). Drive for a couple of miles until you come to a roundabout.

Native Americans have been seen running through the woods. Some appear to be residual hauntings, yet others have interacted with visitors. One visitor reports having had a Native American guide help him find his way out of the wooded area and back to the road. Other people report similar experiences, although some believe the area is a time and space warp. EVPs of voices have been heard, some seemingly in a language other than English. Some people believe there are hundreds of spirits in the woods at this location.

Old Miami County Jail

Peru: 5th and Wabash Streets

Now used as a haunted houseat Halloween, some of the volunteers and visitors to the haunted house say the made up ghosts aren't the only kind in this former jail. Apparitions of men in work clothes and a woman in a 1940s pencil skirt and blouse have been witnessed.

Old Stone House

Peru: 2372 Old Stone Rd.

Now Christian Life Fellowship Church, this home was part of the Underground Railroad. Lights emanate from the home and shadow figures with lanterns are seen running to and from the river. The oldest part of the building burned and was remodeled on the inside.

Peaceful Acres Mobile Home Court

Peru: Lot 3 Peaceful Acres, 5485 Road 31 South

An apparition of a man (sometimes called "the Toothless Wonder") haunts Lot 3 of Peaceful Acres Mobile Home Park.

St. John's Lutheran Cemetery/St. Charles Catholic Cemetery

Peru: End of N Kelly Ave. Only the Lutheran cemetery has a sign.

A stairway appears descending from the white cross in St. Charles Catholic Cemetery.

Seven Pillars
Peru: On old Francis Slocum Trail; 3 miles east of Peru

Used by the Miami Native Americans, its Tribal Council met here to converse with their elders. It was also a trading post. French believed that the spirits of the dead were all around them and had special items to keep them at bay. It used to be a camping and fishing site. Ghosts have been seen walking through the area, in the water. The area has been repurchased by the Miami as part of their efforts to be reestablished as a recognized tribe.

Tillet Cemetery
(aka Tillett's Cemetery; aka Hook man's Cemetery)

Peru: At the crossroads of US 24 and E. Lovers Lane. Go east of US 24 onto the first dirt road to your left. Cemetery is in wooded area.

A mist is always present and always quiet. A cold area surrounds the Hook man's grave. Sometimes he is seen on the lane walking toward parked cars. Photos of blurred apparitions have been captured as well as photos with shadow people.

Wabash River by Jacob Rife's gravel pit
Peru: Wabash River by Jacob Rife's gravel pit. It's across from West City Park (a house sits on the site).

A skeleton was found in the dirt as they excavated in 1927. Jacob Rife's bones were given the to the Miami Historical society. Since then, screams have been heard, mists have been prevalent and pleas for help are heard.

MONROE COUNTY

Binford Elementary
Bloomington: 2300 E. 2nd St.

A cloaked man walks through the school. Electrical problems plague the whole building. The man is believed to be a former school janitor who was killed by three students.

Buskirk Mansion
Bloomington: 520 N. Walnut St.
(aka Porticos)

This former home, now restaurant, was once part of the Underground Railroad. The first home predated the Civil War and this second structure was built in the 1890s. A girl's face is seen in a mirror. The sounds of children's laughter and running upstairs is heard in the dining room. Children are also seen and disappear quickly in other parts of the home. An upstairs dining room was found with broken dishes and glasses, and furniture overturned, yet no one in the restaurant had heard a sound. Wait staff sitting on the second floor couch jumped at the same time because they felt their backs burning. EVPs of children's voices have also been captured. Even the alarm company has monitored the sounds of children which have set off the alarms.

Hardin Ridge Recreation Area
Bloomington: SR446 in the Hoosier National Forrest.

A two legged upright creature is seen around the recreation area. It is reported as 5-6 feet tall weighing more than 200 lbs.

Indiana University- Arboretum
Bloomington: IU has a great map of its campus on its website.

A voice yells "Get off my home!" Shadows follow visitors until they leave. The legend states that a student died in the pond in the 1980s (or 1970s depending on the story teller) and the shadow figure of the person often stands by the pond.

Indiana University- Ballantine Hall
Bloomington: IU has a great map of its campus on its website.

Legend has it that a woman threw herself from a window when she found her boyfriend with another woman. This woman haunts the basement, where she saw her boyfriend. She is heard crying. The ghost of a janitor is heard rattling the doors to the rooms late at night. Doors on the 5th floor have been known to rattle and shake when no one is around. A janitor is also seen on this floor. On the 10th floor, orbs move and whisper in the air much to the surprise of visitors.

Indiana University- Burford Hall
Bloomington: IU has a great map of its campus on its website.

A woman ghost named Barb died of alcohol poisoning in the building. She vomits, flushes the toilet and cries. Whispers and items scraping on the walls and floors are heard.

Indiana University- The Career Center
Bloomington: IU has a great map of its campus on its website.
(aka Phi Kappa Tau)

The area where the Career Center stands is haunted by children who are said to be aborted from illegal operations in the early 1940s. Measured footsteps climb and descend the stairs. People report having been touched by unseen hands. Another legend has the builder killing himself shortly before the doctor moved in. A man seen washing his hands of blood has surprised people in the second floor bathroom. A female apparition fades from view in front of staffers and her cries echo the halls.

Indiana University - Cromwell Hall
Bloomington: IU has a great map of its campus on its website.

A white cross is sometimes seen on the 12th floor where a man committed suicide. A girl later died in the room. The man jumped from the west side in room 1221. Supposedly no one is allowed in the room.

Indiana University- Delta Tau Delta House
Bloomington: IU has a great map of its campus on its website.

A worker died during the construction of the house. He walks around the whole building and talks about the house.

Indiana University- Dunn Cemetery
Bloomington: IU has a great map of its campus on its website.

Moses Dunn deeded the land in 1855 to the Brewster sisters (who are buried there). Eventually the rest of the Dunn land was sold to IU. The sounds of babies crying are heard here.

Indiana University- Eigenmann Residence Center
Bloomington: IU has a great map of its campus on its website.

Suicides abound in this building and murders as well, most notably Susan Clements and Steven Molen, who were shot on the 14th floor by Andreas Drexler, who killed himself in his car. He apparently was stalking Susan. As a result, shadow figures, moving object and feelings such as severe melancholy and anger surge through visitors.

Indiana University- The Folklore Office
Bloomington: IU has a great map of its campus on its website.

Former chairman, Dr. Richard Dorson (1962-1981). After his death the lamp near the building used to stay on all the time. Dorson was seen leaning against it. He has also made appearances in the courtyard.

Indiana University- Goodbody Hall
Bloomington: IU has a great map of its campus on its website.

The sculpture of Donald Duck wearing a mortar board isn't the only odd thing about this building. A sobbing woman in white is seen crying on the steps inside the foyer.

Indiana University- Kelly School of Business
Bloomington: IU has a great map of its campus on its website.

In the large second floor lecture hall, footsteps and the sound of someone sitting in a fold-down chair are heard. A woman's laughter and screams are heard in the stairwells.

Indiana University- The Indiana Memorial Union
Bloomington: IU has a great map of its campus on its website.

Several human apparitions from suicides and a ghost dog are seen. In the old tower, happy laughter, footsteps and moving furniture are heard. A transparent man from the 1950s is seen under the painting of former IU President and Chancellor Herman B. Wells and in the Tree Suites. In the Tudor room, a picture of a child known as Jacob who died in a fire hangs on the wall. His ghost moves things on the tables in the dining halls at night. When his photo was removed, he trashed the room. In the Bryan Room, which used to be part of a hotel, a man turns on lights at night. He is believed to have been a guest that killed himself by jumping from the building and is scared of the dark.

Footsteps and laughter are reported. Lights turn off and on, In the Federal room, an unfinished painting of Mary Burne hangs. She seems to look at it from time to time and her perfume can be smelled, especially during 2-6am. In the Tree Suites, a man in a suit haunts the stairway. He supposedly killed himself in the building.

Indiana University - The Lily Library
Bloomington: IU has a great map of its campus on its website.

An apparition of a girl in blue is seen studying at one of the desks. She is usually seen close to closing time, or is seen from the windows after closing. Additionally, staff has heard conversations when no one is around. Items move from room to room. Some of the exhibits seem to bring spirits with them only to leave once the exhibit moves to a new location.

Indiana University- Maxwell Hall
Bloomington: IU has a great map of its campus on its website.

A figure of a young man glides through the halls at night, knocking on doors and laughing.

Indiana University-Memorial Stadium

Bloomington: IU has a great map of its campus on its website.

Michael Plume died here under mysterious circumstances. He was found hanging on the west side of the stadium. People believe he was killed because he was homosexual. Visitors and staff alike have seen him hanging in the building.

Indiana University-Old Cresent section

Bloomington: IU has a great map of its campus on its website.

The Lady in Black wears Victorian clothes and follows couples and men down the area of Third Street, close to the sororities and fraterniies. Mostly seen around 3 am.

Indiana University-Reed Hall

Bloomington: IU has a great map of its campus on its website.

The Hall is named for Dr. Lyle and Nell Reed. An RA named Paula was under a lot of stress and killed herself in the 1980s. On the anniversary of her death, December 12th, you can hear her. She is also seen entering different rooms in the dorm. Another ghost is a woman with long black hair who is in a bloody nightgown. Her boyfriend was a medical student and hid her body in the campus tunnels. She is mostly seen wandering the halls, particularly the third floor.

Indiana University-Sigma Phi Epsilon

Bloomington: IU has a great map of its campus on its website.

Michael Pfang was enjoying a homecoming carnival at the edge of a street when a cannon on a float backfired. Pieces of it hit Michael and cut his head off. The fraternity believes he haunts their home as he was a pledge at the time of his death. Michael has been seen in the house, especially in the basement. According to records, his last duty had been to clean the basement. People hear running water, cleaning utensils and whistling. Also, items around the fraternity that go missing are blamed on Michael.

Indiana University-Student Building

Bloomington: IU has a great map of its campus on its website.

The Anthropology and Geography departments are haunted by a student who drowned in the pool that used to be in the building. However, according to records, this building never had a pool, so you be the judge.

Indiana University- Union Board Office

Bloomington: IU has a great map of its campus on its website.

Footsteps are frequently heard when no one is around.

Indiana University- Tunnels

Bloomington: Swain Hall, Third Street and the Union Building contain entrances.

The utility tunnels were constructed over 100 years ago and contain steam lines, voice and data communications, as well as chilled water and medium and high voltage. From Third Street to the Union Building to the Old Crescent, one can walk underground without being seen. These tunnels are extremely unsafe. They are hot (many people have suffered steam burns), full of sharp edges and full of cancer-causing asbestos. Not all of the tunnels have lighting and some parts are very small to the point that one has to crawl through them. Homeless people sometimes sleep in the tunnels.

A girl in a yellow nightgown haunts the tunnels. Legend states she was strangled by her boyfriend and dumped in the tunnel. She waits around looking for revenge.

Another legend is that an elephant died while en route through Indiana and animal activists stole it from IU (which was using it for research) and hid it.

Indiana University- Wright Quad

Bloomington: IU has a great map of its campus on its website.

A man broke up with his girlfriend. She was so heartbroken she killed herself. The Lady in Black is seen around the Quad at all hours.

Indiana University- Wells House

Bloomington: IU has a great map of its campus on its website.

In the early days of the university, the legend states a girl had to be kissed at the Wells House to become a coed. Today the legend states if you kiss a girl at the Wells House at midnight, you'll marry her.

Indiana University- Zeta Beta Tau

Bloomington: Corner of East 8th St. and N. Fess. Ave.
(razed)

In 1984 a former student and a fraternity member got into an argument. Zook, the former student, set fire to the Zeta Beta Tau house. Israel Edelman, who had been visiting, died from smoke inhalation. Zook was arrested and the fraternity moved to N. Jordan Ave. A memorial marks the spot of the former house. The smell of smoke and the ghost of a student have been reported on this road. Voices come from the plot of land, now used for gardening.

Kappa Delta Rho Fraternity
Bloomington: 1504 E. Third St.

A girl fell asleep and dreamed Stanley Rice, who had been killed in a car accident, came to her bloodied and disfigured. He came at her with a pick axe in the dream. The girl woke up but instead of being relieved, people heard hear scream, for the pickaxe was in her real life nightmare. When the people in the house came to her room, they saw the axe- which had been missing for six months.

Lake Weimer
Bloomington: Off W. Wapahani Rd.

The apparition of a woman searches for her husband in the lake. At times she walks along the water and other times she floats on the water.

Manann Cemetery
Bloomington: W. of Bowman Rd. on CR 300N

Once part of Miami Nation land, this cemetery has dancing red and green lights near the limestone obelisks. Footsteps are heard and the silencing of wildlife is also experienced.Strange knocks occur on cars and temperature drops are reported.Foul smells and chilling breezes are felt and smelt by investigators. Shadow people dart through the stones and stand at the edge of the cemetery as if keeping watch.Some investigators believe it is the work of Native Americans or even Civil War soldiers.

Matthews Mansion
Ellettsville: S. Edgewood Dr. and Edgewood Dr.

Voices and transparent apparitions of men, women and children are se

Paris Dunning House
Bloomington: 608 W. Third St.

Once part of the Underground Railroad, books fall from shelves, doors open and papers are heard shuffling. Some investigators believe that these noises come from slaves who were killed at the house.

Railroad Tracks
Oakville: Between Trailsend and Bluejay Dr.

The tracks at this location have largely been removed, however, several apparitions are supposed to be seen here. Former slaves who built the railroad track are one set of apparitions. An engineer with a lantern is another. Finally, a girl with a doll is seen running down the tracks. She falls and you hear a scream. She disappears.

Raintree House

Bloomington: 111 and 112 North Bryan Avenue

The Raintree was built in 1882 for the Rogers family. In 1925 Agnes Wells purchased the house and later IU purchased it. Legend claims this was a stop on the Underground Railroad (which can't be true as it was built in 1882). Additionally a woman committed suicide by immersing herself in a vat of lye soap and ingesting it. EVPs here included mention of the basement, and a woman interacting with investigators in response to questions.

Rose Hill Cemetery

Bloomington: Entrance on Elm St. south of W. Kirkwood Ave.
(also part of Dodd's Cemetery)

Once time this cemetery was Bloomington's City Cemetery. Additionally, an old oak tree had the initials "GY" carved in it ("graveyard). Shadow figures, especially around the Evergreen Arbor. surprise and delight people. Hoagy Carmichael and several notable others are buried in this cemetery. Mists and orbs have been captured by investigators. One investigator was pushed onto the ground and couldn't get up. No amount of pulling from his friends could get him off the ground.

Bloomington-Step Cemetery

See Martinsville- Morgan County

MONTGOMERY COUNTY

Ben Hur Nursing Home
Crawfordsville: 1375 S. Grant Ave.

Residents and staff talk about two children who speak to and annoy them. A nurse who used to work there also is seen moving through corridors and checking on patients.

Culver Union Hospital
Crawfordsville: Near 306 Binford St.

(aka St. Claire Medical Center)

Signs of haunting in the morgue area of the hospital.

Davis Bridge
Hibernia: Davis Bridge Rd. near S600W

The land near this home used to host many rodeos. The original house burned down and the ranch home was built in its place. Legend says that people in the area die in threes. Lots of negative energy is felt here.

Lester B. Sommer Elementary
Crawfordsville: 3794 W. US 136

A girl lived on the property before Sommer's School was built. She was tortured and abused by her father and tried to run away. Her father shot her and buried under the house on the property. Today, lights flicker in a restroom and you can see her shoes under the stall door.

Michael Cemetery
Crawfordsville: On W. Offield Rd west of CR S325 W

Investigators capture mists. One investigator walked through a visible mist and felt hands on her face; however, the photographs did not capture the mist.

New Market Trestle
New Market: East of US 231 and south of S 400 W. Trestle is over Offield Creek

A phantom train whistle and the sound of brakes are heard. Several blue figures skirt the water. Some people believe these are the people who died at the trestle. Others believe they are elemental.

Oak Hill Cemetery
Crawfordsville: 392 W Oak Hill Rd

Investigators report orbs throughout the cemetery.

Offield Monument
Balhinch: Offield Monument Rd. Near Spooky Hallow Bridge.

The date on the monument changes on Halloween.

Old Jail
Crawfordsville: 225 N. Washington St.

Doors are heard opening and closing. Conversations with unseen people occur. An "evil" chuckle is heard in the lower level of the building.

Silver Dollar Bar (and Apartments)
Crawfordsville: 127 S Washington St (no buildings in lot now) Corner of Washington and Pike

In May 2007, a devastating fire destroyed the entire 100 block of South Washington Street- including the historic Tommy's Bar (as it was known to Wabash College folks). It was known more recently as the Silver Dollar Bar. Thirteen apartments were destroyed and one person died in the fire. The town was devastated, as the bar was known for its "come as you are" attitude.(Leslie) Eric Largent, a resident of the building, died in the fire trying to save others in the building. The firefighters that battled the blaze had to leave his body in the building as it was too unsafe to retrieve it. They used thermal imaging to detect people and survivors. People in the neighboring businesses have seen him walking through their stores. Additionally, other people have seen him leaning against the neighboring building looking out over the empty lot. When approached, he looks very sadly at the people and disappears.

South West Corner of E. Main and S. Green Streets
Crawfordsville: Building at SW corner of E. Main and S. Green

Originally this building was a bank. A child's ghost haunted this building when it was a restaurant. An electrician would not go in the basement because of the "spooky ghost".

Spooky Hallow Bridge
Balhinch: Offield Monument Rd.
(aka Spooky Hollow)

Several legends exist about this bridge. This bridge is home to the boyfriend who scares his girlfriend by making up a scary story and saying the car died. He gets out of the car and the girl hears a scraping noise. When she leaves the vehicle she sees him hanging from a tree and his hand is scraping the roof of the car. If you go to this location, your car will die.

At one time, this bridge was a covered bridge (a new one was built later). Depending on the story, either a black man or a white woman was hung from it. If you flash your lights three times, you can see the hanging person.

Investigators capture unexplained mists.

Wabash College
Crawfordsville: 301 W Wabash Ave

Investigators have witnessed a young man with an arm that seems to be out of its socket and dangling lower than the other. His clothes are tattered a bit and he seems to acknowledge the investigators but does not talk to them. Obs are also seen.

MORGAN COUNTY

Brick House
Mooresville: 8 E. Washington St.

Visitors have reported hearing footsteps in this old building. Doors slam and windows close on their own.

Draper Cabin
Martinsville: Morgan-Monroe State Forest (6220 Forest Rd.)

Folklore includes a murder that occurred years ago. Another story includes a murderer that has been stalking the cabin for 130 years, waiting for victims. Although these stories have yet to be proven, investigators and visitors have reported seeing transparent wolves around the cabin and a shimmering pink woman walking through the woods at night. The best times to visit this cabin are in early spring and fall when the pink lady makes her most copious appearances.

Gravity Hill
Mooresville: Keller Road off the US70 Monrovia exit

A woman and her son were killed on the road while changing a flat tire. The ghosts of both greet people at the bottom of the hill. People claim if you put your car in neutral at the bottom of the hill, something will pull you to the top. Variations of this include naming the woman as a Native American and her grandson. The child was playing in the road and as the grandmother tried to get to him, they were both killed. People have reported EVPs of a woman screaming, a little boy singing and cries of help.

John Dillinger's old family home
Mooresville: The town of Mooresville has grown around the area and the home has long since been razed.

A ghost group is seen picnicking under a tree. Laughter and shouts of happiness are also heard. On May 22, 1934 John Dillinger visited his family for a picnic before his fateful trip to Chicago which ended his life.

Stepp Cemetery
Martinsville: Morgan-Monroe State Forest (6220 Forest Rd.)

The wife of a local doctor died in a crash on Liberty Loop Rd (aka Mahalasville Rd., aka Cramertown Loop) road in 1936. Her infant died and was buried in Step Cemetery. The woman went insane and spent her time at the cemetery at her infant's grave. Sometimes called the "Black Lady" she is seen shrouded in black, sitting on the stump and rocking her infant. Other times the story is said to be a woman grieving over her husband or daughter. Many people have visited and investigated the cemetery. Some in search of the Black Lady but some in search of Bigfoot. People have reported mists that stall cars and drain electronic batteries. The Black woman is said to chase people, cry and scream. Other versions include a murdered road worker or teenager.

Visitors also experience bad feelings, nausea and vomiting. Temperature changes, strange breezes and a sense of darkness in the sun is also reported. Orbs, apparitions of the woman and streaks of light have been captured on film. EVPs of crying have also been recorded.

NEWTON COUNTY

Body Cemetery
Kentland: 1 mile west of Woodland on E. 1400 North Rd.

(Pronounced BO-dee.) Alfonso's grave glows- it is the only grave you can see as you approach the cemetery. Legend has it that the cemetery was once home to a Native American burial site. It is an interesting cemetery, as it is a sand dune.

Cast Park
Kentland: N. First St. and Old US41

Named for Alvin C. Cast, who was a well respected member of the community, and served as an educator, leader and businessman. The walking paths have been home to shadow figures running between trees. The sound of someone out of breath as if from running is heard and occasionally, a bright green light is seen on the walking paths although no source is ever found.

Kentland Community Center
Kentland: Corner of Fourth and Lincoln Streets

A figure of an old man is seen around the pool. A woman in white walks through the building after dark lighting each room she passes through.

Lantern Lane
Kentland: 1980E and W1200N in Woodland, IL. A mailbox in a cement post marks the lane's location.

A floating lantern greets visitors. Sometimes, it glows a soft white-yellow; other times it is a white hot blue color. One legend centers on a woman who was waiting for her husband to return. When he didn't return after night fall, she went to find him. Neither was heard from again. Some people believe the lantern is held by the woman looking for her husband. When the house they lived in still existed, a visitor decided to take something from the home and it turned hot, burning her hands.

Another legend is that a glut of horse thieves in the area were hung from trees at Lantern Lane and you can see their ghosts on many nights. Some visitors have indicated that when the blue light appears, they can see people hanging from the trees.

Old Gas Station House
Lake Village: Unknown

People hear pounding on the walls throughout the building. Spectral people roam the rooms, emitting bright flashes of light.

NOBLE
COUNTY

Albion Jail Museum

Albion: 215 W. Main St.
(aka Noble County Old Jail Museum)

Visitors have felt hands on shoulders, taps on arms and cold breezes.

East Noble High School

Kendallville: 901 Garden St.

A man is seen in the gymnasium in the bleachers and walking next to people. A girl who died in the science room in the 1980s likes to trick janitors by turning the television on.

Ligonier Public Library

Ligonier: 300 South Main St.

Reports of temperature drops, high EMF readings, and orbs. Staff members have had experiences of the ghost, from sightings to the sounds of footsteps. Books have even flown of the shelves and objects have been moved.

Restoration Lutheran Church

Kendallville: 500 E. Mitchell St.

Unseen footsteps are heard walking up and down stairs. Mirrors show faces from other people and times. Temperature spikes and drops occur. Shadow figures move furniture and sometimes chase you. One person is said to have had scratch marks down her back. The kitchen in the basement has a lot of activity. A dark figure slowly appears and makes you feel very uncomfortable.

Spook Hill

Kendallville: 9663 E 1000 N

A pack-peddler, or traveling peddler who carried his wares in a pack, was murdered by the property owner in the barn over 130 years ago. A mysterious shape could be seen moving from the house to the barn every night after the murder.

Strand Theater

Kendallville: 221 S. Main St.

Built as an opera house in the 1800s, it is now haunted by ghosts of the past. In the balcony and projection areas, a man stands and watches whoever is in the theater. He's been seen for several decades. One owner doesn't believe that the activity is related to ghosts, but could possibly be a source of negative energy.

OHIO COUNTY

Cedar Hedge Cemetery
Ligonier: On First St. off west end of Downy St. (Behind Rising Sun High School)

Spirits follow visitors, and some claim they've blocked their exit out of the cemetery. These spirits have been in the form of full apparitions that have not seemed human, shape and size are too large. The spirits will follow you back to your car.

Empire House
Rising Sun: 114 S. Front St.

Built circa 1816 as a private home by Daniel Brown who operated a general store out of the front of the house. Later, he became a steamboat captain and helped build the fifth floor of the local Masonic Lodge. Various churches also held services in the building. The structure later served as several hotels including the Commodore Perry Inn. In 1885 the home became the Empire House (hotel and restaurant) and has remained so until today.

Several full solid apparitions of men have been seen in the home. One guest retired for the evening and was very surprised to see her door open and a man walk to the front of her room and disappear onto the veranda.

Mulberry Inn and Gardens
Rising Sun: 118 S. Mulberry St.

The Victorian Room has a ghost that likes to play with the plumbing. Several guests report water running in the middle of the night. One guest's shower turned on by itself shortly after she had checked in, brought her bags upstairs, and sat on the bed.

Old National Bank of Rising Sun
Rising Sun: 212 Main Street

Former occupant of upstairs apartment heard noises downstairs at all hours of the day and night. Many times, it sounded as though furniture was moved and scraped across floors. Twice the same occupant heard his name called and someone tapped the floor under his chair. When he spoke to the tenant downstairs, he found no one was supposed to have been in the building the previous day.

Another story is that a man came home and found his wife with another man. He strangled his wife and her lover with chains then disappeared. On the anniversary of the murder, he came back and saw they had been buried together. He was angry and was killed while driving. Some people believe a chain came through the window of his car and killed him. When they buried him, chain links, which signify life and ties to Earth, were included on his stone.

ORANGE
COUNTY

Bond's Chapel (Church/Cemetery)
Paoli: 8625 W. CR810N (West Baden)

A chain on a headstone grows a link each year. The stone was replaced but the chain reappears. The chain represents the love of a man in the Army and woman who waited for him. Their parents kept them from getting married before he shipped out, but his girlfriend waited. He was killed and brought back for burial. The girl didn't go to the funeral but stayed across the street. Today, the chain glows at night. Sometimes you will see a girl in black on other side of cemetery.

A similar story is that an illegal slave owner beat his slaves to death with a chain. One of the slave's wives put a curse on the slave owner. Every year after the slave owner's death a link of a chain is added to his grave, binding him to the graveyard. Legend has it if you touch the chain you will die/go insane/have tragedy in your life within seven years.

French Lick Springs Hotel
French Lick: 8670 W. SR56

This hotel was the place to see and be seen in its heyday. In the 1800s people came for all the sports and other amenities provided by the hotel. But they also came for the healing Pluto water of the springs. In the 1850s, it was a stop on the Underground Railroad. Dr. Bowles, the original owner, died in 1873 and Thomas Taggart bought the hotel. His family operated it well into the 1940s. After WWII, business declined and it was sold and restored by new owners. Most recently, after more years of struggle, it's been restored even further and has been renamed French Lick Spa Resort and Casino.

The hauntings at the location begin with Mr. Taggart. All the elevators are subject to him opening the doors or pressing buttons for people. Sometimes he's heard asking what floor- imagine the surprise of people when they realize he isn't there. The fifth floor, room 521 is host to ghosts who scatter clothing and change on the floor, and turn on the shower when no one is in the room. The sixth floor is host to shadow figures, and unseen presences. Misty figures reflected are in mirrors that make cleaning staff very uneasy. Staff and visitors have been touched, stroked, and one woman was kissed on the neck.

Horse Field
French Lick: Between Ames Chapel Rd. and Cave Quarry Rd. on SR150.
When a severe storm went through a horse field, two black horses and a black colt were killed. If you visit the fields when storms are nearby you are supposed to see the horses under the oak tree where they took shelter.

Mineral Springs Hotel
Paoli: 124 S Court St

This great old hotel has a wonderful buffet including chicken that tastes like it was fried in Crisco, and is served up hot and tasty. Paoli itself is a wonderful place to spend a day. Staff and visitors report hearing noises from the kitchens- pots and pans banging when no one is in the kitchen. A woman in 1910s clothing walks up the stairway. Sometimes she turns and smiles at visitors. Investigators believe she is one of the guests that stayed in the hotel.

West Baden Springs Hotel

West Baden: 8538 W. Baden Ave.

This hotel (now hotel and casino) was host to wild parties, especially in the roaring 1920s. The times were good and the wine, women, and money were in ample supply. When the stock market crashed, at least two men jumped from the building to their deaths, signaling the end of decadence.

For many years, the fate of this hotel was uncertain. However, through investments and donations, this architectural wonder has been restored and is now reopen for business. And so are its host of ghosts.

Rumors of residual hauntings of the 1920 suicide jumps have been reported. Temperature drops occur on the grounds and within the building. Mists and orbs, as well as pale green lights, were reported on the second and third floors. With the renovations, these occurrences are still reported with more vigor. A man in a dark bowler hat in early 1900s clothing is seen walking along the third floor corridor. A woman in an elaborate gown is seen in the Atrium at night. Investigators who have spent several nights in the hotel have also reported EVPs of several people including a man who says "I've lost everything" and a woman crying. When asked why she's crying, the woman says "he's gone, it's gone". A brusque man is heard in the Atrium saying "It's too hot here." Staff members have reported seeing shadow figures and translucent figures in the basement of the building and at night. When the resort has slowed down somewhat, the sound of footsteps can be heard in the halls outside many doors. Guests hear mysterious knocks on their doors; when they open them to see who is there, they find themselves alone. Cold breezes play about the building. Staff and guests have also been pushed and slapped by unseen hands.

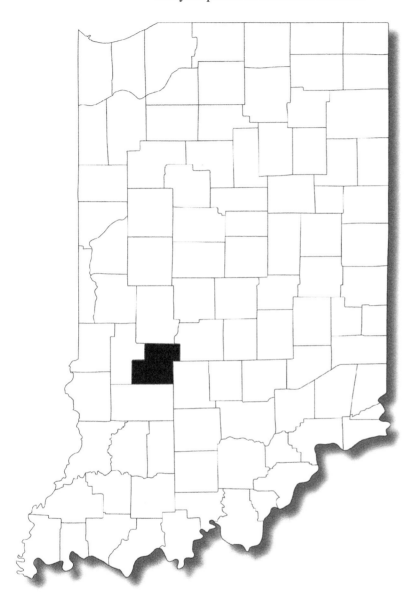

OWEN
COUNTY

Cagles Mill Lake

Cunot: Richard Lieber State Park is right next to it.

(Cagles Mill Lake is bounded on the east by SR243 and on the south and west by SR42.)
(aka Cataract Bridge; aka Cataract Falls Bridge)

Spanning the largest waterfall in Indiana, the upper falls have a sheer drop of 20 feet while the lower falls drop 18 feet. On Halloween 1878, robbers killed a man on his way to Cloverdale. Today, this man is seen on the bridge walking towards his destination. A Civil War soldier was also killed by highwaymen on the bridge. He appears to visitors as a bright light, culminating into a solid or translucent vision.

SR 42 used to run through this manmade lake. A man who lost his fortune in the stock market during the Depression hung himself from the bridge. On dark quiet evenings, walks on the bridge, the rope around his neck. He jumps off the bridge and sometimes he walks alone on the road and watches cars pass by him.

McCormick's Creek State Park Hotel

Spencer: 451 McCormick Creek Park Rd.

Reports claim this building was an insane asylum, which is untrue. From 1888-1914, it was a sanitarium, which treated chronic diseases, including mental health issues. Most times sanitariums were used for people who had the means to pay for the services; otherwise patients would find themselves at home coping with disease or in the case of mental health, in a state hospital. People hear screams, crying and footsteps when no one is around.

PARKE
COUNTY

Beacon Hill Cemetery
Rockville: US 41 and CR 50 W
(aka Crying Baby Cemetery)

Cries of a mother are heard. Sometimes you can hear a baby cry.

Bellmore Schoolhouse ruins
Bellmore: The only thing left of the school is the sidewalks, out houses and a part of the sign that tells the date of the school. There is now a mobile home on the property.

Changes in temperature (from hot to cold) are experienced. Investigators have captured a boys screams. It is believed he was killed in the boiler room. Bricks and dirt fly at visitors.

Billie Creek Village
Rockville: SR36 west to Rockville

This location is a museum and contains several buildings that predating the Civil War all the way up to the early 1900s. The village is full of everything from translucent apparitions seen at night to the odd solid apparitions seen with tour guests. One guest reported staying in the schoolhouse after the other guests left the building. She was looking out one of the windows and saw an apparition of a man behind her. It startled her as she thought she was alone. When she turned, he was gone. The woman turned back to the window to see him behind her again. She heard the man clear his throat, and as she turned to say something to him, she saw quickly him and then his form disappeared.

EVPs of children playing and a woman talking about needing more flowers have been captured by investigators.

Bridgeton Bridge
Bridgeton: Near CR 780 S

This 245 foot red double-spanned bridge witnessed a horse throwing a buggy and its female rider into one of the arches, killing her. Additionally, bootlegger Willie Aikens was hung from the structure. Orbs signifying spirit activity have been captured. EVPs of a moaning man have been heard. The frightened cries of a woman and her spooked horse have also been recorded.

Diamond
(See Brazil, Clay County)

Mansfield (town)
Mansfield: On SR 59 between CR 43 and CR 324

People walk through this town as ghosts from a different time. Wagons and horses are heard. Visitors hear murmurs of conversation. Rocky Fork is known for its green light bridge ghost.

Mecca Tavern/Mecca Bridge
Mecca: 4854 W Wabash St (CR 275 S)

Visitors see and photograph orbs at this site where bootlegger Willie Aikens died (he was hanged from the bridge.)

Missing Death Tracks/ Harrison's Rosedale Tavern
Rosedale tracks: West and Middle Streets. The old tracks have been removed but ran just west of West St. across Middle St.
Tavern : 113 Middle St
(aka Rosedale Tracks)

In the 1960s a woman was hit by a train while walking by the freight tracks. She was found later by her husband. The woman comes back to replay her death, and also frequents the nearby tavern she and her husband owned. Sometimes she talks to drunks and then disappears.

Sim Smith Bridge
Montezuma: On CR 44/ W40 N, south of US36

Built in 1886, this bridge is home to a Native American girl was run down by a horse on the bridge. She appears as a residual haunting replaying her death about halfway through. This bridge, which spans Leatherwood Creek, and was once a main road between Rockville and Motenzuma, also hosts a Native American spirit with a papoose. Reports indicate this ghost will walk with visitors or will disappear as it approaches people. EVPs of horses hoofs, jangling bridles and a man have been caught. Many unexplained photos have been taken.

Turkey Run State Park
Marshall: Turkey Run State Park on Sugar Creek (off SR 47)

Turkey Run is named for the wild turkeys that used to congregate in the canyons (called "runs"). In the early 1900s, Johnny Green, an old Native American, used to go to people's homes and tell tales of old Native American conflicts with the settlers. One day, he went to Goose Rock at the mouth of Turkey Run. Mr. Pruett, a disgruntled husband of a woman he had told stories to, shot him. He fell and was trapped under the rock—his spirit is said to roam the shoreline.

PERRY COUNTY

Fox Ridge Cemetery
Kitterman Corner/Siberia: Off Chaplin Rd, west of SR145 and north of I64

John Davidson was hanged for kidnapping a girl, although he proclaimed his innocence. Two weeks after he was hanged, the girl reappeared-married. The men who hung Davidson were never convicted. The cemetery is home to Davidson's body, with a fieldstone that has a noose on it and the statement "Vengeance is mine, saith the Lord." Investigators at the cemetery have heard an angry voice speaking. Asked if it is Davidson an affirmative answer is given. Asked what can be done to help him the voice states, "Liars".

River Road
Cannelton/Tell City: River Road (CR 334) can be accessed through the Ohio Scenic Byway near Cannelton or via Boundary St. in Tell City.
(aka Brazee's ghost)

A horseman with a whip was seen in 1858 by the Brazee/Schuster wedding party. Thirty-two years later, a boy was riding the same stretch of road and saw a horseman brandishing a riding crop. Today, reports of a phantom horse and rider are still reported, most noticeably by the sound of hooves, the snorts of the horse, and the sound of the whip. The figure has been seen in the moonlight as a pitch black apparition.

Tell City Library
Tell City: 2328 Tell St.

The intercom buzzes when no one is waiting. Books appear out of thin air, and fly from the shelves. Mysterious figures seen throughout the library. Footsteps are heard on second floor.

Virginia Place
Cannelton: 205 Taylor St.

Moving orbs are recorded. The ground floor living room is the most active room. An apparition was caught behind an investigator in photo. Child ghosts playfully move items. Faces of children, men and women have been caught in multiple pictures- children, men and women. It is believed that the ghosts are that of Isabella de la Hunt, her husband, Civil War Officer Thomas de la Hunt, and their children, who lived in the home during the late 1800s until the early 1900s. Reports of square orb sightings have also occurred. Legend has it that Thomas killed the son of a black maid, because either he was the father of the boy, or he was jealous of the man who was. EVPs indicate that Isabella was not abused, but that her husband did commit the deed, have also been recorded. Furniture is sometimes shaken in the home. Other spirits

include a little girl, a little boy, a black dog, a pretty woman and a mean-looking man.

PIKE
COUNTY

Austin Arnold Road

Winslow: Austin Arnold Rd.

An old man destroyed his own property when coal mines contemplated moving out toward his land. Later, he shot his dog and eventually himself. Some versions of the story state the man killed his family as well. One building remains on the property. Cold spots and feelings of unease and heaviness are felt at this location.

Blackfoot Cemetery

Spurgeon: 2.5 miles NW of Spurgeon on CR900S, southeast of Meridian Rd.

The cemetery dates from mid 1800s. Strange lights have appeared- blue, green and red. Much ado centers on a gravestone that is completely separate from the others in the middle of the cemetery (although this could be due to the age of the cemetery). A witch is allegedly buried in the cemetery and local folks believe this is her grave

Gullick House

Petersburg: 9th Street and Main Streets (razed)

The Gullick house was built by a local merchant, Jackson M. Kinman. Richard, the son of Jackson, was killed during the Civil War. His mother wouldn't allow him to be buried and instead put him in the attic. Eventually, she relented and her son was buried. The Case family rented the home from Kinman. The two Case girls, Hattie and Sarah, used the attic as a playroom until they saw Richard's shadowy figure in the corner. He watched but never spoke to them. Eventually, Sarah married and moved out, leaving Hattie and her husband Mr. Gullick in the home. When the house was razed in 1941, Hattie told several people about the ghost and wondered what had become of him.

Some local people believe he is still around. He is seen at various locations on the corner where the house stood, looking sad. Two investigators tried to speak with him when they saw him, but he disappeared immediately. No EVPs or photos have been captured..

PORTER
COUNTY

Bailey Homestead
Chesterton: Mineral Springs Rd. between US 20 and US 12

The house was built by Honore Gratien Joseph Bailly de Messein who helped settle the Calumet region of Indiana. His trading post was known far and wide as a fair place for both white and Native American people. Ghost children play with the children who visit. A young man walks through the property during the day. He wears a white shirt and rough sewn breeches.

Baum Bridge Road Inn
Kouts: 1092 South Baums Bridge Rd.

Once a stop for people traveling through the Kankankee River Valley, this paranormal hotspot includes orb sightings and EVP activity. A man with an aura light around him is seen in the Inn. When you look for him, he will automatically appear in front of you.

Brown Mansion
Chesterton: 700 W. Porter Ave.
(aka Westchester Township History Museum)

In 1885, George Brown built this home for his family. Very prominent in the community, he married Charity Carter in 1855.

A short year after they moved in to the Brown Mansion, George Sr. and George Jr. were very ill. George Sr.'s son James contracted typhoid in 1888. In 1889 his son Charles died at 18 of complications of typhoid fever contracted at age two. Charity had cancer in 1894 and was confined to a wheelchair until her death in 1895. Daughter Anna, who was married in the home, was divorced less than 8 years later. In 1899, George died. A year later the house burned but was salvageable.

The mansion was once turned into apartments, and the ballroom used as storage for the museum. Eventually the house was sold to Dr. Gustafson from Indianapolis who rented it out. In the 1950s, Bill and Jeanne Gland rented the home talking about their ghost "Ebbie".

Camp Lawrence
Valparaiso: 68 E. 700 N.

Legend states that in the 1970s the maintenance director Joseph John O'Connell was killed. Witnesses claim it was a creature such as a yeti. This creature has been seen around the area since.

Campbell Street
Valparaiso: Campbell St.

Annabel went against her parent's wishes They wanted her to be a schoolteacher in the area. She met a man and went courting, and got married. As soon as she had a baby boy, she quit teaching. Her husband drank a lot and money stress didn't help. She escaped with her child, making her way over the fields in the cold night. She died in the snow. Now people see her in the trees next to the road asking for help. Sometimes you can hear her yelling "Help me," and walking as a white figure.

Chellberg Farm
Chesterton: Mineral Springs Rd. between US 20 and US 12

This 1885 homestead is now a museum. It was built by Anders and Johanna Chellberg, who were part of the Swedish community. A ghost woman, who is very particular about the house, tends to tell people to wipe their feet and be tidy while in the house.

Court Restaurant
Valparaiso: 69 Franklin St.

Built in 1885 as an undertaking establishment, it changed to a furniture store, funeral home, a barber shop, an American Legion hall and finally a restaurant. The names have changed over the years, Royallee Retauarant and Lounge, This Side Up, Court Restaurant and 69 East. But the people haven't changed. Cold drafts are felt (especially in the men's restaurant), lights turn on and off as well. Footsteps are heard and orbs have been captured on film. The scent of roses and tobacco are also experienced. A woman named Marsha says hello to visitors.

Crisman School
Portage: 6161 Old Porter Rd.

The school is haunted by several apparitions of teachers who have passed away.

Dewey House
Valparaiso: The Dewey House is no longer standing. It burned to the ground in 2000. Today, what people believe is the Dewey House (at the curve of 650 N and 125 W) is actually a private residence (it's now been razed and there is a newer home in its place). The Dewey location is to the west of this on the north side of 650 N.

(aka Dewey's House; aka Old Man Dewey's House)

One of the most widespread legends in the Valpo area, the story goes that in 1954 Mr. Dewey lost his job because of alcohol. He killed his family and chopped their heads off, staking them on the gate posts near the road. He then hung himself in a grain silo. Today, many people believe you can still see blood on the walls and the hounds of hell guard the gates to the house. Other people report seeing red eyes and orbs in the woods.

Part of the legend occurs after Mr. Dewey died. Someone bought the house and started to remodel. One of the workers fell through the floor and landed on a pitchfork. Although there is no concrete evidence of this story, there was a similar murder in another state in April 1955 in which a Mr. Duncan died in prison before his trial. Mr. Dewey Babcock (his real name), died in 1986 in Whispering Pines Nursing home. His wife died after him.

Diana Of The Dunes
Chesterton/Porter: 1600 N. 25E
(aka Ogden Dunes)

Once uninhabited, what is now the Dunes State Park was open dunes. Fishermen and locals would occasionally see a nude woman on the beach, or swimming in the lake. With comparisons made to the Greek goddess, Diana, her name was born. In reality, the woman's name was Alice Marble Gray, the daughter of a well to do Chicago physician. Legend tells us that she went to the dunes to soothe her broken heart, but in reality, she was going blind. So she moved into a fishing cottage and lived a simple life. In 1920 Alice met Paul Wilson. At best he was a skilled nautical man with a checkered past. They were happy together until a man was found beaten and burned on the beach. Wilson was suspected of the murders. Although the crime wasn't proven, the couple moved to Michigan City. Although Alice had two children with Wilson, he beat her and made her life miserable. After the birth of her second daughter, she either killed herself or died of uremia poisoning. Wilson disappeared but was later found in a California prison, serving time for theft. What became of Alice's daughters is a mystery. To this day, Alice returns to the dunes to ease her soul.

Devil's Bridge
Michigan City: County Line Rd. near LaPorte and Porter County line

The mob buried bodies here in the 1920s. Visitors capture orbs and see a transparent man who disappears.

Gray Goose Inn
Chesterton: 350 Indian Boundary Rd.

A litte redheaded girl appears to guests. She smiles and interacts. One guest said she threw a ball to her, then disappeared. The guest was left with the ball. She put it on the table beside her bed. In the morning, it was gone. Other guests hear a child's laughter.

Hebron High School
Hebron: 307 S. Main St.

On a Halloween night in the 1930s, a girl waited in the gym for her date. He never showed. She got some rope from the janitor's close and hung herself in the bathroom. Today, visitors see her hanging in the bathroom during many times of the year

Hebron Train Depot
Hebron: 127 S. Main St. *(the Depot is right next to the museum)*
(aka Stagecoach Museum/Panhandle Depot)

The majority of Hebron worked at a train station in the 1800s. A hobo haunts the depot. In October 1903, a head on train crash killed a hobo. He was buried in Hebron Cemetery. Later the Depot was known as the Whistle Stop Ice Cream Shop. A young man went to work here one day angry, as he had had an argument with his wife. He was careless and was hit by a train. Today his ghost throws pots and pans around the kitchen and turns off ovens. No business has been able to stay long. The Historical Society moved and converted the building where strange noises and footsteps are experienced.

Historical Society of Porter County Old Jail Museum
Porter: 153 Franklin St.

Visitors see orbs and people have gone missing as if in a time warp. In the rope room an entity is seen and heard. A child haunts the children's room. Downstairs a woman is seen. A helmet that is part of the collection has been known to get hot where a bullet pierced a hole. Voices are heard throughout the house, especially when only one staff member is present or when staff members are separated by floors. The keys to the cell are known to move on their own.

Housing Subdivision
Portage: The area is south of U.S. 20 and west of Swanson Rd.
(Note: The area is now a new housing subdivision.)

On site at the former Nature's Friends Nudist Colony, an excavation team unearthed Mathias Perner's cremated remains in 2005. (He was a machinist who died in 1937 and was reburied in Blake Cemetery.) A second urn was damaged at the time of excavation. The ghosts of two men are seen rising from the area where the urns were found.

Inn at Aberdeen
Valparaiso: 3158 S. SR2

Items such as combs and socks go missing. The specter of a girl suspected of taking them is seen at various times and locations. In Room 305, the fireplace comes on by itself.

Luther Cemetery
Valparaiso: North of US30 on Murvihill Dr.

Orbs have been captured here and voices are heard.

Maplewood Cemetery
Valparaiso: South of US30 on S Sturdy Rd. and Penna Hill Dr.

Orbs have been captured here. A young woman's voice is heard saying "Maud". Orbs have been captured on film. Maud

Dau, the niece of Col. John Wheeler, who died at the Battle of Gettysburg, is buried in the cemetery. She died of TB at 15. Cemetery restorers have heard the voice and had a mischievous spirit touch them in the cemetery. One worker had her apron untied. Another worker had her bucket of ammonia tipped over.

Old Farm House Antiques
Hebron: 409 S. Main St.

A woman says hello to visitors. Curtains have been pulled down.

Old Porter County Home
Valparaiso: South US30 on IN2

Visitors see children playing in the home.

Old Porter Road
Portage: Between Portage and Burns Harbor that line Old Porter Rd.

This area has seen its share of bad happenings. Many deaths and injuries have happened on the road and on the railroad tracks. Shadow figures are seen on the train tracks especially in the winter. Phantom dogs are also seen walking beside the road, just to disappear before your eyes. A devil dog is also spotted with yellow eyes and a semi-human form.

Old Roller Coster Road
Portage: Ransom Rd
(Note: Sycamore Rd in South Bend is also nicknamed Roller Coaster Rd. Many locals have said that Sycamore Rd is the real Old Roller Coaster Rd.)
(aka Ransom Road)

Transparent and solid apparitions of automobiles chase people on this road, then disappear as quickly as they appeared. In 2002 John Blosfield was killed on this road. Some visitors say he is seen walking beside the road.

Old Train Tracks
Hebron: Unknown

The tracks are the site of an alleged train crash. Its victims supposedly haunt the area

Porter County Court House
Valparaiso: 16 Lincolnway

Orbs and feelings of dread are sensed in this building. The elevator moves from floor to floor without any reason. EVPs asking for help, asking if you've seen certain people have been captured.

Porter House
Porter: Waverly Rd.

An old lady looks out of the front room upstairs. She is rumored to hate children. She has touched and dragged several people Shadow figures who like to play tag hasc been reported.

Rasz's Gathering
Portage: 420 E. Commercial Ave.

Cold breezes, whispers and orbs have all been experienced at this local establishment. Televisions and lights turn on by themselves. The bar's ghosts includes the former owner Benny Lynch, who appears after closing time, and other assorted shadow figures.

Spring House Inn
Porter: 303 N. Mineral Spring Rd.

A ghost boy and his mother haunt the inn. They interact with guests by smiling, approaching them, and by waving to them.

Stagecoach Road
Portage: Stagecoach Rd. off US12 near Ogden Dunes

Visitors see apparitions of former residents in the area. One investigator caught a mist on film.

Stereo Bridge
Valparaiso: US130 at railroad tracks south of W370N

Visitors hear the residual crash when two trains collided on the same track. You can hear the whistles blow and hear the crash and screams of agony.

Troll's Bridge
Valparaiso: CR175W, south of 650N

A troll makes an appearance when you stop and talk to it.

Valparaiso City Hall
Valparaiso: 166 Lincoln Way

Investigators report orbs and a feeling of being watched.

Valpo University – Alumni Hall
Valparaiso: 1700 Chapel Dr.

Two children run around the hall at night. Sometimes they interact with people and talk about playing outside or playing tag. Sometimes the elevator moves from floor to floor for no reason.

Wolf Mansion/ McCool Cemetery
Portage: CR700N (7 Mile Rd.) and CR450W (Wolf Rd.)
McCool Cemetery is at Central Ave. and McCool Rd.

Lights have been seen inside the mansion. In one instance a candle was lit and a shadow blew it out. A solid apparition of a man with a gun has also been reported. Visitors have captured orbs and one worker felt breathing on his neck in the basement of the building. People have been followed inside the home. The legend is that Josephus .'s children died of typhoid fever or small pox in the 1800s. Because of this, he hung himself in the cupola and now haunts the house.

(Note: The story would seem to be false. Josephus McCool died of cancer on March 8, 1895 and is buried in McCool Cemetery. His wife Susan died in 1903 and is in the same cemetery. Nonetheless, it is a part of Indiana folklore.)

POSEY
COUNTY

Griffin (town)
Griffin: Griffin off of I64 and SR69

The town was almost destroyed during the Tri-State tornado on March 18, 1925. It killed 58 people and injured 202. In the days after the tornado, you could only reach the town by boat. Only part of the schoolhouse was left. A year later, the school, the church, the grain elevator, and most of the homes were rebuilt.

In town, various people- men, women and children- are seen walking. Sometimes screams and moans are heard. There has been some speculation that Sydney Hyatt is one of the spirits. He was found under piles of bricks between the only restaurant in town and the general store. Other possible ghosts could be that of Clarissa and Vera young, sisters aged 14 and 9 respectively who were killed during the tornado.

New Harmony (town)
New Harmony: On SR66 next to the Illinois/Indiana boarder.

As the home to two historic attempts at communal living, New Harmony has a rich history. From 1814-1825 the Harmonists under Johann George Rapp and from 1825-1928 under John Owen, worked and prayed together in a utopian-like setting.

The town in general is the site of many paranormal events. Groups of shadow figures are seen in the local cemetery. Translucent groups of people walk from the south side of North St to the north side. The Working Men's Institute is home to several odd occurrences, including a man in blue who is seen walking with a book in his hand.

EVPs recorded include chanting and speaking in German. The EVP is believed to have said, "We must pray now" and loud laughter from a male voice. Lights throughout the town mysteriously turn on and off. It is not uncommon to feel cold breezes pass you even when it is very warm outside.

Poseyville Library
Poseyville: 55 S. Cale St.

The first library was established in Poseyville around 1825. The second was part of the town hall in 1901. The third came from a Carnegie endowment in 1905. In 2000 the library was renovated and expanded. As part of that process, the Hansbrough Inn (built ca. 1890) was demolished. The library staff and patrons believe now that they are haunted by the ghosts that moved in from the Inn.

The library owned the old Hansbrough Inn, which closed in 1910. The library had apartments in the building. The basement of the old inn was a dining room for train passengers. Cleaning staff, who normally lock themselves in the building, hear the opening and closing of the main entrance doors, although no one was found in the building. The consensus is that the library's ghost is a female and wants to be a caretaker of the library. The ghost has been seen in the basement of the library as the mist of an older woman from a different time. Other staff members have seen her as a grey mist in the basement, and on the northeastern corner.

One reason for the haunting could be that room was recreated using an historical picture. Computer issues and lighting problems abound. Installed programs uninstall, lights burn out in an unusually short amount of time. Disks go blank and DVDs become unplayable, despite having been played previously. Usually it is the computer room that has lighting issues first, then the Carnegie section, on to the Lamar room and then the hallway.

Robin Hill
Mount Vernon: 917 Mill Street
(aka Popcorn Hill, Ferndale, and Belden Place)

Built in 1837 (or 1838 by some accounts), one legend states the original owner, William Lowery, helped slaves on the Underground Railroad. When his daughter fell in love with and became pregnant by a former slave,, he killed the man and his daughter in her room. The room is supposed to contain blood stains and a residual haunting of this event. Every time people paint over the spots they reappear. Supposedly the daughter collected porcelain dolls and the dolls are still in her room.

Lights passes through the upper window. A baby giggles in the basement and people whisper throughout the house. Toilets flush and general noises are heard at night.

PULASKI
COUNTY

City Park
Winamac: E.Washington St. east of S. Riverside Dr.

Two brothers were in the Civil War. One never returned home and the other lost his mind, walking along roads and creeks looking for his brother.

Investigators have captured mists by the creek. Some people have reported seeing a handsome young man walking along the creek.

Moody Lane/Francesville Lights
Francesville: Division Road to Meridian Road to W150S (E Moody Rd)

The legend goes that two brothers were riding in a buggy. One brother fell out and a wheel cut his head off. The surviving brother never recovered, or gave up the search for, his sibling's head. The orange-red light that is seen is that of the other brother looking for the dead brother's head. Many times the light is seen moving row by row in corn fields.

Drive down the lane and back, and then drive down again, and park. Flash your lights three times and shut them off. The searching light is supposed to cross in front of you.

Many people claim to have experienced the legend. They also get lost without an exit and lost in a nearby cemetery (Smith Cemetery).

(See Smith Cemetery, Francesville, Pulaski Co. and Moody Lane, Rensselaer, Jasper Co.)

Old St. Anne's Cemetery and New St. Anne's Cemetery
Monterey: West of Monterey on E700N north side of road; off of E800S on S600E.

A praying nun with a glowing halo carries a baby in this cemetery. Witnesses have seen her mouth moving as if in prayer (or possibly talking to the baby). Sometimes, visitors have heard the baby crying. Witnesses have seen the nun sitting on the roof of a barn nearby old St. Anne's.

Smith Cemetery
Francesville: Corner of W100S and CR300W. Technically, this is in Jasper County

The graveyard is near Moody Lane, where a man and a woman were killed on opposite sides of the road. At midnight they cross the road to see each other. People have experienced seeing a woman dressed in tattered clothes cross the street with her arms outstretched.

PUTNAM
COUNTY

Boone-Hutcheson Cemetery

Greencastle: North of CR600S east of S CR375W

(aka Boone Hutch Cemetery)

A police officer from the 1950s carries a blue light through the graveyard. A nearby cave that runs under the cemetery has a ghostly figure protecting it.

Known to locals as Sellers Cave and University Cave, legend has it that the cave at the cemetery runs to DePaw University. A house on campus allegedly has a sealed up tunnel to the cave. Some people believe this legend is confused with the University's involvement in the Underground Railroad. Still, some people believe that John Dillinger used the cave as an escape route and hiding place.

Brick Chapel

Greencastle: 5 miles north of Greencastle on US231

One of the best-kept ghostly secrets is a piece of property behind Brick Chapel north of Greencastle. An old brick house stood there until recently. This site received national attention in 2000 on an ABC special, "World's Scariest Ghosts."

Two well-known paranormal investigators named Guy Winters and Terry Lambert worked for ABC Television. They shot still photographs and videotaped footage of the old brick home. Several photos showed a woman in pink glowing in an upstairs window of an empty room.

However, there are some who claim to have parked along the side of the field and seen pink balls of light dance across the field. The driveway is currently gated and locked. No Trespassing signs are posted.

Cloverdale Cemetery

Cloverdale: South side of SR42 at CR175E

A couple of women were driving at midnight through the cemetery and saw a man bent over a casket under a tarp. He turned to look at them and they got scared. When went back for a second look, the man had disappeared.

Seven sisters are buried here. If you go around their graves seven times your wish will be granted. Several people have broken pieces of the headstones; when they try to put them close to the bigger stone, it is like a magnetic opposite polar effect is occurring. Temperature changes and strange cold spots are also reported. A hooded black figure appears out of nowhere.

Some investigators have reported taking "something" back with them. The begin having issues at their own homes, including seeing shadow figures and smelling rotting flesh.

DePauw University
Greencastle: DePauw University has a great map of its campus on the university website.

This university was founded in 1837. At least three janitors from different decades have quit because of the hauntings.

In the library, Governor Whitcomb watched over his rare book collection until it was placed in a restricted area.

The library is haunted by a very possessive spirit. In the early 1900s, a student at the old library took a book called The Poems of Olson. A ghost appeared to the student demanding its return. And so it was. This has been reported by many students over the years.

Dick Huffman Bridge
Reelsville: West of US231 on US40, turn south on CR450W. The bridge is east of 600W
(aka Wetky Bridge)

This bridge was built in 1880 and is 265 feet long. Originally it was known as the Wetky Bridge because a mill of the same name was nearby. An old man haunts the bridge. He got drunk one night and fell off the bridge thinking he could fly or walk on water.

Edna Collings
Clinton Falls: Outside Clinton Falls
(aka Edna Collins Bridge)

This 80 ft. bridge was built in 1922 by Charles Collings after the original concrete bridge washed away. Edna Collings liked to swim in the water and jump off the old bridge. Her parents would pick her up when it was time for her to leave. One day the girl drowned. When her parents came to pick her up, they were devastated. Another version of the story says she was raped and killed. If you honk your car horn three times, she will get in the car with you. She is also heard splashing and laughing. Cars have been pushed and door locks flip up and down uncontrolled. The girl has also been seen looking at you from outside the car.

Fern Cliff Nature Preserve
Reelsville: Unknown
(aka Reners Quarry)

An explosion the mine killed over 40 people. The sounds of the explosion and dying men are still heard. This area is near the cliffs in the nature preserve.

Forest Hill Cemetery
Greencastle: Cemetery Rd. to Forrest Hill Cemetery

Pearl Bryan haunts the cemetery. She was killed in 1896 by Scott Jackson and Alonzo Walling after a failed abortion attempt. Pearl told her friend William Woods that she was pregnant by a mutual friend, Scott Jackson. When Jackson found out, Pearl was subjected to a chemical abortion (substance unknown) and an abortion by dental tools. When it was clear she was going to die, Jackson and Walling killed her, then dumped her body in Fort Thomas Kentucky. Her head was never found. She is buried in Forest Hill Cemetery. It is said she walks around the cemetery trying to find her head.

Four Arches
Greencastle: Located west of Greencastle not far from Fern Cliff

The body of a murdered woman buried in the cement when it was built of the train trestle/tunnel. Her figure is seen walking through the tunnel. At other times a phantom train runs through the tunnel. Reports have been made of hearing the whistle echo and feeling the wind blow through the tunnel, although sometimes it is not seen.

Locust Hill
Greencastle: Six miles north of Greencastle on US231
(Note: This building is a private home.)

James O'Hair (O'Hara) built the home and it was in his family for 153 years. Notable guests include William H. Harrison, Miami Chief Cornstalk, and Squire Boone (Daniel's brother). Today it is an antique shop. The ghost of the man an O'Hair daughter fell in love with inhabits the house, along with other spirits. Rocking chairs and candles have levitated and been thrown by unseen hands. A Confederate soldier is often seen as have two women in long white dresses.

RANDOLPH COUNTY

Greenville Pike

Bartonia: On Greenville Pike: At the stop sign turn right at the first gravel road turn left

A headless horseman rides over the bridge. He is said to carry his head in his hand. As he passes by, he laughs maniacally. He's also reported as very good looking. Before his appearance, several women report feeling someone kiss their hands. He also chases you over the bridge and disappears.

Mobile Home

Randolph County: 1475 S. Randolph County Road 750W

A woman named Angela was either murdered or shot herself in the head inside her mobile home. Her ghost is said to roam the area. An EVP was heard asking where Veronica was. (This is one of Angela's daughters.)

Ridgeville Road

Ridgeville: Ridgeville Rd.

A house in the woods is rumored to have blood on the walls. Legend states that several murders happened in the house. The nearby cemetery has a bridge and a creek that runs through it. The man who murdered his family drowned them in the creek. The woman is supposed to appear as an apparition or her wedding ring falls onto the bridge.

Sleepy Hollow Road

Ridgeville: This location is tucked away in between fields. Between W800N and W700N (the north and south boundaries) and N400 W and N300W (the east and west boundaries). There is a small lane on the W700N side that takes you back to a grove of trees, on the NW side of those trees is another path that takes you to a larger grove of trees. Both areas are considered Sleepy Hollow.

People have reported being chased by zombie-like creatures, suspected to have been a part of a non-descript accident in the early 1970s.

RIPLEY
COUNTY

Bonaparte's Retreat
Napoleon: 8961 N US 421

This building has been a variety of businesses, including a tavern and inn and was once a stop on the Underground Railroad. A female apparition appears to guests in the eatery and on the stairway. Her perfume can be smelled in the basement where fugitives were hidden during the Underground Railroad years.

Devil's Elbow
Osgood: N. Delaware Rd. and N. Milan Versailles Rd. SW of SR129

This local road is inhabited by evil spirits. A man was killed many years ago on the road, but the hauntings have predated his murder. Some people believe it is the evil spirits that provoked the murder.

Glowing red eyes, a milk-white figure of a woman, and a baby crying have been reported. This area affects your car; it will either stop working, or the headlights will dim without assistance.

Central House
Napoleon: On the square (Main Street)
(aka Newman House; aka Hicks House)

Built in 1838, this historic building has been used as an inn, a doctors office, several saloons, apartments, restaurants, and a stage coach stop. Several paranormal events occur which are tied to a girl named Jessica, who died from chicken pox, in 1865 at the age of 13.

She plays in the child's room and laughs. During tours, the rocking chair rocks, books move from shelves, and cold breezes whirl around the stairs. The clock in the house also has a habit of striking outside of normal times in abnormal ways.

Jessica also likes it when people play music in the house, especially the organ. She hums and sings to the music. The organ also plays when no one is using it. The lights in the house move and sway for no reason. Investigators report seeing orbs, doors closing and doll heads moving.

St. Louis Cemetery
Batesville: East of S. Mulberry St. at the end of Schultz St.
(Note: Batesville is in Franklin and Ripley Counties)

The cemetery is part of St. Louis Catholic Church. Burials began about 1869 in the cemetery. An Indian woman is said to haunt the cemetery. She was chased by the townspeople and buried alive. Her tomb is supposed to have a stone door as a top marker with a fence of iron bars around it.

Silver Bell Nursing Home
Versailles: 6996 S. US421

This 29 bed patient facility was a hotel before it was a nursing home. Lights go off and on in empty rooms; the staff hear children playing and people whistling when residents are asleep. The presence of invisible people is felt throughout the building. A nurse's aide was locked in a laundry room by an unseen presence and had to climb out a window.

Sunman- Guildford Park Bridge
See Dearborn Co.

Versailles State Park
Versailles: Off of US50 near Versailles

A soldier named Silas Shimmerhorn deserted the Confederate army and became one with the wolves around Versailles. He feasted on farm animals and shared his lot with the wolf pack. Eventually, the farmers got wise and found his hideout in the Bat Cave (now in Versailles State Park). Silas and the wolves were not there. Now people report seeing the pack of wolves at night, sometimes accompanied by a man. They hear the yelps of the pack as they approach.

RUSH
COUNTY

State Road 44 Slaughter
Rushville: SR 44 three miles east of Rushville

On November 15, 1941, a Greyhound bus crashed head-on with an automobile. Nine people were killed in the fiery crash. Investigators have recorded orbs and orange mists in the areas, especially around the anniversary of the crash.

Three Mile and Carthage Roads
Carthage: Three Mile and Carthage Roads

A farm hand for the Stevens family who owned the land was robbed of his weekly wages and killed at the intersection of Three Mile Road. Locals began to see his ghost at the intersection counting his money.

Some believe this is not the true story, but rather a rug salesman, Sam Abood, was robbed for $700 (but not killed) at the same location.

People who have investigated the location have reported a mist and have captured orbs on film. No one has spoken to the farm hand or the salesmen…yet.

ST. JOSEPH
COUNTY

Adams Road Cemetery
South Bend: On Adams Rd. west of Orange Rd. just past the lake.
(aka Adams St. Cemetery)
(Note: Some investigators have confused Porter Prairie Cemetery on Adams St. in Niles, MI (a short drive from South Bend, IN) for the Adams Rd. Cemetery)

This old cemetery is said to contain unexplained mists that seem to hang over tombstones.

Children's Campus- Indiana North Hall
Mishawaka: 1411 Lincoln Hwy. W.
(aka Famly Child Center)

In 1992 North Hall was used for helping teenage girls. One nurse saw a green helium balloon near the ceiling. This type of item was forbidden, and as she was on night shift, she couldn't leave to remove it. The other staff members said to just leave it for the day shift to dispose of. The two nurses on staff did their bed checks as necessary and went about their other tasks. The balloon remained in the room with them. At 2 am, the balloon seemed to be deflating. One nurse thought that she'd dispose of it once it was finished deflating. When she looked up again, the balloon had shifted in the hallway, going through a doorway and again, popping up to the ceiling. It continued on this way until it moved back toward the nurse's station. As the nurses watched it reenter their area, it sped up and dove towards them. After it had sufficiently scared them away from the area, they watched as it went back out the way it came-under a desk, scooting along the wall of a kitchenette, and making a 90 degree turn, and then going around the room to the back of the kitchen, and droppping to the floor behind the trashcan.

One of the rooms it had stopped at was number 6, which is believed to be the room in which that a 15 year old resident died in from improper restraints in the 1980s. Odd feelings have been felt for years in this location and in the basement laundry room. In the parking lot, the staff has been bothered by knocking on cars, yet no one is around.

Copshaholm
South Bend: 808 W. Washington Ave.
(aka Oliver Mansion; aka Northern Indiana Center for History)

Katherine Oliver haunts the Oliver Mansion. She moves items throughout the house. If you listen closely enough, you can hear her whisper to you. Also, Mrs. Standfield who was an early curator, is said to haunt the museum.

Dreamworld
South Bend: N. Michigan St.

A woman with a dog walks the railroad tracks. Legend has it she was hit by a train and killed. EVPs of her calling for her dog have been captured.

Hacienda Mexican Restaurant
Mishawaka: 706 Lincoln Way West (100 Center)

At one time, the location used to be a mansion. The owner had an affair with a maid. She confessed to the owner's wife and who wanted nothing to do with her. The maid was sent packing. She hung herself in the attic. Now she's seen throughout the restaurant. The owner is said to have shot himself in the basement. One manager of the restaurant turned off the lights and alarm and when she would looked back, the lights would be on. She decided to take the light bulbs out of the lights. The lights still came back on; the bathroom lights would do the same thing. The water turns on as well.

Harrison Street tracks
Walkerton: Harrison St.

A railroad worker was hit by a train. Today he's seen as a blood-splattered apparition. The ghost of a girl who killed herself on the track is also seen.

Haunted House
Lakeville: Off U31 on 6C Road, around a curve on the left side.
(Note: Home has been razed.)

A lonely woman hung herself from a dining room chandelier. The house has been torn down, but a barn still remains. When the house still existed, people reported footsteps and moans. Also, there were reports of seeing a pair of bodiless feet, and sounds of the back door slamming.

Highland Cemetery
South Bend: Portage Ave. and Lathrop St.
(aka Council Oak Cemetery)

A mysterious spectral horse is seen running through the cemetery at night. His eyes are as blue hot as a fire. He is said to have a fog precede his arrival.

Holiday Inn City Center
South Bend: 213 W. Washington St.

A ghostly flight attendant visits guests in their room. The same person is seen in mirrors throughout the hotel. Legend has it that a pilot killed the flight attendant.

Hotel
Mishawaka: US 933 (Lincoln Way)

This abandoned hotel is supposed to be a place to make things disappear before your eyes. Sometimes the hotel itself is said to disappear in a time warp.

Juday Creek (Railroad) Bridge
South Bend: East of SR933 N and north of W. Cleveland Rd.

A train engineer who was being replaced by someone younger killed himself on the bridge. Today you can see him standing there, holding a lantern.

Lincoln Elementary School
South Bend: 1425 E Calvert St

Legend has it that this was once a children's hospital. In the restrooms the faucets turn on and off randomly and the lights flicker. This seems unlikely as the school is very new.

Mishawaka City Cemetery
Mishawaka: West of Main St.; South of W. Jefferson Blvd.

William Aldrich (lived at Main and Lawrence Streets), who died of TB, was buried sitting up in this cemetery. After much fanfare, and a stint on "Ripley's Believe it or Not," the casket and all of Aldrichs' possessions have disappeared. He is said to walk the cemetery and the area around his old house in search of these belongings.

North Michigan Avenue
South Bend: North Michigan Ave. and Douglas Street.

A phantom, driverless car is seen speeding down the avenue, only to disappear as quickly as it was seen.

Old Central High School
South Bend: 330 W. Colfax Ave.
(aka Central High Apartments)

The ghost of a woman and her dog haunt this area. She was run over by a train while walking the dog. At different times of the day, you can see her cross the intersection. The old school auditorium, now used as apartments, is rumored to be haunted by students.

Old Roller Coster Road
South Bend: Sycamore Rd.
(aka Sycamore Road)

(Note: Ransom Rd in Portage is also nicknamed Roller Coaster Rd. Many locals have said that Ransom Rd is the real Old Roller Coaster Rd)

Transparent and solid apparitions of automobiles chase people on this road. They disappear as quickly as they appeared.

Old St. Joseph Hospital
Mishawaka: 215 W. 4th St.

The Sisters of the Order of the Handmaids of Jesus Christ cared for the sick in the early days of the history of St. Joseph Community Hospital in Mishawaka. They treated the poor in economically underdeveloped areas. In the hospital as we know it today was born. It opened with 40 beds and 5 nuns as nurses. The facility was renovated in 1993 Many patients report being made comfortable or waited on by nuns in old fashioned habits. The fifth floor surgical wing is particularly active. A phantom shadow of a man is also seen. Patients report a nurse visiting them and feeling much better afterwards, only to find later no living nurse had been to see them.

Park View Tavern
South Bend: 515 E Jefferson St.

Built in 1862 this structure has long been a tavern, and is reputed to have had gangland ties. The spirits are numerous in this building, including Marly, a liquor delivery driver (who later killed himself), a boy who died in the basement and several ghosts that move as shadows from room to room. Ashtrays and other items have flown off tables and crashed into walls. A n apparition of a man floated above the loading dock. A male ghost was seen near the manager's office and voices have been heard in various locations. Mists and orbs have been photographed and seen and hisses have been heard on EVP recordings.

The State Theatre lounge was bought by Ken Allen. It is haunted by a 1920-ish beautiful woman with brunette hair who is clad in lavender and white. She is mostly seen in the projector room.

Potato Creek State Park /Porter (Rea Cemetery)
South Bend: 25601 SR 4

Drowned children haunt the park with their cries and calls for help and for their mothers.

Primrose Road
New Carlisle: Primrose Rd. off of old Cleveland Rd.

Visitors have reported an odd amount of tire damage and other car troubles on this road. No one seems to get cell phone signals on this road either. Ghosts of long gone people tell you to leave the road and not to come back. A farmhouse is said to appear from nowhere, and a woman in white will answer the door. A pond nearby has a rock in the middle nicknamed Blood Rock. It's said to move to different locations in the pond. Horses are heard running intently on the road and in the woods. A woman is said to have been killed and thrown in the pond. She's seen walking out of the pond on foggy nights.

St. Mary's College
South Bend: SR933

A girl who hung herself in Le Mans Hall haunts the building. Blood spots from another girl who died appear.

State Theater
South Bend: 214 S. Michigan St.

A woman haunts this location. She is described alternately as a vaudeville actress, a flapper, and a chorus girl. She appears to enjoy a change of clothing. The woman wears a white, blue, or lavender dress. She appears often when blues music is played. The theater is currently closed.

Tippecanoe Place
South Bend: 620 W. Washington St.
(aka Studebaker Mansion)

This restaurant used to be a stately home to the Clement Studebaker family, famous for building wagons and cars. It has entertained some of the finest families including President Benjamin Harrison. It has been used as a home for deaf children and as a Red Cross Hospital. It's believed Clement Studebaker killed himself in the home. Today, the home doesn't seem to like disbelievers of the paranormal. When a waiter was asked about the ghost, he said he'd never had an experience, which caused glasses to fly off shelves.

Pictures move on the wall as if moved by unfelt wind. In one of the old nursery rooms, (now a bar on the second floor) a bottle of liquor flew off the shelf and fell to the floor at the feet of a very surprised bartender who had just declared he didn't believe in the paranormal. The security alarm consistently goes off; when the police are called, they find nothing missing, but see and hear dishes being thrown around in the basement of the building.

Other paranormal events include cold breezes, and shadow figures. Phantom restroom goers use the facilities at will.

The University of Notre Dame
Notre Dame: Notre Dame has a great map on its website.

- The Potawatami lived on the original university grounds. Washington Hall on the campus is haunted by Native Americans as well as George Gipp, a former football player, who died of pneumonia after staying out past curfew and getting locked out. He has been seen in all areas but mostly resides on the stage and greenrooms. He has also pushed students, and played music. Gipp's footsteps are heard all over the building. Additionally, Washington Hall is home to a steeplejack who died during installation of lights.
- Columbus Hall is also haunted by Native Americans. Horses have been seen on the grounds outside the building and riding down the front steps.
- The Administration building is home to Father Sorin, the founder of the university. He is seen as a residual haunting.

Uniroyal Plastics
South Bend: N. Hill St. was the site location.

Now razed, this company was founded in 1922 as United States Rubber Company. Building 3 was very haunted. On the fourth floor one security guard was startled by a very ordinary looking man wearing pinstriped overalls, and carrying a tool belt slung on his shoulder. The man smiled at the guard and walked out of sight into the next room. When the guard followed, he found himself alone. Despite a search, the man in overalls was not found. That same night the guard's flashlight stopped working. All security lights went out on the floors he visited, but the elevator was waiting for him. When he returned to his post and told his story, his flashlight worked again and the security lights were back on in the building.

SCOTT
COUNTY

Austin High School
Austin: 401 S. US31

A Spanish teacher who died in a car accident roams the school. Teachers, staff and students have seen her walking the halls, mostly at night. She was supposedly very fond of the Beatles and as the story goes, if you play their music, she will come. Custodial staff have quit after door handles to rooms they clean start rattling, and the area turns freezing cold.

Old Railroad
Blocher: Between N. Blocher Railroad and N. Blocker Main Sts.

A woman was killed on the track and a ghost train replays her death. As you watch, you'll see the woman appear. Her foot seems to lodge in the track. As she tries to free it, the train runs through her and you hear her scream.

Bridge Water Cemetery
Scottsburg: East end of E. Bridgewater Rd. near Kinderhook Lake

Legend states that Civil War soldiers were buried in the cemetery. African-Americans were not allowed to be buried there. Some African-Americans were hung in the cemetery. At night, handprints appear on your car and shadow figures move mysteriously through the tombstones. Temperature fluctuations are felt and several people report having been followed by a transparent white horse.

Investigators and visitors experience temperature drops and see glowing eyes in the trees. EVPs of spirits telling people to leave are frequently recorded. Other visitors speak of a demonic presence with glowing red or yellow eyes. Many investigators have had their electrical equipment and cars die without warning. Others have seen a night watchman in the cemetery. The transparent man is supposedly buried in the cemetery and his headstone glows as people enter the cemetery.

Haunted Slave House
Scottsburg: Liberty Knob Rd. (CR500S)

An old house rumored to have housed slaves sits back in the woods. Visitors have reported feeling sick and feeling malevolent feelings in the house. Some visitors claim to have been scratched and poked hard enough to leave marks. At least three people claim to have gone through a time warp in which they have seen African-Americans chained and lined up in the house "like cattle".

Liberty Knob Rd. and Bloomington Trail
Scottsburg: CR500S and S. Bloomington Trail. Taylor Rd. Between Liberty Knob Rd. (CR500S) and S. Bloomington Trail.

A misty fog appears bringing with it Confederate Civil War soldiers. The sound of metal on metal and the scent of gunpowder, leather, and sweat are also sensed. Some visitors hear fighting with the sounds of guns firing, swords clanging and the sounds of men screaming in agony.

Not everything is war-related. One man who lived nearby was in his barn working and felt he was being watched. Looking up, he saw a soldier, who has since reappeared many times. Once, while riding late at night, the same soldier guided the man back to his home, telling him to be careful, as he was about to hit a tree branch.

One person reports having her car stall on that stretch of road. She was aware of the legend and as she was walking back to town, she felt very uneasy when she heard a horse behind her. Turning, she saw a transparent Civil War soldier on horseback. He asked her if she needed help. Stunned, the woman stuttered, "Yes" and she was instantly lifted onto the horse. As the horse trotted off, she reports, "I don't remember the trip back to town. All I remember is being dropped off at the outskirts of town." She was able to stop at a friend's home and solve her car issues, but it will be something she never forgets.

Scott County Home

Scottsburg: 1050 S. Main St.
(aka Scott County Heritage Center and Museum)

This former county poor farm was originally built in 1879. In 1892 this building was replaced by the brick one that exists today. Many a family who had lost all money and hope moved into the farm. To stay on the farm, they were expected to work. Today, the building is the Scott County Heritage Center and Museum. Many of the people from the original farm are still seen walking around the property

Babies cry, lights turn on and off, and strange smells permeate the area. Footsteps sound on the upper floor when no one is in the area. Bells ring without anyone pressing them and no one is there. The front door opens and footsteps entering are heard. Employees hear their names called and feel a woman's presence. A mental patient named Mary lived there her whole life so they named the ghost after her.

SHELBY
COUNTY

Boggstown Cabaret
Boggstown: 6895 W Boggstown Rd.

This cabaret is full of family entertainment. The building itself is from 1873 and a Red Man's Lodge. Next door was the Seventh Day Adventist Home for Unwed Mothers. It was also a general store and barber shop.

Investigators have captured orbs, and video of shifting shadows. One family who took pictures at the cabaret found a strange mist in a photo. It appeared in a shape of a short person standing next to their daughter.

E River Rd.
Waldron: E. River Rd., SW of Waldron

A transparent male apparition walks along the road asking for help.

Electric Bridge
Rays Crossing: Off of E. Union Rd. on E. Short Blue Rd.

People report seeing a man on the bridge. He disappears when approached.

Kopper Kettle Inn
Morristown: 135 E. Main St.

Known for chicken dinners, this former tavern and hotel was once a stop on the Underground Railroad (the tunnel leads to the house next door). The building was originally the Old Davis Tavern, then the Valley House, and in 1923 given its current name. The Big Brother, Yellow New, and Music Rooms have reported paranormal activity. Women in Victorian and prairie style clothing have been seen. In the Big Brother room voices as if from a party have been heard, and in the Yellow New room, an indelicate burp was recorded.

Lady Victoria Hamilton House
Shelbyville: 132 W. Washington St.

 A little girl haunts the entire building, which used to be Italians Gardens. She was in a black dress and liked to knock pots and pans off tables and open drawers, throwing utensils around. Now and then she likes to scare you by screaming as if she's throwing a temper tantrum. For a time, the third floor was a living area with an old rocking horse that would move on its own.

Private home
Waldron: Unknown location

The home was built in the 1920s. Mysterious figures are seen darting around the home. Children are found playing in dining room. Three people from original family died and had funerals in the home. Two children who lived in the home had nightmares in which one of the apparitions that had been seen by his parents entered his dream. Footsteps are heard upstairs when no one is there. Feelings of dread precipitate the paranormal events.

Tanglewood
Shelbyville: Unknown location

Paul Tindall used to play an organ in his home. After his death, people swore he was still at home playing the organ and the lights in the home would come on at odd times.

Twins House
Shelbyville: Unknown

The location of this house is unknown. Some people believe it is the Federal style house on Polk across from the courthouse. Other people believe it is the house on the north east corner of Franklin and Miller Streets.

Many theories A father killed his wife. Twin boys killed their dad. On July 4, 1940 the boys stabbed each other. Supposedly on July 4 you can see the reinactment of this. Throughout the year the boys are seen at the windows of the house.

Union Road (Haunted House)
Shelbyville: IN44 NE to Rays Crossing. Turn left at N 600E to CR250N and turn left. Follow road around curve (Now N 575 E) to E. Union Rd. Turn right. You'll go over 2 bridges. About 5 miles down E Union Rd, a boarded up white house with barbed wire stands.
(aka the KKK House)

Several legends are associated with this house. One story is that a little girl was accidently shot in the house. The second story centers around two teenage boys that went insane after their father killed their mother. On July 4, 1940 the boys who stabbed each other to death. Other history about this home centers on KKK activity. A Klansman lived in the house with his daughter. She was dating an African-American. The father caught them and he killed both of them. Still another story says the girl killed herself after her father killed her boyfriend. The bloodstains are supposed to be in the upstairs bedroom. Other legends include KKK members killing people in the house and in the basement. The basement is supposed to have nooses in it.

If you stand next to the house, you can hear scratching from inside as if something was digging its way out. Murmurs are also heard inside the house. You can also hear two young men screaming in pain. Mists are seen in the house, and gunshots are heard.

Waldron Junior-Senior High School
Waldron: 102 N East St.
(aka Waldron Middle School)

Three boys were playing in the school and they locked one inside a closet with chemicals. The boy drank the chemicals, thinking they were water. By the time the boys remembered to get him out, he was dead. Now he walks around the gym. Sometimes he is seen in the closet.

Werewolf Hollow
Rays Crossing: IN44 NE to Rays Crossing. Turn left at N 600E to CR250N and turn left. Follow road around curve (Now N 575 E) to E. Union Rd. Turn right. Turn left on N575 E again. At 400 N turn right (turns into Short Blue Rd. Drive to bridge.

Growls are heard from 7-10 foot tall beasts with grey, white or black hair. A ghost of a man will scratch your car if you get too close to him as you pass by. He will sometimes warn you not to go back down the lane. Orbs are present. Orange and yellow mists occur. Another story says a boy went to the mailbox near the hollow and he was hit by a semi while crossing the street. Today he still crosses the road looking for the mail. Finally, a couple pulled off the road near the creek. They heard scratching on the car door. The man got out to see what was going on. Suddenly the woman heard screaming. She drove away and her boyfriend was never found.

White House
Shelbyville: Off 250 North on Union Rd.

A girl killed herself in the house. A permanent blood stain seeped into the floor. People hear scratching, footsteps and eerie laughing.

SPENCER COUNTY

Eureka Road

Rockport: Eureka Rd. (later W. CR50S) is off of S. 9th St. in Rockport. Note: No train tracks currently exist on this road, which runs to the IN-KY border.

Reports of different residents hearing men having a conversation and a spectral train when there is none on the tracks. They have also heard a man calling their name and the televisions turn themselves on and off. Children have also complained about toys moving across the floor, and of seeing horses running through the upstairs.

Mathias Sharp House

Rockport: 319 S. 2nd St.

House is a home for Katherine Sharp who went from farmer's daughter to well off matron. Both husbands, Mathias Sharp and Mr. Batchelor, (whom she married after Sharp) became ill from supposed food poisoning and died. Although she was acquitted of both deaths, the Sharp children continued to believe she killed her husbands.

The documented haunting go back to at least 1916 when it was documented that on wedding nights, breaking glass was heard by the occupants. Some people have witnessed the event. Additionally, Katherine's black clad figure is seen walking around the house inside and out muttering about how she was "robbed" of her home.

Rockport Inn

Rockport: 130 S 3rd St.

This bed and breakfast is over 100 years old. One owner's wife died there. She can now be seen in the rooms, and heard walking and humming.

Sunset Hill Cemetery

Rockport: SW of old SR 45, bordered by S CR25 W and WCR100 S

Visitors see a demonic presence wearing a dark cloak.

STARKE
COUNTY

Bass Lake (Cemetery)

Bass Lake: The Bass Lake Cemetery Association is at 6726 E. Kitty Ln. The cemetery is across the street.

According to legend, grass turns blood red, visitors hear evil laughter, and a werewolf roams the grounds in the evening, but there is no Bass Lake Cemetery in Starke Co. However, several spirits are seen around the lake. A man fitting the description of a pilot and a woman fitting the description of his passenger are seen at the lake (Stephanie Nottke and Bruce Groen). The smell of smoke and fuel are often sensed by investigators. The apparitions shimmer on the water and walk toward the shore.

Craven's Factory

North Judson: End of Sheridan Ave. close to 502 Sheridan Ave.

James Messer killed himself in this factory. Around 1:30am, people have reported being pushed to the ground and spit on.

Dog Face Bridge

North Judson: Take IN421 south to 500S turn right. Take the second dirt road on the right. There will be a sign that says bridge out and one that says road closed. Go to the bridge turn your car around facing out and get out of you car with your keys. Take US421 to 500S and turn West on 500S. Go a little ways and you will come to a stop sign. That road is 1100W. Turn North on 1100W and follow it about 1/2 mile. You will come to the bridge and a dead end.

A dog ran in front of a car carrying a couple honeymooning. The couple drove off the bridge and killed the dog in the process. The woman and dog lost their heads in the accident. The body of the woman and the head of the dog were never found.

The bridge is no longer there, but a few decaying supports mark the spot where it was. When you approach the bridge, the woman appears wearing the dog's bloody beaten head. If you don't make it back down the path to the road and past the first bridge (see directions) she will kill you.

Investigators have seen mysterious cars while investigating yet when they've listened to their evidence the sounds of the cars were not heard. Oranges and lemon verbena are smelled. Temperatures drop quickly. Electronics have lost all power, although fresh batteries and charges were verified before the investigation.

Highland Cemetery

North Judson: Located on CR10 at S300W

People have reported being grabbed on the leg, and neck.

Old Haunted Hospital
Knox: 102 E. Culver Rd.

This is the site of an old hotel. In the basement of the hospital, crying and screams are heard. Footsteps echo in the silent night. A janitor is still seen in the basement, mopping the floor. Patients who have passed on are still seen on the second floor.

San Pierre Cemetery
San Pierre: San Pierre Rd.

In the back right side of the cemetery, in the woods, there are more stones. Visitors see figures of people walking through the woods.

STEUBEN COUNTY

Covenant Cemetery

Fremont: North of Clear Lake on Ray Clearlake Rd. (e 750 N) and N 700 E.

In the north west part of the cemetery, a two children appear. They walk to the middle of the cemetery and disappear.

Lakeside Cemetery

Fremont: South of Freemont. East of N. SR827. If you get to US80/90, you've gone too far.
GPS: 41.739182, -84.932304

Strange lights dance in this cemetery, which is surrounded by woods and bogs. Some people speculate that these are fairies or elementals that live in the woods. Others believe these are the spirits of the dead from the part of the cemetery that was relocated 25 years ago.

McNaughton Family Cemetery

Fremont: NW corner of CR 700E and Ray Clear Lake Rd (CR 750N)

When you walk between the tombstones, you levitate although you are still moving forward. Cold spots and mysterious brushes with unseen people

Old Circle Hill Cemetery/ Circle Hill Cemetery

Angola: Old Circle Hill Cemetery (East of Wohler St. off of W. Stocker St) Circle Hill Cemetery(Circle Hill Cemetery Rd.)
(Note: Some people are confused as to which Circle Hill Cemetery these events have taken place.)

The old Circle Hill Cemetery was established in 1874. Several black hooded figures have been seen in the old Circle Hill Cemetery. The figures have been known to chase people.

Sigma Phi Epsilon house (at Tri State University)

Angola: 115 S. Darling St. (House is scheduled for demolition)

Established in 1884, Tri State University is a privately funded, higher education institution which grants baccalaureate and masters degrees. Sigma Phi Epsilon fraternity began using the house in 1968 although a new building at South Darling and S. Gale St. is currently being built. In the current building, a girl who died there several years ago haunts the home. She's been seen as an apparition, she's touched and kissed several men in the home and she's also known for taking items, but returning them in odd places later.

Town Circle/Strand Theatre
Angola: 49 S Public Sq.

If you go the town circle at night and look at the Strand Movie theatre building, you will see a man with a long red beard walking around the top of the building. Some reports this man scream for a woman named "Marie" to return.

Wing Haven Nature Preserve
Angola: E. of I69 on north side of W 400 N

The original part of Wing Haven was a gift from Helen Swensen received in 1983. With other sections added to the complex it now totals 264 acres and has about a mile of trails. For the last 30 years, a story has circulated about rituals being performed at the site of the nature preserve. They believe this ritual has released a being (e.g. demon, spirit, etc) into this world. The being is supposed to be contained within the stream but when you approach the stream, it will make contact with you. Visitors have experienced unexplained flat tires, electrical problems with cars, electronics, and phones. Some people have reported suicidal and other violent urges overtaking them in this section of the preserve.

SULLIVAN COUNTY

Antioch Cemetery
Cass: East of N CR800E on E CR100N (at junction of N CR875E)

On foggy nights around 1:30 am, a man dressed in a dark colored suit with flowers in his hands can be seen looking down at a grave. Witnesses also see shadows of people flashing past and over their vehicles, accompanied by scratching and tappings heard.

Bethel Cemetery
Hymera: On SR48 east of S. Church St.

The Nathan Hinkle grave and monument (Revolutionary War soldier/casualty) glows. If you call his name, he will talk with you or manifest in the form of a mist.

Free Springs Bridge
Ferree: CR 175 W across the railroad tracks at the bottom of the hill.

Many murders took place over the years at this bridge. A headless man roams around looking for his head. A phantom hobo that was ran over by a train is also seen. A couple had a car accident in which she was killed. The man was never found. He is heard calling her name throughout the area around the bridge.

Encyclopedia of Haunted Indiana

SWITZERLAND COUNTY

Schenck Mansion
Vevay: 206 West Turnpike St.
(aka Shank Bed and Breakfast)

This home has two legends with the truth somewhere in between. A woman named Sarah lived in a cabin and took in Civil War soldiers. When she took in Confederates, the militia came in, tied Sarah and a soldier up and burnt the cabin. After their deaths, no one seemed to know the Confederate soldier's name- until it appeared written in the dirt. Once the ghost was named Ed, the writing in the dirt stopped.

When the current Victorian home was built, it stood empty for a long time. It didn't help that the ghost would bother the African-American workmen in the home. When the family moved in, the son of the owner felt someone touch him and pinch his "bum". Male visitors to the home have seen a solid apparition of a young woman and report kisses bestowed upon them. One woman witnessed the apparition as well.

Another variation of this story is that a husband and wife lived in this home until the husband was sent off to war. During the war, his wife cheated on him. When he returned home, he found his wife and her lover in bed. He killed them and himself. They replay that fateful day many times throughout the year in the evening. Additionally, the woman touches men who enter the house. The husband yells to get the men to leave.

TIPPECANOE
COUNTY

Baby Alice
Lafayette: 13th and Elizabeth Streets

In May 1857, a blue light was reported. It was nicknamed Baby Alice for a prostitute who was killed in her place of business. Today, the light is witnessed in late Fall and early Spring. Blue lights float through house and grounds. Some saw Baby Alice after her death from congestion due to poor health and consumption carrying a pitcher (or some said her heart and lungs) in her hands.

Battle Ground Cemetery
Battleground: NE on Main St. (turns into Pretty Prairie Rd.)

A red eyed demon haunts this cemetery. The demon has been witnessed during the day and night walking on two hooves. With the upper body of a human, it has a face like leather. People say for each soul he takes in the cemetery, an open sore appears on his face. One scared investigator saw the demon and as he was backing away, he witnessed fewer than five open wounds on the demon's face.

Black Rock
Lafayette: Near Lafayette on east of CR N 1100 E on CR E 350 N
(Note: This is a defunct town that is now little more than woods.)

The area, once inhabited by Native Americans, was the site for a mission and a church. Native Americans are seen here and along the river. A farmer named Fred has been seen around the area as well. He is suspected as having died of a heart attack. Another spirit named William likes attention, but has a hard time showing himself on film or EVPs. According to some investigators, William doesn't know he's dead. Other spirit is of a woman named Emma. A little boy also walks the woods in the area. Cold spots are felt and unfelt breezes make trees sway.

Blue Bridge
Battleground From SR 25, turn left on 275.
(Note: This is very close to Prophetstown.)

A man chased by the mafia couldn't get over the bridge so he went under it. The mafia followed but mistook each other for the man and killed themselves. Today you see the residual haunting of the shooting.

Cumberland School
West Lafayette: 600 Cumberland Ave.

A transparent man is seen in the window.

Deadman's Curve

Lafayette: CR 450 S and CR 450 E (7 miles SE of Lafayette)

(aka Culver Station)

Thirty people were killed in a train wreck on Halloween evening 1864, when a 16 car cattle train and an 11 car passenger train (carrying hundreds of Union soldiers) collided. The speeding trains and impact, as well as cries of the injured and dying, can be heard.

Eisenhower Bridge (Lafayette)

Lafayette: Eisenhower Rd. before N 400 E

A ghost of a woman with a shotgun haunts the bridge. The legend states you must flash your headlights and she will appear to talk with you.

Harrison Cemetery

West Lafayette: Behind William Henry Harrison High School at 5701 North 50 West in West Lafayette.

(aka St. Joseph Cemetery, aka Lafayette Catholic Cemetery)

Ghosts here cry and moan in the night hours and throw rocks, sticks, and other objects. Occasionally there are sensations of being followed. Headstones move to different locations. People have been touched by icy hands.

Historic Five Points Fire Station Museum

Lafayette: 1511 Main St.

Captain Nimrod Jones lives in the old No.3 fire station at Five Points. He was there when it was built in 1921, and continues to live there today as a spirit. Although no apparitions have been seen, voices have been reported as well as walking in the late evening. A new station planned for 1710 South St. replaced the existing Five Points station which, for 79 years, has stood at the hilltop where Main, 18th, and South Streets come together.

Greenbush Cemetery

Lafayette: 1408 N. 12th St.

Lights dance over the tombstones in the cemetery, especially on foggy evenings. On the far east side, a lot of paranormal activity is noted around a black stone of a man who was killed on his motorcycle. His voice has been heard and cameras have stopped working. On an erroded hill full of children's grave markers, the children are seen playing and running. People often leave gifts and trinkets for the kids.

Lafayette Jeff High School
Lafayette: 1801 S. 18th St.

A former student who died in a car accident is said to walk the halls. Footsteps are heard and the person is seen along the corridor leading to the north side classrooms.

Lahr Hotel
Lafayette: 117 N 5th St. at Columbia St.
(aka The Moon Murder)

James Moon, a Quaker farmer and blacksmith lived about 10 miles south of Lafayette. Once, he rented a room at the Lahr hotel- room 41. During his stay, a lot of banging occurred. After assuring the hotel manager that he'd pay for damages, James continued his secret work. A few days later, he left his room and met friends. The next morning, he was found dead in his room. He was killed by an ax chop from his home-made guillotine.

The hotel has now been turned into apartments, but that doesn't stop spirits from roaming the building's halls. Residents and visitors report feeling uneasy in what was the old lobby. Doors open and close on their own. Whistling and voices are heard in several apartments.

Moses Fowler House
Lafayette: 909 South St.
(aka Tippecanoe County Historical Society)

Shadows are seen moving through the home and distinct voices are heard.

Old City Wharf
Lafayette: Banks of the river between the Wabash & Erie railroad trestle (south of E. State St) and Union St.

Lafayette was a bustling hub for settlers in the early 1800s. By the 1830s, the city had a wharf along the river just a block away from the thriving downtown courthouse. As wares were transported down the river, they would be offloaded at the wharf. Not always the most savory of areas, many untold murders occurred along the banks of the river. Numerous bodies have been found floating along the waters.

In recent years, the area where the wharf stood has been redeveloped by the town. Lafayette wants ready to make "the Levee" a profitable commercial area. At night, visitors to the river bank have heard muffled conversation and have witnessed strange mists.

Pierce Cemetery
Lafayette: W 600 N and N 50 W

Investigators have captured orbs and mists. A small girl in a pink and white checked pinafore skips through the darkness.

Pythian Home

Lafayette: 1501 S. 18th St.

This building was erected in the 1920s for the families of the Knights of Pythias and then it was turned into an orphanage (1928) and later a nursing home (1930s). Lights turn off and on. Ghosts touch you by walking next to you or tapping you on the shoulders. Odd smells occur, such as roses and lavender. Legend has it that someone was murdered in a bathroom. After cleaning it up, they left the room and came back in just to find it as blood filled as it had been before. Another version of the story is that a woman hemorrhaged to death. Many people from the nursing home are said to have taken their lives. Safety station 13 has a door that leads to an attic, and the door opens by mysterious unseen hands. The safe in the hallway of the mansion (it weighs 600 lbs) moves on its own as well. Today, on the anniversary of the murder, the crime scene returns. Every year the Jefferson Memorial High School puts on a haunted house in the building. Screaming and banging has been heard in the elevator. Once when this happened, it got louder and louder to the point that the doors popped open, the sounds stopped and no one was in the elevator. Voices are heard; orbs captured.

Purdue University

West Lafayette: Purdue Airport (Hangar 1); Earhard Residence Hall: NE corner of McArthur Dr and 1st St. Dr.

Airport (Hangar 1): Amelia Earhart haunts the hangar. Mechanics have seen a three-dimensional figure of Earhart in the hangar. Known for her lust for life and desire to know everything about aviation, Earhart is still on the job, watching mechanics work on planes and perform other tasks.

Earhart Residence Hall: Students and staff feel and see paranormal activity in Amelia's first floor corner room. They feel cold drafts, see the windows open and see a shadowy figure of Earhart in the room. They also hear the tappity-tap of an old typewriter. Snickers bars are said to appear out of thin area and sometimes Amelia Earhart appears holding one.

Purdue University-Owen Hall

West Lafayette: Owen Hall on the campus of Purdue University

Wade Steffey, a freshman at Purdue University, went missing on January 13, 2007 after attending a fraternity party. For weeks, the police suspected foul play and the campus was searched except for one area, a high voltage utility closet. He was discovered by a staff member. Eventually his death was ruled an accident. Apparently he was trying to retrieve a jacket he'd lent to someone and found his way into the closet instead.

Today, students cannot go by this area without feeling a cold chill. One student claims that the body was not found in the corner, as reported, but that the utility worker opened the door and the body fell out. Students and staff alike have felt a severe feeling of depression and anxiety associated with the area. Additionally, staff members don't like going into that area because they say they've seen shadowy figures lurking about.

An interesting side note, after Wade's body was found and the funeral was over, his parents took a much needed break and went to Florida. While on a beach, his mother tracked something floating in the sky, which eventually made it into the water and onto the beach. It was a Spider-Man balloon. She believes even though he wasn't a huge Spider-Man fan, "sometimes you have to use what is available" and he sent the balloon to let them know "he knows we're there, he knows we're working on ourselves" and that eventually they would get through the painful situation.

White Wolf
Lafayette North of SR 25 near Spring Vale Cemetery and Eel River.

William Lingle wrote about the haunting of his home. As early as 1872, he wrote that a blue light morphs into a white wolf appears at this location and then changes into a water beast before becoming the image of a Native American.

William Henry Harrison High School
West Lafayette: 5701 N 50 W

This school is named for the man who was instrumental in killing Native Americans during the War of 1812. A teacher who died is seen in the cafeteria and in the hallways.

TIPTON
COUNTY

Old Factory
Sharpsville: E. Elm St by old train tracks

There are reports of women looking out the abandoned factory windows. The banging of metal on metal can be heard. People can be heard talking when no one is around.

Tipton Courthouse
Tipton Town Square

Security and visitors report a man who was imprisoned in the basement dragging his leg and walking up the stairs. One woman was rudely slapped in the face before a wind blew past her.

UNION
COUNTY

Hanna House
Dunlapsville: 3130 S. Old Dunlapsville Rd.

Not to be confused with Hannah House (see entry in Marion County), this early 1800s home was built by Captain John Hanna. A woman named Jenny haunts an upper bedroom. She is seen in a long white dress. She appears in many pictures taken by visitors in the form of mists and orbs.

VANDERBURGH COUNTY

112 Franklin Street
Evansville: 112 Franklin St. *(razed)*

This incredibly active location had a portal in the living room. It has now been razed because no one would stay in the house for long.

123 Michigan Street
Evansville: 123 Michigan St.

An older woman is seen in the windows when no one is home.

24 Monroe Street
Evansville: 24 Monroe St.

The basement of this home had a painting of woman knocking on door holding a lantern with flowers in it. The painting covered the whole wall next to the stairs.

Investigators saw an entity in basement, and painting on the basement wall. Suddenly, something under the stairs grabbed one person's legs leaving red marks. The attic had a pentagram drawn in charcoal on the wooden floor. The area seemed charged with negative energy.

205 Florida Street
Evansville: 205 Florida St. *(razed)*

The home has rooms under the attic eaves. On the stairs to get to the rooms, a dark entity pushes people down. A child saw a man in black who was not nice and laughed very evilly. Once, when one of the occupants was left alone, she had a feeling she needed to leave but stood her ground to finish vacuuming. She told the negative force she would be done soon and to leave her alone.

In an upstairs room, many people reported hearing "get out" by unseen people. A residual haunting of a man getting a haircut was seen in the upper story kitchen. The home also had a woman who would cry in the upstairs bathroom. Psychics said that someone had committed suicide. Footsteps are heard on the porch. The person who rented the upper apartment for many years felt that the majority of the spirits were protective because the people in the apartment below were drug dealers. On another occasion, a man kneeled next to a Native American who was visiting the occupant. He told her the man was a spirit guide who was just checking in with him. One child who lived in the apartment watched a bird come in the window and said it talked to her, telling her things that only her family would know.

The child's mother believes it was her grandmother, who always wanted to come back as a bird. Another male occupant heard his name called and heard his uncle call his name as well- his uncle was not in the house. Another occupant who was crying saw the presence of a woman behind her as a reflection in the mirror- the entity had her arms around her and wanted to know why she was crying.

A humorous incident involves dishes flying out of the cabinet. The apartment occupant told the spirits, "If you want me out, get me a winning lottery ticket!"

One eerie incident involved a woman waking up and seeing her husband standing by the windows. She called to him, sat up and saw not her husband, but a demon with red eyes and a crisp pointed robe (not like the KKK). She stared, blinked, and it was her husband again.

578 Baker Street

Evansville: 578 Baker St. *(razed)*

This apartment had a furry black shadow figure in its back apartment. Upstairs, there was one room that was not part of any apartment. The curtains in this room would move all the time. Many times men were heard fighting on the stairs, occupants would open the door to find out what was going on and no one would be there. One ghost figure of an old lady used to walk up the same stairs with a ghost cat in her hands.

649 East Maryland Street

Evansville: 649 E. Maryland St.

Late at night cards could be heard shuffling in the kitchen, as if someone were playing a game. There was also a transparent woman seen in the kitchen at the sink looking out the window. The house also had an extraordinary infestation of odd, abnormally large, spiders of many species. Two other women ghosts walked through the living room area while staring at a renter. They then moved into the next room and disappeared through the wall, which was once a door leading outside.

814 E. Franklin Street

Evansville: 814 E. Franklin St.

The Victorian house was built at the turn of the century, and later used as apartments. A male entity walks the main hall downstairs in the early evening and late at night. It sounds as if he is pacing and waiting, and he seems to be wearing older style heavy soled boots. Pots and pans would clang and bang when no one was in the kitchen downstairs. This continued nightly after the tenants vacated, leaving the upstairs renters all alone with the spirits, boot steps, and noisy cutlery. A woman in white is seen in the upstairs in several rooms, and a cold, strong breeze was felt by the upstairs renters teen daughter when she was home alone. No one stayed in the apartments for long because of the activity.

1929 Stringtown Road

Evansville: 1929 Stringtown Road

Parents died here and now haunt the location looking for their children.

7831 Seminary Road
Evansville: 7831 Seminary Road *(razed)*

The old farm house that used to sit on this glorious hill is now gone. Inside lurked several people. An older man was seen sitting in a chair just as transparent as he was. An older woman used to look out the front window. The front door would open of its own accord, even though it was locked. Although it is not certain, investigators believe these ghosts were former owners who have just chosen to stay in the area.

8513 Rainier Drive
Evansville: 8513 Rainier Dr.

Owners see the ghost of a tall man in a black suit with bowler/jazz hat who carries a suitcase. Many times he walks into the bathroom and disappears. The children have also seen the "suitcase man" walking through the home, going up or down the long hallway. Additionally, a black shadow haunts one of the rooms. It casts a bad feeling about the home.

The area around this home is generally haunted. The woods next to the mobile home park are haunted by shadow people and a dead local farmer, which adds to the atmosphere. A trailer sits near the property on which a girl was raped and brutally beaten by her mother's boyfriend.

Angel Mounds
Evansville: 8215 Pollack Ave.

Native American sun worshipers lived at this location for hundreds of years. It is unknown why they left or were wiped out, no indication of a great war has been found. Unusual graves have been discovered. Visitors have seen residual hauntings of people who lived there in former times. A procession of people carrying a small body has been seen. Crying and laughter have been heard on the grounds, as well as chanting and mysterious drumming.

Big Ditney Hill
Evansville: Big Ditney Hill is surrounded by Weyerbacker Rd, Greenbrier Rd, Wasson/ Lilly Pad Rd. and Seven Hills Rd. Two roads come off Lilly Pad Road that lead to access of the hill.

The Irishmen who built the Wabash and Erie Canal got very ill and many died. A mass grave was dug. The ill who would probably die were thrown in with the dead. One intrepid man clawed his way out one evening, and it's said he killed the foreman for allowing such a thing to happen. The foreman is said to roam the hill on moonlight nights and is known as the Ditney Man.

Boehne Camp Hospital

Evansville: Boehne Camp Rd. *Privately owned and torn down in 2007. The buildings across from the old hospital are being renovated into apartments.*
(aka Evansville TB Hospital)

Ghost patients roam this old TB hospital grounds. The ceiling of the old hospital was known to drip blood. A rocking chair in the building would rock by itself. One explorer found himself without the use of a thumb after a visit. Patients are still seen although the hospital has been razed. Sometimes visitors have heard tortured screams as if someone was in pain.

Carpenter House

Evansville: 405 Carpenter St.

This home was built by Willard Carpenter in 1849. Staff and visitors hear strange noises and see items levitate.

Dogtown (town)

Cypress: Dogtown Tavern: 6201 Old Henderson Rd

Dogtown has the reputation for being a very haunted area. The river bottoms are full of stories about the dead rising from the waters. Stories of mob and gangster burials along the banks of Dogtown are also told. In the dark woods around Dogtown are many unknown gravesites left to be reclaimed by nature.

Three most notable haunted places are:

Haunted School House: A man raped and killed two girls in the basement. You can hear the girls screaming at night. Additionally, the abandoned homesites on the way to this location are full of shadow people and orbs.
Dogtown Tavern: The doors open and close on their own and the lights flicker. A couple of transparent men sit at the bar from time to time. (Note: Tavern is now closed)
School: Drive along Old Henderson Rd. until you get to a gravel road. Follow this road until you're about to go into the woods. The house is privately owned and under renovation.

Eastland Mall

Evansville: 800 N. Green River Rd.

A security guard was killed at the mall. You can still see his transparent figure walking around checking the stores.

East Mary Street

Evansville: East Mary St.

A Lakota man had been adopted by a white man and his Hispanic wife. He grew up in this house. He sometimes stayed there since his mother needed help and had become disabled due to the disease lupus. "Ron" was sitting in his old room very late one night listening to the radio when the music changed to a show about the death of JFK. Ron's mother really liked JFK and there were several pictures of him around the house, in Ron's room. Ron looked at the picture of JFK in his room and it was glowing. Ron heard the picture say, "I am not gone."

Evansville Christian Life Center
Evansville: 509 S Kentucky Ave.

Formerly the Monastery of St. Clare, it is now home to a not-for-profit organization dedicated to the "restoration of people".

Legend has it that on June 8, 1985 construction workers came in to removal. The DNR came in to remove burials from the monastery. As they finished up their work, a bad storm came through. Ten years later at the same time, another bad storm came through (1995). Every 10 years on the anniversary date of the removal, a bad storm is said to come through. People believe the nuns are unhappy that their burial place was disturbed.

Today, people say they hear footsteps walking behind them and they feel entities watching them. Staff and residents have also seen the shadow figures of nuns walking from room to room throughout the building.

Evansville County Courthouse
Evansville: Fourth and Vine Streets

On January 18, 1973 Anne Kline was stabbed 19 times in a basement alcove of the courthouse. She was a math teacher at Lock Year Business College and was conducting courses down in the courthouse basement because the college had suffered a fire. The crime is still officially unsolved.

Visitors to the old courthouse have felt a "desperate" presence in the building, especially in the area of the murder. Several investigators have had to leave the area because of the negative energy. People have reported feeling ill as well. One investigator saw a pool of blood on the floor and tried to take a picture of it. When he saw the picture, it didn't contain blood, but it did contain a white mist that had not been visible at the time the picture was taken.

In the catacombs, Investigators report electromagnetic field disturbances. On one investigation a bottle of clippings of news stories about murders and missing people was found. A spirit has been seen floating in the same room. When approached, it runs by the witnesses, leaving them with a feeling of dread. Temperature spikes and cold spots are also felt.

Evansville State Hospital
Evansville: 3400 Lincoln Ave.
(aka Southern Indiana Hospital for the Insane; aka Woodmere)

This mental hospital was commissioned in the 1880s and established in the early 1890s. It followed the same destructive path as the other state institutions- overcrowding from day one, a lack of knowledge about the budding mental health field, and therefore untrained staff. Later it also suffered from lack of trained employees even after more became clear about the field of mental health. In 1943 several older buildings were destroyed by fire, but the newer buildings remained. In mid-2006 the remainder of the old buildings were razed with only a small section of modern buildings left.

When the burned buildings were still partially erect, staff and patients would see lights go on in the buildings, when there was no electrical hookup. Shadow figures would walk the campus, the burned buildings and even in the newer 1940s buildings. One patient saw the distinct figure of a person going from room to room, turning on lights and bending down as if they were checking patients. He said it went on from one floor to another until he could no longer see the person on the opposite side of the building.

In the 1940s infirmary, trays rattled when no one was around. On Ward 8 (B8) on the third floor, something that sounded like a bowling ball rolling across the floor above it was heard- it would hit the wall and start over again. The odd thing is that there was nothing but roof on that floor.

In the same building, in 1989, in the corner room, phantom footsteps were heard walking through the building. Staff and patients alike reported seeing shadow people walking behind them and beside them. Staff and patients also felt a presence, as if something was not quite right in the building.

In the G/H building (newer building with fence) a patient felt like something evil was watching him in the mirror, as if it didn't want the man there. He later found out a different patient committed suicide in the room. In G ward basement, a white ball of light bounced through the rec room and went through the windows and outside. The staff and patients watched it move across the lakes and go towards St. Mary's. It went across Lincoln Ave over the buildings there and disappeared.

Several suicides occurred in the buildings and several patients jumped from windows. Some of these patients could be seen as ghosts reenacting their demise years after their deaths and their screams could be heard.

Now that the buildings are gone, some of these patients can still be seen as mists, orbs, and apparitions on the grounds. EVPs of screams and insistent cries for help have been captured.

Hangwell Tree and surrounding area

Evansville: Hangwell tree and old man sighting: Godeke Rd. (CR 550 N) Corner of Schultz Rd.

A strange coldness and cloying dread falls over this area. Recently someone has built a house by the old maple tree. Legend has it the tree cannot be cut down. Old timers know of this tree and the legends, but no one can provide history or why the area is so haunted.

Visitors see people hanging from tree. A male ghost walks the road in front of the tree. The Beast of Hangwell roams the fields around it. Full body apparitions appear in and around the tree. Shooting stars are seen gathering at the tree. As one group approached the tree around 2:00 am, one June, a full-blooded Lakota Indian saw the surrounding trees turn into lion's heads and he would not approach the tree. Other visitors approached the tree and saw a red-headed woman hanging from the tree in a long, pink, sheer gown. Under the tree leaves, dark shadows of "a 100 other people" hung with the woman. These people held books, and wore trousers, shoes.

Another visitor on the expedition remembers playing ball with a little boy in knickers , and who had a little dog with him. Some of the visitors came a few hours later at daybreak and went by a house (see below) where a man was leaning against a stop sign. They told him they were going to visit the tree and he nodded- disappearing before their eyes. On the way to the tree, viewed across several acres of plowed fields, was a glowing gold skull on the tree trunk. Upon close examination, there was no patterning on the trunk to give this illusion.

During another visit, shadows played over the ground, blocking the exit from the area. As the group tried to move away from the tree, the shadows followed them. Finally one member of the group distracted the shadows and the rest headed to the road. Eventually the other member was able to run and escape the enclosing shadows.

Henry Reis School
Evansville: 1900 Stringtown Road

A shop teacher died and now haunts the school. Tools turn on and off. Hand tools disappear. Students report ghostly footsteps and cool breezes.

Home near the Ohio River
Evansville: SE First and Monroe Streets *(razed)*

Occupants saw a bleeding Revolutionary War soldier in basement room under the front living area. The home is no longer there but the agonized cries of a man are still heard.

Howell Wetlands
Evansville: 1101 S. Barker Ave.

Investigators have seen a woman in a pale pink frilly dress by the banks near the bridge

No 6 School
Evansville: SE corner of No. 6 School House Rd. and Big Cynthia Rd.

The apparition of a man is seen in the windows.

Little Ditney Hill and Gander Cemetery
(aka Little Ditney Cemetery; aka Lockyear Cemetery)
Evansville: Booneville-New Harmony Rd. and Gander Rd. Go north on dirt road. Gander Cemetery is on Little Ditney Hill

Note: Some visitors mistake Gander Cemetery for Young or Youngs Cemetery (which is on the Boonville- New Harmony Rd.)

The Gander and Lockyear family cemetery sits on Little Ditney Hill. The interments date from 1899, although because of spotty records, these could go farther back. A pterodactyl-like creature roams the area. So does a band of Native Americans. The Indians are reported as dark shadows with white outlines. An unidentified man in black walks through the trees.

Pidgeon Creek

Evansville: Located at Diamond Ave. and Pidgeon Creek. Park at Garvin Park and walk on grass near levy. If you go down Heidelbeck and go next to levy, you'll have to drive into gravel. Go from First Ave. to Heidelbach Canoe launch, along Pigeon Creek Heidelback Ave to Negly Ave to Baker Ave to road that goes to creek.
(Note: Now the creek has overflowed, and is overgrown with random types of trees.)

In Garvin Park a demon lies in the ravine. Visitors hear screams. A group of visitors investigated one night and one asked the demon to present itself. Shooting stars appeared and a sinister fog rolled in, circling the group. A "flat paper man" with a bowtie smiled and danced sideways between the levy and creek with his arms moving. He split into two people- one white with black bowtie, black with white bowtie—both danced towards each other. One investigator got a severe headache and saw native people dancing around the tree.

Two big rock-shaped moving tannish-brown mounds with sharp razor teeth were coming for them. Moving along the creek, behind tree, coming up the dirt road. One investigator warned another. Grass started moving without wind. As the investigator got on the road, creatures start moving slowly. A little tree next to them (now has a copper fish hanging from it), started swaying like dancing. One investigator saw something in the old cotton wood tree- a grey fog mass sparkling on edges. It rises up, gets past the top of the tree, turned into a moon shape with soft edges, bursts, and twinkly stuff falls into tree to the ground. They decided to leave, as fog was very close to them, and one investigator was pregnant.

Pollack and Lodge Streets
Evansville: Pollack and Lodge Sts.

This property was once one of the area's most prolific farms, boasting many barns and a very large grand house with two wings. The family spent many wonderful years there till tragedy seemed to strike all of them all at once. The gentleman took his older son with him into the Dubois County area to sell some cattle and buy a couple of horses. The man and his son conducted business and stayed at an inn, where they were both killed in their sleep for their cash and the two grand horses they had purchased. No one was ever convicted of their murders. The father and son lay in state before burial at their home on Pollack Ave. It was a hard winter and the widow had seven more children to care for with no husband and no older son. It was cold and the widow shut all of them into one room on the second floor to keep warm. A lamp tipped in the night, or a chimney fire started, burning part of the house, and the family suffocated to death.

Another the burned portion was rebuilt, the house was sold. The house kept changing hands frequently, even after it was turned into apartments. Renters wouldn't stay. Every two or three years, the former burned section would catch fire, and then it would be rebuilt. Owners and renters would see a shadow man in the backyard smoking a pipe. You could smell the cherry tobacco. Frequently children could be heard laughing and playing, small pranks would occur to the living. On

Christmas every year the smell of popcorn would permeate the space of the house. Apple pie could be smelled as well. Late into the evening sounds of laughter and many guests partying would be heard. Glasses clinking, laughter of adults, murmured conversations, and carols being sung could be easily heard as well.

In the last ten years the rest of the land and barns were sold off for a subdivision, and the old house is still there as a four-plex apartment building.

Residual haunting near Hangwell Tree
Evansville: S. Newmaster Lake Rd. Stop sign on curve.
(See Hangwell Tree entry. Past Hangwell Tree around the next curve.)

The man burned to death in house. It's said the man killed wife in home. He was abusive and she fought back. He raped her with a stick of firewood. These acts are a residual reenactment.

Reynolds House
Evansville: 611 Harriet St
(Now a medical clinic in downtown Evansville-Doctor's plaza)

A ghost of a 19-year-old named Oscar haunts this house. He died in 1922 and has been seen and heard ever since. He runs up the stairs and shuts windows during storms. One 12 year old girl saw him on the stairway and later in the room where he died. He is said to have followed the Reynolds when they moved to their new home, yet he has still been seen in the area by people visiting downtown.

Salems Kirche
Evansville: South Welborn Rd.

Former renters report phantom church bells ringing at five in the morning, but upon going outside, the bells become silent. The abandoned church also has a misty ghostly woman who sits in the front of the church as if still in prayer. The antique piano in the church will play mysteriously at dusk and dawn. There are graves of several pets beside the church, but the stones are usually overgrown by weeds. One of those pets was a much loved canine of the former renters. He is seen as a misty wolf like form at the edge of the woods. A shadow man is seen exiting the church from the back door and sometimes the wider side door. He is usually hunched over as if he is dragging something heavy.

There is a clearing to the north of the church where an old barn and forge stood. You can sometimes hear the whinny of horses and the stamp of their hooves during the day. Shadow figures of men and women are sometimes seen in the surrounding woods which abound with deer.

Another ramshackle barn is at the end of the long driveway. Strange footprints have been found in and around the barn, similar to those of a large bird or reptile. The pond down the hill from this barn is home to a little boy spirit. During the Depression era he drowned there trying to rescue his pony. The pony had become entangled in some barbed wire near the pond and couldn't get loose. The pony drowned there too. Sometimes late in the evening you can hear both of them thrashing about in the water.Sometimes hear the boy's cries for help can be heard.

South Sweetser Avenue 1700 Block
Evansville: S. Sweetser Ave. 1700 block *(razed)*

Former renters report a crawl space hatch in the floor of the kitchen. It would never stay shut. Growling could be heard late at night when a person was brave enough to venture into the kitchen for a glass of water. One fateful night the utilities quit working, then would come on and off at random intervals. The renter's dog and hamsters were going crazy with a nervous frenzy. The floor hatch started to bang up and down, cold spots and breezes were felt in the house. The occupants went outside to await a brother-in-law who was coming to work on a car. As the brother-in-law arrived, a horrible, evil groaning could be heard coming from the house to the front yard. Whatever it was tried to coalesce as a grey mass floating ten feet above the ground, then it landed with a very loud band on the hood of the non working car.

There was also a boarded up upstairs formerly accessible by a wooden staircase outside the house. It too was boarded over. A local man had been dealing drugs and child porn from the apartment upstairs. One night someone came, argued, and shot him. His blood stain remained on the floor upstairs, and on the downstairs ceiling. His footsteps had been heard upstairs as well as a weekly reenactment of the shouting and shooting.

A year or so later investigators went to the house. The landlord did not show up with the keys, but the neighbors said the house had caught fire each time it was rented in the previous year. The last time caused the utility company to completely disconnect the house from all wiring. The back was open, and there was a foul decomposition odor coming from the kitchen. The house was in very bad condition and the blood stain was still on the ceiling. Bumps and bangs were heard upstairs, and a tenant recorded an EVP saying "No, no, don't."

Tekoppel Elementary School
Evansville: 111 N. Tekoppel Ave

Three young girls at day camp went to the girls bathroom and got an odd vibe from the storage room located there. Several people have reported bad vibrations from spirits that are said to haunt the building. The maintenance area holds spirits of children and a mean adult man. The lower level is the most haunted. Investigators captured lots of orbs.

University of Evansville- Paint Studio
Evansville: USI has a great campus map on its website.

Items move in the studio. At night, soft misty figures are seen in the studio and hallway. At present, it is not known who the entities are.

Willard Library
Evansville: 21 First Ave.

Willard Carpenter opened the library in 1885. He was a successful businessman with a daughter, Louise. Legend states when Carpenter died, his daughter was so bitter that the fortune was left to the library and not her, she is trapped there as a spirit.

Women's Restroom (basement): When the library was still on coal heat, a man who came in every morning to shovel coal for the day saw the grey lady watching him- he left and never came back. In the women's restroom. Conversations from bodiless people are heard here, doors open and shut without occupants, and the water turns on and off.

Childrens' section: Books have flown off shelves, aimed at adults and children. Some of the stuffed animals have moved their heads and talked to children and investigators. Additionally, one child and her mother saw the dollhouse lights come on- although it has none! Visitors feel cold spots and the rocking chair rocks on its own. Sometimes the mist of the grey lady appears. Visitors have also reported smelling the scent of lilacs.

Main area: Louisa is believed to be the grey lady seen in the library and on its webcam both in the main area and children's area.

West Side Sportsman Club
Evansville: 1000 N Peerless Rd.

Ghostly children play by the lake. No one knows if these were children who came to the club, or if they were children who died on the property at an earlier time.

VERMILLION COUNTY

Ernie Pyle State Historic Site
Dana: 120 Briarwood St.

The tracks by grain elevator are home to a transparent man. He will spit at you and yell if you follow him.

Helt's Prairie Cemetery
Newport: One mile west of IN63 on 1050 S. Rd. (south side of road)

This cemetery was started about 1817. It was donated by the family of Rev. William James. Notable burials are Antoinette Stover (Grandmother of Pres. Dwight D. Eisenhower), and the only person ever executed in the county. During the day, small children dart between the headstones and at night, an older, stooped gentleman is seen walking through the cemetery.

Lake
Cayuga: IN63 and E. Maple St. in the curve

The area around the lake is haunted by several children who are seen walking. Legend has it that the children died of illness in the mid 1800s. Their parents were overcome with grief and could not be consoled. Several mothers killed themselves here. Investigators believe the children are stuck between this world and another, are looking for their parents. When the children manifest, the temperature drops between 10-20 degrees even on warm days/evenings. EVPs of children talking about school and chores have been captured. One EVP captures a child asking, "Where are they? Where is mama?" another child answers "They're gone. They left us."

Thomas Cemetery
Newport: 2 miles north and west of Newport, Indiana on SR 71 and Hopkins Rd.
(aka Newport Cemetery)

Named for Philemon and Catherine Thomas, the first burial was Eli Thomas in 1831, the father of Philemon. The cemetery has six additions in all, and covers almost 17 acres. A family in Victorian clothing has been seen sitting next to a gravesite in the first addition (south side). They do not interact with people; rather it seems they are celebrating a family member at the gravesite.

VIGO
COUNTY

1100 Seventh Avenue

Terre Haute: 1100 Seventh Ave.

A man nicknamed Uncle Seddy, George Sedwick Mankin is seen in this home. He was a coalminer who died in this home, August 10, 1928. He is buried at Highland Lawn Cemetery. His figure has been seen gliding from room to room and sitting in the living room. Temperature drops occur when he makes his appearances.

2425 6th Avenue

Terre Haute: 2425 6th Ave.

Once an orphanage annex for African-American children, many strange occurrences have happened in the home including seeing small children. The ghost of a 9 year old boy haunts the house. He is very mischievous and hides items. He is also very curious and likes to rummage through drawers and boxes.

Fontanet

Du Pont Powder Company *(aka Fontanet Brick Plant)* : 2 miles north of Fontanet. It is an unmarked woods.

Fontanet: North of E Rio Grande Ave on N Baldwin St.

(aka Fountain, Fountain Station, Hunter)

On October 15, 1907 sparks fell on some loose powder and the Du Pont Powder Company exploded at 9:15am. The first explosion came from the glazing mill. Three other explosions followed. At 9:45am, a second explosion came from the press room and another one in a smaller mill building. At 10:45am the heat from the fire caused the thousands of barrels of powder at the powder magazine to explode.

Seventy to eighty people were employed at the mill. When the second explosion at the powder magazine occurred, it injured physicians who were trying to triage the injured. People who died in the explosion didn't all die immediately. Dr. Carroll, who was burned to a crisp begged to "be shot". Superintendent Monahan was blown to bits and burned. His wife was burned to death in the home they lived in at the mills. Two half sisters escaped.

In Fontanet all the buildings were smashed to the ground, although no one was hurt in the town. A brick schoolhouse a quarter mile from the scene was damaged and many children were hurt. Windows as far away as Brazil and Terre Haute shattered. In all over 40 people died and 250 were injured. People in Cincinnati felt seismic waves from the blasts.

Interestingly, Fontanet was a mining town that was operated by the Coal Bluff Mining Company. Coal Bluff was two miles north east of Fontanet.

Alfred I. duPont had remarried that unfortunate day and interrupted his honeymoon to survey the damage. He vowed to rebuild it all, and so he did, with the exception of the mill itself. The people left in the town begged him not to because they were scared.

The place where this plant was now looks unnatural. It is a wooded, private piece of property. A large amount of dead trees litter the place. The area is haunted. If you visit the location on the day of the accident, you can see the glow of the furnace and fires, hear the explosion and hear the screams of the dead and dying. Visitors also report feeling intense heat, smelling burning flesh, and being touched by hot hands.

Fontanet has a bean dinner every year to commemorate the explosive event.

Fruitridge Avenue and Hulman Street

Terre Haute: Fruitridge Ave. between Hulman St. and Margaret Ave.

Young men and fast cars are nothing new in any town. Fruitridge Ave in Terre Haute has seen its share of late night competitions. One has become legend. As two cars challenged each other one hot summer night, and a nameless young man blew a tire near Hulman Street. His car spun out of control and crashed into a huge brick wall. The boy was thrown through his windshield and smashed face first into a wall. For many years now, some say you can still see the face of the youth staring out of the rock where his life ended.

Highland Lawn Cemetery

Terre Haute: 4520 Wabash Ave.

A dog, Stiffy Green, and his dead owner, John Heinl, walk the cemetery at night. The dog was in the mausoleum of the owner but the cemetery staff removed it because of people roaming the cemetery after dark. Heinl died in 1920 and soon after, despite care of local residents, the distraught dog died as well. He was added to the mausoleum to be with his owner.

Honey Creek Mall
Terre Haute: 3401 S. US41

A very pale man in an old-fashioned suit, carrying flowers is seen in many shops, sometimes by multiple people at the same time. He doesn't interact with anyone. Some people believe he is a ghost from a different time. Other people believe he is an incarnation of Death. He is also seen exiting the mall quickly. Usually it seems he is following someone who recently exited as well. When curious visitors follow him, the figure simply disappears.

Indian Orchard
Terre Haute: Oakcliff Rd. and Wabash River

The Delaware Indians occupied this area from the early 1700s. A girl living among the Native Americans, Lena, had been taken from white parents in Pennsylvania when she was a child. A time came when white captives were to be returned. Lena was asked to leave, although she'd been raised by a chief. The person who was to take her away, Nemo fell in love with Lena. When she was reunited with her brothers and sisters (her parents had passed) she couldn't forget Nemo. Eventually the two snuck away and took vows before the Great Spirit.

When they returned to the tribe at Terre Haute, they found that her village had been destroyed in a tribal fight. As they settled in the area, one evening warriors from the Miami tribe tried to kill Lena and her son. Nemo fought to save his family, but succumbed to the enemy arrows. Lena threw her son to the Delaware men and killed herself with their knife. The Miami raised her son in honor of her bravery.

This battle can be seen reenacted along the banks of the Wabash.

Indiana State University
Terre Haute: Indiana State University has a great map on its website.

Blumberg Hall: Students report items missing and moved. A woman who threw her child down a trash chute haunts the building. The Resident Advisor gave birth in the residence hall but got rid of the baby because she didn't want to lose her place at school and on campus.

Malloy's Pub
Terre Haute: N .7th and Lafayette Streets

Visitors see orbs and moving objects. Investigators report batteries dying while on location. Visitors also feel as if they run into something solid, like another person even when nothing is standing in front of them. Owners and customers have also detected a spirit of a railroad worker, and a child named Sarah, who likes to play tricks on customers.

Old Mill Dam
Markles: Off Rosedale Rd. and Mill Dam Rd.

This was part of the Underground Railroad. A small transparent girl stands by or in the creek.

Pi Kappa Alpha House
Terre Haute: US 40 and Scott Ln.
(aka Glenn Orphan's Home)

In 1987, the Pi Kappa Alphas had no clue what awaited them in the former orphanage. The fraternity makes its home on part of a 26 acre wooded property, with more than a half-dozen buildings. Members of the fraternity see the front door of old dormitories open and close, yet no one appears.

The main building of the fraternity was built in 1896, and the majority of the other buildings followed soon after. Although some buildings have been destroyed and others added over the years, it is now a property full of the best and brightest people at Rose-Hulman.

Opening doors aren't the only tales. Visitors hear children splashing in water and laughing when no such child is around.

Something knocks on the front door and when answered, no one is there. This phenomenon has happened quite a bit. One young man took to his room when he heard the knock at the door and found no one. As he closed the door, he heard the knock again, except it came from a room under the staircase.

Some of the orphanage buildings do not belong to the fraternity, but they are haunted, nonetheless. Children have been seen playing outside the property, bounding in and out of trees. Their laughter for some students is sometimes deafening.

Preston House
Terre Haute: SE side of 13 1/2th and Poplar Streets' Fowler Park 10654 Bono Rd *(razed)*
(aka Dewees Mansion)

Originally from France, Major George Dewees was a harsh man by nature. When his son was scalped and killed, he began to guard his house with hungry dogs. Depending on which story you hear, Dewees was either a Underground Railroad operator or rumored to have a thriving slave trading business. Regardless of the outcome, Major Dewees threw himself into his work. When his marriage failed and his wife, Matilda, wanted to leave, she became mysteriously "out of town" for an extended period. Eventually people began to suspect foul play and upon inspection, it was believed that the Major interred his wife in the walls of the house. Dewees was never investigated, but the house was never more unlucky. It was rumored after his death that the home was part of the Underground Railroad, but no evidence of that has been found. Several times the home was targeted by fire bugs. Eventually, it was left to crumble. When the home was eventually razed, the workers were told to look for the body. It was never found. Parts of the razed home including stone and woodwork, are now part of the gristmill in the Pioneer Village at Fowler Park.

Legend has it during Dewees time and for many years after, his wife's spirit was seen coming from the fireplace into the room or she was seen sitting on the chimney, sometimes accompanied by a blue light. Still today, the now-empty lot is home to a woman believed to be Matilda. She appears as a white apparition, sometimes crying and is surrounded by a blue light. Although no connection with the underground railroad was historically made, investigators have captured EVPs of spiritual songs while investigating the lot.

Interestingly enough, the Fowler Park gristmill has its share of paranormal activity. People claim to feel a very angry presence in the mill during different times of the day. Additionally, the angry voice of a man has sent people running when he tells them to leave. Finally, several visitors report running into an invisible form as they've walked around the structure. Could this be the Major, unhappy that his home was torn down or used for other purposes?

St Mary of the Woods College
St Mary of the Woods: Located on Hwy 150 just outside of Terre Haute in St. Mary of the Woods, Indiana.

- Theatre: This is home to an apparition best described as a floating nun that on occasion can be seen late at night, as well as hearing footsteps of someone running up and down the stairs when there is no one else in the building.
- Tunnels: under the campus (sad to say they are closed to the public): Spirits have been seen and heard.
- O'Shaughnessy Hall: Blood stain that looks like is a face in a wall. The stain came from the early days of the school in the 1800's when a nun took her life. Many attempts to remove the stain have been made. When it appears

to have been cleaned it mysteriously re appears days later to the same form and color which it was before. Note: This hall is no longer there. A new dining hall with the same name is in its place.

- Foley Hall: A nun who was an art teacher didn't get to finish a painting before her death. The face of her subject wasn't finished. She is said to haunt the hall without a face. Late at night, in the cold 2nd floor art studio, other girls see her but can't see her face. Sometimes it is clear that you can't see her, other times she stands in shadow. Footsteps and noises as if a skirt is rustling have been heard. Torn down in 1987 but she is said to migrate.
- Guerin Hall: This is probably the most active building on campus. Particularly rooms 333, 334, 346. An invisible nun tucks students in at night. Her measured step precedes her touch.
- LeFer Hall: Lights turn on and off. Shadowy nuns in old habits are seen flittering around the dorm.
- Grotto: The Virgin Mary puts in appearances during the Fall
- SMWC Cemetery: Shadow figures abound throughout this cemetery. At times, they are interactive or shift into different colored mists. One investigator reports seeing a shadow figure shift into a light pink figure which then morphed into a wispy mist that came toward her. As she backed out of the cemetery, it followed her until she reached the grotto.

Shadow Beasts

Terre Haute: Off US40 on 675W. Turn left at the end of the street, you'll see shadow beasts run with the car on this road.

Shadow figures and a beast run next to your car. When you try to shine lights on the beast, it disappears. Yet when you shut your light off, the shadow figures and beast return, moving with your car.

Terre Haute Country Club Golf Course

Terre Haute: 57 Allendale

Apparitions and orbs appear nightly. At the 6th hole, a child named Alex walks. As the legend goes, Alex got drunk, passed out and died. He vomits and screams for help.

Terre Haute Regional Hospital

Terre Haute: 3901 S. 7th St.

Nurses see deceased patients. Room 540 has a cancer patient who is seen (west end of 5th floor). Nurses tried to track her down as a wandering patient, but when they went to find her, she had disappeared.

Vigo Co. Historical Museum

Terre Haute: 1411 S. 6th St.

Orbs and mists are captured in pictures. The orbs tend to stay around the main staircase. At one time a private home, this building has been home to a halfway house, and is now a historical museum.

The old crib in one of the upstairs exhibits moves occasionally, even though the area is closed off.

WABASH COUNTY

104 East 2nd Street

North Manchester: 104 East 2nd Street (Brick house with apartments)

Not much is known about this location. It has two attics and hidden passages, as well as at least two known ghosts. One spirit is a tall skinny Amish-looking man in 1800s clothing. Multiple people have seen him. He does not interact but walks up stairs, and walks by visitors and residents. The second ghost is a red headed boy that walks with the man down the basement stairs.

207 West 4th Street

North Manchester: 207 W. 4th St.

Not much is known about this location, except four houses including this one caught fire and burned down. The old house had attic space without an access point. There is now a Victorian house built in its place.

Two ghosts seem to be the same or similar man at the 104 E. 2nd street location. Visitors experience feelings of a presence, feelings of dread. Doors open and close without a reason, especially if you entered a room. Pictures fall off the walls. Phantom footsteps are heard. Mother of a former tenant has been seen in a bedroom and going up stairs. Picture of same woman levitated. Doors lock without provocation. Steps are heard in living room.

Gravel Pits

Disko: Travel west out of Disko on IN 114 , first right turn after E. Center St.

A woman clad in purple rags is said to roam the local gravel pits.

Mississinewa Battle Grounds/Graveyard/Lake/Forest

LaFontaine: Mississinewa Lake/Forrest: 5613 E. Mississinewa Dam Road
Battleground: Off SR 15 north of Kem Rd.
Graveyard: SR 13 and Palmer Rd. (W 850 S)
(aka Hobbitland)

Apparitions are seen running between headstones. Blood appears on tombstones when the figures run through the cemetery. Mysterious sounds come from the woods, ranging from groans to growls and high pitched sounds. This area was closed off by the state for unknown reasons.

Liberty Mills Public Access

Liberty Mills: On the south end of town is a public access site onto the Eel River. The stretch of the Eel River running by Liberty Mills is known for its canoeing and listed in several canoeing recreational guides.

Several years ago a car load of teenage girls were driving on the road. The driver lost control going around a curve, hitting several trees and ejecting the girls from the car. People said that on that night they could hear the screams of the some of the girls as they died. One even hung in a tree-a branch piercing her midsection. To this day if you go to the public access site you can hear the girls screaming and crying for help. Witnesses report hearing faint cries.

Moonrock

Wabash: 3647 Old SR24 between 2 trees

Wy-nu-sa, a beautiful Native American jumped from a cliff after a duel between two men. Her favorite, was killed. Indian dancers are seen dancing around the rock.

WARREN COUNTY

Cicott's Trading Post Park

Independence: East Independence Road and N800E (aka CR650N). A Trail of Death marker notes the location.

The Trail of Death went through Independence. Zachariah Cicott had a trading post on the site of the park in 1816. He was married to a Potawatomi woman and founded Independence. He is buried in the town cemetery. As someone who loved to party in life, so he does in death. He is seen walking through town, on the side of the road. He has crashed a couple of parties in the park by stealing beer and extinguishing lights. Girls report being "gently and sweetly" kissed by unseen lips- and have reported the taste of alcohol afterwards, although they do report enjoying the flavor.

Devil's Kitchen

Williamsport: Center of Williamsport, under the falls.

A legendary black stove sat in the cave that runs under Williamsport. Locals believed if you went in the cave, the devil, demon or ghost would cook you in the oven. Reportedly, a child named Damon Hoffmeister died at this spot.

Indiana Springs Company

(aka Mudlavia Lodge; aka Mudlavia; aka Hotel Mudlavia; aka Mudlavia Spa)

Kramer: Take E. Kramer Rd. (CR225E) out of Kramer. You'll come to a point in the road where E. Kramer Rd. veers left and there is a smaller road that leads right. Go to the right (E. Hunter Hill Rd.). You should see the ruins of the spa on the right.

Samuel Story discovered the springs in 1884 when he was suffering from rheumatism. Once he drank from the spa, his condition improved. Henry Kramer, for whom the town Kramer is named, developed a hotel on the site. Known as a world-class spa in the early 1900s, it burned in the 1920s. At the time, mob activity was suspected. Mobsters are supposed to be in the pond next to the former hotel.

Today harsh voices are heard. Some people have been scratched, poked and chased by unseen people running after them. Temperature drops occur. Feelings of sickness, tightness in the chest and dizziness are experienced. Orbs have been captured. The sounds of parties from mobster days are heard.

Rumors state that it burned three times, the second time killing everyone inside. People have also reported feeling someone malevolent follows them. Other visitors to the basement report a spirit who was killed in a shooting during a party.

Locust Grove Cemetery

Locust Grove (NE of Tab): South of CR850N on 600W

Locust Grove never got very big. In 1913 it was reported as having fewer than 100 citizens. Now a defunct town, only the Locust Grove Church and Cemetery remain. Sounds of armies walking have been heard. Some believe it is Civil War soldiers. Other people believe it is Harrison's troops moving to the Battle of Tippecanoe.

Mound Cemetery
N600E and E700N NE of Chatterton
(aka Round Cemetery)

This mound-shaped cemetery is about 30 feet high. Originally a Native American burial ground, the Martindale and Little families owned the land and helped establish a "white" cemetery on site. Today, the cemetery is surrounded by a road and experiences much unrest. Native American chanting is frequently heard during the day and night, especially when it is very quiet around the area.

Legend has it that anyone who disturbs the burial site of Native Americans will have bad luck. Investigators have reported having the Native American burial site curse befall them when they've entered the site. Investigators report everything from car trouble to marital issues after they've visited the site. Additionally, misty images are often caught on photos around the upper portion of the mound.

WARRICK COUNTY

Heilman Road
Chandler: Heilman Rd.

There is a desecrated cemetery that sits on a hill top off the gravel road. EVPs captured include moans and wails as if someone were dying. A black shadow chased investigators out of the area one evening. When they returned the next day to retrieve equipment, they found recordings on their cameras consistent with the wailing and moaning heard by others. Unseen hands are moving the video camera through the area until a dark figure appears with glowing white eyes. It comes toward the camera and the camera drops to the ground, leaving the watcher with screaming.

Mt. Carmel Register
Mt. Carmel: 115 E. Fourth St.
(aka Dailey Republican Register)

An old ghost named Caesar haunts the building. Papers go missing and visitors hear footsteps and voices when no one is around.

Scales Lake
Boonville: Off of S. Parklane Dr.

Black Annie is believed to haunt this lake. Black Annie (or Annis or Agnes) is a witch/crone-like woman who delights in killing people, children in general. This is a Celtic legend which has crossed to our side of the pond.

Silent Room
Boonville: Unknown
(note: This location is sometimes attributed to Tennyson, Indiana, but it is in Boonville)

The story goes that 5 women were killed in a shed off this road by the land owner. People feel watched and an overwhelming feeling of despair surrounds the place. Supposedly the shack was soundproofed for the murders and you are unable to scream inside the shed. Additionally, some people feel that they've been pushed and clawed at inside the building.

Warrick Publishing/Boonville Standard
Boonville: 204 W. Locust St.

People feel strange vibes and feel as if someone is running past them. Investigators hear tapping noises in the basement. An EVP captured asked the spirits what their favorite color was answered with the word "green". Investigators also felt touches on their arms and backs and saw shadow figures move through the building. Investigators and staff also caught orbs on film. Investigation equipment malfunctioned on site, leading some investigators to believe spirit activity was afoot.

Yankeetown Bridge

Yankeetown: Yankeetown Rd. bridge over Little Pigeon Creek

A woman hung herself from the bridge. Investigators have been able to hear her jumping and the crack of her neck and the swinging of her body from the bridge.

WASHINGTON
COUNTY

Bradie Shrum residence
Salem: E. Hackberry St. (You can't miss this one- it is a three story brick, Gothic, Italianate home)

Home is supposed to be made up of bricks from the second Salem courthouse. An elementary school teacher is said to haunt the building, going about her daily business but never interacting with people.

Crown Hill Cemetery
Salem: The closest road is St. Michaels Rd. SE.

A stone of Caddy Naugle is of a little girl by one of the gates. Her stone was carved by an unknown stone mason. She had gotten sick and died. Caddy haunts the cemetery in search of the mysterious man who showed her daddy kindness in carving the stone.

Not to be confused with the Crown Hill Cemetery in Indianapolis (see entry), this cemetery is located in a wooded area bounded by Buck Creek. No standard roads lead to it.

(East) Washington School (Middle School)
Pekin: 1100 N. Eastern School Rd.

This school has several areas that are said to be haunted, although the school has no explanation for them. In the third floor girls bathroom, lights switch on and off at will. Many students have seen the switch move by unseen hands. Additionally, the toilets flush on their own and the stall doors open, close, and lock without anyone being in the restroom. In the old gym on the basketball hoop, a handprint that looks like blood is said to appear and disappear. Some students believe the handprint appears before sports games as a sign of bad luck. Custodial staff has also witnessed the events, and have heard footsteps echoing the hallways when no one else is in the building. Cold spots precipitate these footsteps.

French House
Pekin: 8178 S SR 335

Items move around from one spot to another. A little boy about eight, with dark hair, overalls, and no shoes roams the home.

Goose Creek
Salem: South of SR 56, close to Mill Creek Rd.

A woman spends her time throwing rocks in the creek. When you approach her, she'll
give you an annoyed look and disappear. A man with severe head wounds walks through this area as well. He doesn't interact with you.

Henderson Park

Salem: Henderson Park Rd. into park. Take gravel road to creek.

Local lore states that in the 1970s, three girls were murdered by a cult in the cemetery. A man took the three girls to the cemetery on the promise of a party. Instead the girls were sacrificed, leaving their souls to haunt the Henderson Cemetery, which is said to be on park grounds.

According to local historians, no such cemetery by that name exists in the county. The Old Smedley Cemetery (Mount Pleasant-Old Smedley Cemetery) is on the grounds of Henderson Park.

In the park on the path near the creek, investigations and visits have turned up mists, voices and feelings of dread and discomfort, although nothing has been recorded as hard evidence.

Indian Spring

Indian Spring: S. Mill Creek Rd. between W. Fort Hill Rd. and W. Wilson Ln.

Although her identity is a mystery, a woman with a switchblade sticking out of her back is seen walking along the road. Some people speculate she is a settler, but others say she was an unsolved murder case from the mid-1900s.

Katie's Lane

Salem: E. Farabee Rd. at S. Eastern School Rd.

A drunk man tipped a tombstone on himself and died. The police have ruled it unsolved and were puzzled that he could tip over a one ton stone. Legend states that a house exists across from the Blue River Baptist Church and that before the house was built, strange lights were seen and odd noises were heard.

Old Blue River Cemetery

Salem: Bounded between SR135 and S. Blue River Church Rd. This cemetery has no main roads to it and is in a wooded area.

Civil war soldiers have been reported standing against trees in the cemetery with their guns next to them. When approached, they nod to you and continue smoking. The closer you get the more they fade away. When they do disappear, you can still smell tobacco smoke.

Rotary Springs Camp

Hitchcock: Between N. Cox Ferry Rd and N. Rush Creek Rd.

A female ghost spends her time stacking rocks. She's been captured as a mist on photos.

Salem (Town)
Salem: Gas stations of Salem

A dead delivery man is said to visit two of the gas stations in town. Although he pumps the gas, he has yet to pay. Apparently one gas station employee was ready to call the police when the car that was pulling away disappeared in front of his eyes.

Smith Miller Cemetery

Salem: Much debate concerns where the real 13 graves is. Many versions of this story exist all over the US and the UK. This one is Smith Miller Cemetery at the end of Baker Rd. on the banks of Blue River. To get to this cemetery go to the end of Baker Rd. You'll have to go through a field, into a gully and across a wooded area. It is private property, so you'll need permission to visit.
(aka 13 Graves)

Legend says that if you go through and count the graves one way, you'll count 13. When counting the other way, you'll only count 12. Once you've done this, one of the grave inhabitants is supposed to appear.

WAYNE
COUNTY

Blue Clay Falls

Centerville: North end of Abington Rd.

Reports of a group of people with lanterns wearing late 1800s clothing are seen walking on the road and across fields. Many investigators have reported watching them pass en mass without any member of the group acknowledging the investigators. EVP evidence includes male and female voices urging someone to continue, singing, and crying. Some investigators have speculated these are Native Americans, however, some investigators believe these are displaced people from some other source.

Crying Woman's Bridge

Dublin: Heacock Road, which is parallel to US40. The bridge is gone but where it stands is now blocked at both ends for safety reasons. The location is hard to find in summer due to overgrowth.

A woman lost her baby in an unidentified accident on the bridge. Visitors report hearing a baby cry and a woman wailing and calling for her child. Investigators have reported the names Johnny and Will.

Other variations include the woman driving a car with her baby girl next to her. Rain began to fall and the woman, unfamiliar with the roads, ran off the bridge. The woman's body was found, but not the child's. The mother's remains were reportedly buried in a Potter's field with her baby's pink blanket and pacifier.

Still other people have reported that the woman made sure the child was safe and then died, haunting the area and killing children. (Reportedly several children have drowned in the area.)

When couples used to park on the bridge, they claimed they would hear the woman's fingernails on the car and find scratches in the paint later.

Doddridge Chapel Cemetery

Centerville: Abington Township Line Road and Chapel Rd
Currently the Doddridge Chapel Cemetery Association sells copies of the cemetery records to keep the grounds and chapel.
(aka Chapel Road Cemetery and Church)

Phillip Doddridge donated the four acres for the church/cemetery and was the first person buried there. In 1816, Doddridge built a log cabin for worship in the SE corner.

Reportedly, if you park your car in the church driveway and shut off your lights and ignition, you will hear a dog whining. The temperature will drop inside the car, even during the hottest months. Other reports include adult sized handprints on car windows and vehicle, and shape-shifters outside the car that will appear on one side, disappear, then to reappear on another side.

Earlham College
Richmond: 801 National Road West

Library: Genealogy room is home to mysterious shadow figures
Grounds: Transparent figures of men and women in Quaker garb are seen walking through campus. Legend has it that on Halloween night 1857 that two students were walking across a pipe in the creek and hit their heads. They passed out and died in the shallow water. Today, if you visit the creek on Halloween night, you hear screaming and splashing in the water below.

Goshen Cemetery
Richmond: On SR 227 north of Turner Rd.

A lady in white disappears when you approach her. Footsteps follow you throughout the cemetery. Shadows and white lights dart through the area. The northeast section contains a large amount of children. Odd thumps, bumps and temperature drops occur.

Old Burial Ground
Richmond: S. Seventh and E Streets
(aka Swicker Park)

The first non-Quaker cemetery in Richmond is home to quite a few ghost sightings. While Burials stopped in 1870, and by 1881 the cemetery was in shambles. It became a dumping ground for anything and everything. In 1881 when South E Street was extended, workers cut through the cemetery sending bodies, bones and coffins into the air. By March 1881 a ghost was seen walking around the cemetery and going to homes and tapping on windows. In April 1881 the ghost, now seen as an old man, was asked by a man named Al Bogart, "'What disturbed you?' The ghost answered, "We are on strike," replied the specter. "We have seen our graves neglected, our last resting place desecrated and made places for the living to sneer at and avoid; our tombstones are covered with moss until the inscriptions are hidden; our graves are sunken in until they are all but holes in the ground; weeds and grass grow over us and wrangle at our unfortunate condition until even the birds of the air avoid us. We are going on strike! We want shorter grass, better fences, less pasturage for cows and horses over us..."

"'We seek treatment as if we had once been human beings who helped build Richmond and make it habitable... Wandering horses and wayside cows and errant pigs disturbs us! We rest uneasy in our narrow houses, not knowing what is to come... Fences are cheap, labor is plentiful, ground is obtainable, yet we are left after our years of toil and trouble on earth, with actually not a place to lay our heads! That is why we go on strike in Richmond!'"

Once the South Side Improvement Association heard of this exchange, they offered anyone who wanted to move their family should do so. The Cemetery became a park. However, only a handful of people relocated relatives. In 1894, the workmen removed the headstones, and left the bodies. In September of that year, the newspaper reported workmen stumbling on remains. The Evening Item reports: "Upon numerous occasions the workers have come across remains; this morning marks the climax. In the huge bank that is being cut down about the center of the place, a metallic casket was dug out... The casket is five feet and four inches in length, is of solid iron and old style in shape. At the head a small iron door opens back and beneath a thin pane of glass the features of a woman are plainly to be seen. The face is in a good state of preservation. The hair, which is brownish color, is smoothed as straight across the forehead as if it had been combed but yesterday. The identity of the person is unknown... Residents on that end of town say that it has been 25 years since anybody was interred in the old cemetery, and it is possible that the body found today has been there twice that long. Hundreds of people visited the place today and were permitted to gaze... into the window of the past."

As the workman converted the site, the gravestones were recycled into south side walkways. Four years later, grass was sown. In 1899 the dedication of Swicker Park was made.

Throughout the 1900s ghosts of the graveyard have been reported and it is believed it is Richmond's early settlers unhappy with what has happened to their resting place.

Richmond Downtown
Richmond: Around 6th and Main Streets

On April 6, 1968 a natural gas explosion killed 41 people and injured over 150. It was caused by a gas leak under Marting Arms Sporting Goods. A second explosion was caused by gunpowder. Twenty buildings were torn down as a result and Richmond downtown was rebuilt.

From that time, the ghosts of these people have been seen on the street and in the new buildings. Many investigators believe these are residual hauntings from people who were not ready to go.

Richmond State Hospital
Richmond: 498 NW 18th St.
(Note: This hospital is still in use by various organizations and patients receiving care are still on the grounds. If you do visit, be respectful.)

Nearly every old mental asylum has ghost stories attached to it and Richmond is no exception. Throughout the older buildings you can hear strange things. Wheels of a phantom cart are heard, as are mysterious moans and screams. Legend has it that in the old powerhouse a room in the middle, there are bloody handprints.

It's been reported that the greenhouses around the hospital are also haunted; however, this seems to be more legend. A small office with a phone is supposed to be on the grounds. If you pick up the phone and listen, an operator asks you who you want to speak with. This story also seems to be legend or the phone is no longer on the grounds or accessible.

Star Piano Building
Richmond: White River Gorge Park

This area is rumored to have been built on a cemetery, but that is nothing more than legend. The building has now been turned into an outdoor concert and event hall.

Richmond is widely known as the birthplace of jazz. As part of that birthright, the Star Piano Company, which opened in 1872, began recording records in 1915 using old equipment from a bankrupt company from Boston.

The recording company was named Gennett, thereby avoiding confusion with the piano side of the business. A groundbreaking company, Gennett recorded both black and white artists. Some of the best known jazz artists, including Louis Armstrong, recorded at the studio. History reports that the recording studio was at the south end of the company complex and when trains would roll by, all recording had to be suspended because of the noise. Eventually, Decca bought the rights to some of Gennett's recordings and in 1997, Richmond began preserving this vast jazz legacy.

Two buildings remain- the concert hall and a smaller, unkempt building. In the smaller building, there is evidence of graffiti and squatters, and the remains of some of the workers. Many people have reported male and female office workers walking in the area of the buildings in 1920s clothing. One visitor stopped to talk with a full color solid female entity and chatted about the company. The woman was quite knowledgeable. When the visitor mentioned how sad she was that there was no one specific place to get the Gennett records, the entity was puzzled, saying they were available through the company and at music stores. When the two said their goodbyes, the woman walked into one of the concert hall towers and disappeared.

WELLS
COUNTY

Apostolic Christian Church

Bluffton: East of Sunrise Way at 630 E. Dustman Rd. Locals indicate the playground was under the current parking lot

An older gentleman ran a playground for kids on the site of the Apostolic Christian Church. The children loved him, but apparently the adults didn't approve of the playground- or of him. The man was found under a red bridge in the Wabash River.

People hear children laughing and a pounding on the bottom of the bridge. An older man is seen walking in the area. Sometimes he is seen sitting on a bench that does not exist.

Markle

(See Huntington Co.)

The Rittenhouse

Bluffton: 218 S Main St.

Now a restaurant, the building was once home to a morgue/funeral home. Some visitors claim you can still smell the chemicals and death in the home. Mysterious occurrences include seeing spirits, presumably of the dead who passed through the building. One visitor reported walking in the upper gallery and seeing a transparent man weave his way through the guests below. He turned abruptly and smiled at her. EVP reports include disembodied voices asking for help, unintelligible murmurs and loud conversation.

Vera Cruz (town)

Vera Cruz: SR 301 (S700E) and SW Center St. as well as near the bridge SW of town.

A man from the 1800s shot himself in the kitchen. He has been seen from the time of his death until present day walking into town and back out, and up the lane to the old house.

In the original home, a babysitter claimed to have seen a headless man walking up the lane to the house. The original house is no longer standing. A new home is under construction. Workers claim to have seen the same headless man, as well as the man seen in town.

Zanesville United Methodist Church

Zanesville: 11811 N Wayne St

During a renovation, workers felt as if they were being watched. One worker was touched by an unseen hand. Ever since, the people are uneasy about going to the upstairs area of the oldest part of the church.

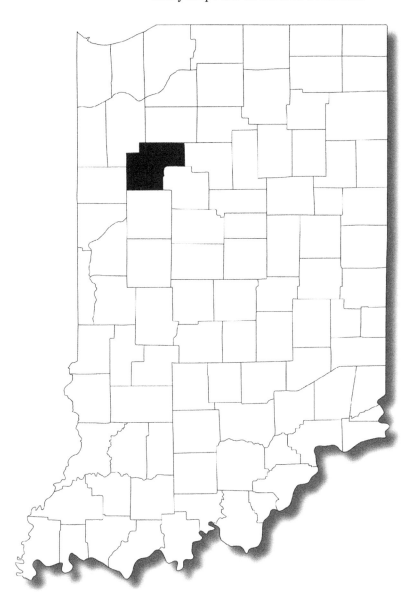

WHITE
COUNTY

Cedarwing Park
Brookston: Bordered by S. Wood St., South of 8th St. E., 11th St. E. and S. Brackney St.

Misty white shapes have been reported running through the yards of neighboring homes. On calm days and nights, cold strong breezes have been experienced by paranormal investigators. Other people have reported interruptions in electronics (e.g. radios, video cameras, photo cameras).

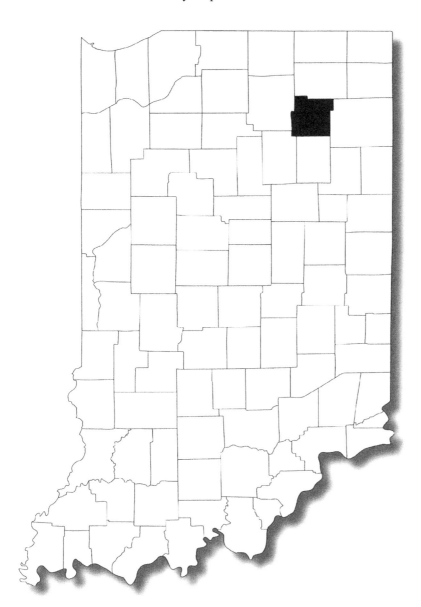

WHITLEY COUNTY

Hazelcot Castle

Columbia City: Marker on east side of Johnson Rd. north of De La Balme Rd. and Johnson Rd. (base only remains)

Dr. Eli Pierce and his wife Sarah moved with his family to Hazelcot in 1835. They lived a rich social life until Sarah died in 1840. In 1874 Dr. Pierce was found on the road to Ft. Wayne, dead of a heart attack. People said after his death that they saw Sarah in the library of the home. People who camped out in the home were awakened by a hand around their throat or by violent shaking.

In 1893, the home was destroyed by people scared of the paranormal. Bits of it were reused in other homes- who knows what they hold?

Old Train Tracks

South Whitley: N. State St. at railroad tracks

Apparitions of girls are seen walking, and talking. One sometimes is seen holding a teddy bear.

Old Whitley County Sheriff's Home and Jail

Columbia City: Corner of Market and Post & Mail Streets

This old jail and home was built in 1875 and designed by J.C. Johnson, who designed many Indiana Courthouses and jails. The beautiful stone masonry was completed by William Carr. On the 10 most endangered landmarks list, this building is home to spirit activity.

History shows Charles Butler murdered his wife Abigail and is said to haunt this old jail, which is no longer used for incarceration. It is sometimes used as a haunted house during Halloween, yet real paranormal activity occurs as well.

Employees and visitors have experienced hearing footsteps and scraping on wall. The building also has one door that will not stay closed no matter how many times it is shut. On the third floor, a woman's footprints appear on the wall as if painted in ash. If you mention Abigail's name on the third floor, unexplained activity, such as lights turning off or on and items moving, occurs.

Shadow figures are seen peering out from windows. Lights are seen in windows at night. A woman had a conversation with an older man who was standing outside the building, taking care of the lawn. He talked to her about the history of the place. She turned to look at the building for a second and when she turned back to him, he was gone.

Parkview Health

Columbia City: 353 North Oak Street

Part of this facility was an old funeral home. The electrical system seems to short out at odd times. Chairs and other equipment move by unseen hands. The activity increases in the evening and during the Fall. Various people, including children, have seen people that others could not see.

Whitko High School
South Whitley: End of W. Wayne Street at Big Blue Ave.

Legend has it one student dies every year. An old woman forewarns people of this each year when school starts.

Index

Addresses

Made in the USA
Middletown, DE
02 April 2021

36385103R00250